The Channel Islands

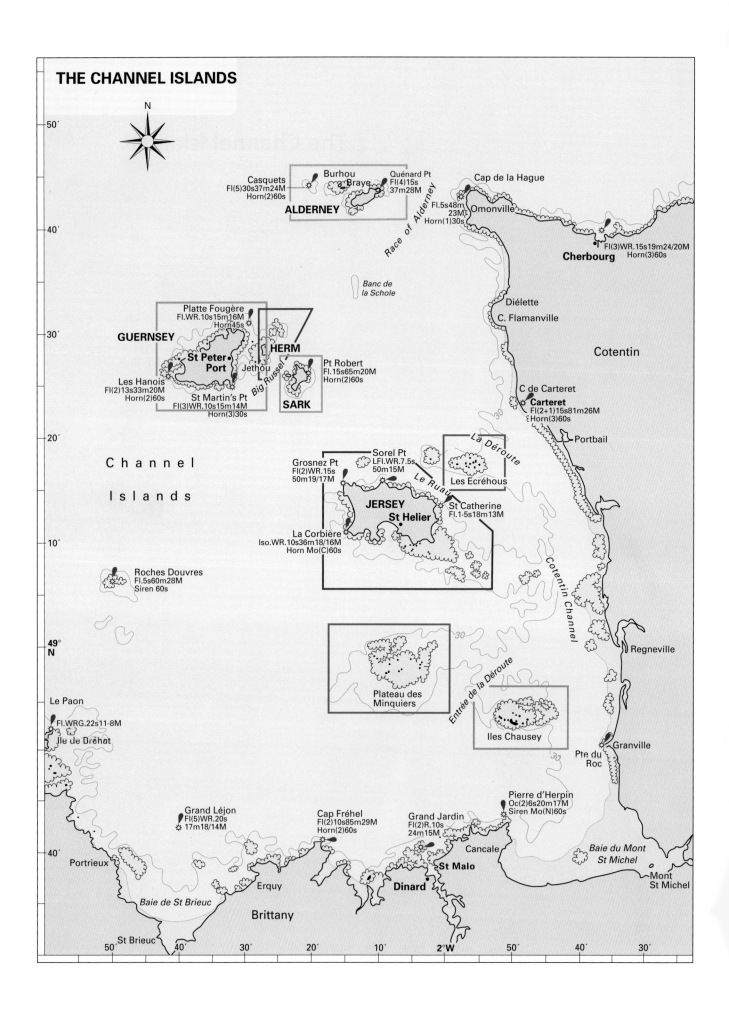

THE CHANNEL ISLANDS

N

Casquets
Fl(5)30s37m24M
Horn(2)60s

Burhou
Braye

Quénard Pt
Fl(4)15s
37m28M

ALDERNEY

Cap de la Hague

Omonville

Fl.5s48m
23M
Horn(1)30s

Race of Alderney

Banc de
la Schole

Diélette
C. Flamanville

Cotentin

Cherbourg

Fl(3)WR.15s19m24/20M
Horn(3)60s

Platte Fougère
Fl.WR.10s15m16M
Horn45s

GUERNSEY

HERM

St Peter
Port

Jethou

Big Russel

SARK

Pt Robert
Fl.15s65m20M
Horn(2)60s

Les Hanois
Fl(2)13s33m20M
Horn(2)60s

St Martin's Pt
Fl(3)WR.10s15m14M
Horn(3)30s

C de Carteret

Carteret
Fl(2+1)15s81m26M
Horn(3)60s

Portbail

C h a n n e l

I s l a n d s

Sorel Pt
LFl.WR.7.5s
50m15M

La Déroute

Grosnez Pt
Fl(2)WR.15s
50m19/17M

Le Ruau

Les Ecréhous

JERSEY

St Helier

St Catherine
Fl.1·5s18m13M

La Corbière
Iso.WR.10s36m18/16M
Horn Mo(C)60s

Roches Douvres
Fl.5s60m28M
Siren 60s

Cotentin Channel

**49°
N**

Regneville

Le Paon

Fl.WRG.22s11-8M

Ile de Bréhat

Plateau des
Minquiers

Entrée de la Déroute

Iles Chausey

Granville

Pte du
Roc

Grand Léjon
Fl(5)WR.20s
17m18/14M

Cap Fréhel
Fl(2)10s85m29M
Horn(2)60s

Grand Jardin
Fl(2)R.10s
24m15M

Pierre d'Herpin
Oc(2)6s20m17M
Siren Mo(N)60s

Cancale

Baie du Mont
St Michel

Portrieux

Erquy

St Malo

Dinard

Mont
St Michel

Baie de St Brieuc

Brittany

St Brieuc

2°W

The Channel Islands

ROYAL CRUISING CLUB
PILOTAGE FOUNDATION

Peter Carnegie

Imray Laurie Norie *&* Wilson

Published by
Imray Laurie Norie & Wilson Ltd
Wych House The Broadway St Ives
Cambridgeshire PE27 5BT England
☎ +44 (0)1480 462114
Fax +44 (0) 1480 496109
www.imray.com
2006

Plans are derived in part from material obtained from the UK
Hydrographic office with the permisssion of the UK
Hydrogaphic Office and her Majesty's Stationery Office.

First edition 1997
Second edition 2006

ISBN 0 85288 790 6

British Library Cataloguing in Publication Data.
A catalogue record for this title is available from
the British Library.

Printed in Singapore by Star Standard Industries

CORRECTIONAL SUPPLEMENTS

This pilot book will be amended at intervals by the issue of
correctional supplements. These are published on the internet
at our website www.imray.com and also via www.rccpf.org.uk
and may be downloaded free of charge. Printed copies are also
available on request from the publishers at the above address.
Like this pilot, supplements are selective. Navigators requiring
the latest definitive information are advised to refer to official
Hydrographic Office data.

www.rccpf.org.uk may include additional photographs of
interest, or of changes if they occur during the life of this
book.

CAUTION

Whilst every care has been taken to ensure that the information
contained in this book is accurate, the RCC Pilotage Foundation, the
authors and the publishers hereby formally disclaim any and all
liability for any personal injury, loss and/or damage howsoever
caused, whether by reason of any error, inaccuracy, omission or
ambiguity in relation to the contents and/or information contained
within this book. The book contains selected information and thus is
not definitive. It does not contain all known information on the
subject in hand and should not be relied on alone for navigational
use: it should only be used in conjunction with official hydrographic
data. This is particularly relevant to the plans, which should not be
used for navigation.

The RCC Pilotage Foundation, the authors and publishers believe
that the information which they have included is a useful aid to
prudent navigation, but the safety of a vessel depends ultimately on
the judgment of the skipper, who should assess all information,
published or unpublished.

WAYPOINTS

This edition of the *Channel Islands* pilot includes the introduction of
waypoints. The RCC PF consider a waypoint to be a position likely
to be helpful for navigation if entered into some form of electronic
navigation system for use in conjunction with GPS. In this pilot they
have been determined by actual observation. All waypoints are given
to datum WGS 84 and every effort has been made to ensure their
accuracy. Nevertheless, for each individual vessel, the standard of
onboard equipment, aerial position, datum setting, correct entry of
data and operator skill all play a part in their effectiveness. In
particular it is vital for the navigator to note the datum of the chart
in use and apply the necessary correction if plotting a GPS position
on the chart.

The attention of the navigator is drawn to the *Safety note* in the
Introduction.

We emphasise that we regard waypoints as an aid to navigation
for use as the navigator decides. We hope that the waypoints in
this pilot will help ease that navigational load.

POSITIONS

Positions given in the text and on plans are intended purely as an
aid to locating the place in question on the chart.

PLANS

The plans in this guide are not to be used for navigation – they are
designed to support the text and should always be used together
with navigational charts. Even so, every effort has been made to
locate harbour and anchorage plans adjacent to the relevant text.

It should be borne in mind that the characteristics of lights may be
changed during the life of the book, and that in any case
notification of such changes is unlikely to be reported
immediately. Each light is identified in both the text and where
possible on the plans (where it appears in red) by its international
index number, as used in the Admiralty *List of Lights*, from which
the book may be updated when no longer new.

All bearings are given from seaward and refer to true north. Scales
may be taken from the scales of latitude. Symbols are based on
those used by the British Admiralty – users are referred to
Symbols and Abbreviations (NP 5011).

Contents

THE RCC PILOTAGE FOUNDATION

In 1976 an American member of the Royal Cruising Club, Dr Fred Ellis, indicated that he wished to make a gift to the Club in memory of his father, the late Robert E Ellis, of his friends Peter Pye and John Ives and as a mark of esteem for Roger Pinckney. An independent charity known as the RCC Pilotage Foundation was formed and Dr Ellis added his house to his already generous gift of money to form the Foundation's permanent endowment. The Foundation's charitable objective is 'to advance the education of the public in the science and practice of navigation', which is at present achieved through the writing and updating of pilot books covering many different parts of the world.

The Foundation is extremely grateful and privileged to have been given the copyrights to books written by a number of distinguished authors and yachtsmen including the late Adlard Coles, Robin Brandon and Malcolm Robson. In return the Foundation has willingly accepted the task of keeping the original books up to date and many yachtsmen and women have helped (and are helping) the Foundation fulfil this commitment. In addition to the titles donated to the Foundation, several new books have been created and developed under the auspices of the Foundation. The Foundation works in close collaboration with three publishers – Imray Laurie Norie and Wilson, Adlard Coles Nautical and On Board Publications – and in addition publishes in its own name short run guides and pilot books for areas where limited demand does not justify large print runs. Several of the Foundation's books have been translated into French, German and Italian.

The Foundation runs its own website at www.rccpf.org.uk which not only lists all the publications but also contains free downloadable pilotage information.

The overall management of the Foundation is entrusted to trustees appointed by the Royal Cruising Club, with day-to-day operations being controlled by the Director. All these appointments are unpaid. In line with its charitable status, the Foundation distributes no profits; any surpluses are used to finance new books and developments and to subsidise those covering areas of low demand.

RCC PILOTAGE FOUNDATION PUBLICATIONS

Imray
The Baltic Sea
Norway
North Brittany and the Channel Islands
Faroe, Iceland and Greenland
Isles of Scilly
The Channel Islands
North Biscay
South Biscay
Atlantic Islands
Atlantic Spain & Portugal
Mediterranean Spain
 Costas del Sol & Blanca
Mediterranean Spain
 Costas del Azahar,
 Dorada & Brava
Islas Baleares
Corsica and North Sardinia
North Africa
Chile

Adlard Coles Nautical
Atlantic Crossing Guide
Pacific Crossing Guide

On Board Publications
South Atlantic Circuit
Havens and Anchorages for the South American Coast

The RCC Pilotage Foundation
RCC PF Website www.rccpf.org.uk
Cruising Guide to West Africa
South Georgia
Supplements
Passage planning guides

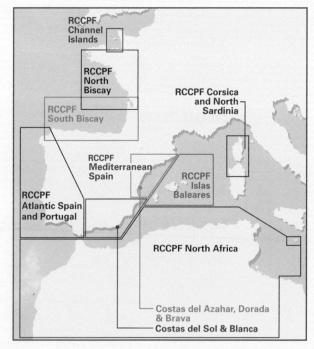

Foreword

Thousands of yachtsmen visit the Channel Islands, either to cruise or to seek a pleasant haven en route between England and France; however, mindful of the strong tides and currents, comparatively few explore off the beaten path. Those that do, have the chance to exercise their pilotage skills (or make full use of local expertise) and are rewarded with fascinating and fast-changing seascapes and interesting anchorages away from the tourist bustle.

The origins of this book go back to the work of Malcolm Robson who generously gave copyright of his pilot books to the RCC Pilotage Foundation with the request that they be revised as necessary. Nick Heath rose to the challenge and produced his book in 1997. Peter Carnegie lives on Jersey and knows these islands well. Writing any pilot book is a demanding task but this complex area provided an enormous challenge. The Pilotage Foundation has been fortunate that Peter has been prepared to devote so much time and meticulous care to develop this new book. He has repeatedly sailed and flown the islands and has recorded not just the main passages but, in conjunction with local experts, has worked the tides to travel and identify the more remote routes. His text is enhanced by his own carefully positioned photographs from the sea and the air and the plans have been updated to WGS84; they now include some waypoints for ease of reference.

I congratulate Peter Carnegie for presenting pilotage information of this complicated area in such a logical fashion, Ros Hogbin for her editorial assistance, and Willie Wilson and his team at Imray who have devoted so much time and expertise to bring this edition of the Channel Islands to publication.

Martin Walker
Director
RCC Pilotage Foundation
June 2006

Preface

It was with some trepidation that I took on the task of compiling the new edition of *The Channel Islands* as a successor to Nick Heath's comprehensive work published in 1997. The area has since seen further development of yachting facilities with several new and improved marks. In May 2004 The Hydrographic Office published a new set of charts compatible with WGS 84 datum. A demand for information in Iles Chausey, now that secure visitors' moorings are available, prompted the decision to extend the pilot to include this French archipelago.

With dependence on GPS as a means of navigation now more or less universal, the aim in writing this pilot has been to steer a middle course between waypoint navigation and traditional methods. Situational awareness through visual observation continues to be a vital element of pilotage and good seamanship.

Referring to the complexity of some of the pilotage described, a reader suggested an alternative title for this pilot might be 'How to get lost in The Channel Islands'. In a sense I can recommend no better place for doing just that than among these unique islands. My hope is that this pilot will assist those who take up the challenge of discovering new harbours and anchorages to achieve their objective safely.

Peter Carnegie
June 2006

The author has sailed all the marks described in this pilot with *Caprice*, a 42' sloop with 65hp auxiliary and 1.6m draught.

Herm harbour

Acknowledgements

The author is grateful for the assistance of Channel Island yachtsmen and professional seafarers in the preparation of this book. The following require special mention and thanks.

Alderney
Steve Shaw, harbourmaster, lifeboat coxswain and pilot
Dave Prince, charter skipper *Voyager*
Annabel Finding, RCC

Guernsey & Herm
Captain Robert Barton, harbourmaster 1997–2005
John Frankland
Roddy Ray, pilot
David Nicolle, charter skipper *Friendship Rose*
Buzz White, charter skipper *Access Challenger*
Stuart Carnegie, RCC

Sark
Jo Birch
Dick Adams, pilot instructor
James Briggs

Jersey
Captain Brian Nibbs, Channel Island Air Search
John Searson, Jersey Meteorological Department
William Coom, South Pier Marine
John Nugent
Nick Bailhache, RCC
Bob Wright and Robert Brown, Jersey Aero Club pilots
James Carnegie
Fuji Photo
David de Gruchy

Iles Chausey
Peter Colback
Chris Fairbairn

Channel Islands Air Traffic Controllers

Julia Carnegie for word processing and computer input.

Introduction

The Channel Islands, with their unique blend of French and English culture, have always held a fascination for yachtsmen. As a cruising ground, the islands themselves and the neighbouring coasts of Normandy and Brittany offer a great diversity of harbours and anchorages, more than can be explored in a lifetime. A climate milder than in the UK and spread over a longer season, and a lack of air and sea pollution, adds to their appeal.

Getting to the islands will, for many, mean a Channel crossing. In suitable conditions this can be a straightforward 8–10 hours' sail from the UK south coast. Braye Harbour, Alderney is a popular port of entry where visitors first experience the friendly atmosphere of the islands and meet with a minimum of formalities. Further south the marinas at Beaucette and St Peter Port, Guernsey and at St Helier in Jersey provide a secure base for those wishing to enjoy attractions ashore and day cruising to nearby anchorages and beaches.

From St Peter Port it is a short sail to Herm and Sark and for the experienced there are the spectacular LW anchorages in the protected sites of Les Ecréhous and Les Minquiers off Jersey. Vessels able to take the ground can retreat to drying harbours such as Herm, Creux (Sark) or St Aubin and Gorey in Jersey.

History

The coastal forts and defences of the islands, many of which serve as pilotage marks, are evidence of centuries of struggle between England and France and in more recent times the German occupation from 1940–45.

The traditional firing of a cannon from the ramparts of Castle Cornet in St Peter Port signals midday

How the islands came to be included in the British Isles but not in the United Kingdom, or the European Union, is the result of a quirk of history. Originally part of the Duchy of Normandy, they were annexed to England at the time of the Norman Conquest in 1066. Following the loss of the Duchy to France in the reign of King John (one of William the Conqueror's successors), Channel Islanders had to decide where their allegiance lay. In 1204 they chose to remain loyal to the English crown. They were rewarded by an exemption from all taxes made by Parliament and given the freedom to govern themselves. Such privileges have been confirmed by successive sovereigns – there is still no VAT in the Channel Islands!

Pilotage around the Channel Islands

With its rock-strewn waters and some of the most powerful tides in the world, the Channel Islands offer something of a challenge. Seasoned locals will refer to their home waters as 'a cruising ground but not a playground' and talk of currents twice a boat's speed, overfalls, fog-banks that roll in without warning and tricky pilotage. While it is true that safe sailing here calls for a degree of alertness and unremitting care, the basic requirement is a good working knowledge of sound coastal navigation. There are three golden rules for survival: know the weather; know the tides; know where you are.

Today, first time visitors to the islands enjoy a head start unknown to earlier generations of cruising yachtsmen. Over the past twenty years the system of buoyage and marks has been greatly extended, the area has been comprehensively charted by both British and French authorities, and yachtsmens' guides and pilots abound. Dedicated visitors' moorings will be found in most islands as well as a choice of marinas in St Peter Port and St Helier. With weather bulletins regularly beamed to all corners of the area and navigation revolutionised through GPS, there are fewer excuses for getting caught out or lost.

Finding an island is one thing; getting safely in is another. Pilotage is that element of a passage concerned with the conduct of a vessel into and out of a harbour or anchorage, and is often a test of the navigator's skill. The yacht will be in relatively shallow waters and in close proximity to rocks and other hazards. Visibility may be reduced and inshore streams unpredictable. At such times the rocks are your 'friends' providing vital signposts. Since time immemorial they have played a key role in Channel Islands pilotage. (See *Appendix. Channel Island Rock Names.*)

This pilot is intended as a resource and backup for those with limited local knowledge. It belongs in the cockpit along with other tools of the pilot's trade: binoculars and a handbearing compass. It is *no substitute for up-to-date charts of suitable scale* which should be thoroughly consulted when passage planning, together with the tidal atlas and tables.

Weather

Despite the Channel Islands being tucked away in the most southerly corner of the British Isles they are still subject to the 'mishmash' of English weather. Atlantic depressions are borne in on the prevailing westerly flow, punctuated by ridges or longer-lasting highs. Air is funnelled from all points of the compass, providing a wide range of conditions to keep yachtsmen on their toes.

The islands can claim to enjoy more sunshine on average than elsewhere in the British Isles. Spring comes earlier, summer hangs on longer and winters are mild. One only has to compare BBC shipping forecasts for Portland sea area with local bulletins to appreciate the difference. Depressions tracking across northern sea areas may bring dismal conditions to the English Channel while those in the islands will often be moderated, offering pleasant sailing. Within the area itself there are subtle variations due to the surrounding French mainland. The Cherbourg peninsula provides shelter from easterly winds but with less effect around Alderney and Guernsey. There will often be a regime of fresh northeasterlies accompanied by a fine spell early in the season. In such situations, however, the peninsula can be responsible for a localised low, which develops to windward of the islands, causing a narrowing of the isobars and resulting in a stiff afternoon breeze (Force 7) strongest in the southern isles. Elsewhere there may be little more than Force 5. See Figs 5a and 5b.

The Brittany peninsula to the S gives shelter from winds from that direction, the degree of which is shown in Figs 1 and 3.

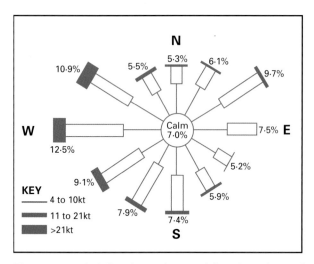

The average wind direction and strength based on observations at Jersey Airport Met Office over the period 1971-2000
Courtesy of Jersey Meteorological Department

S and SE winds are the least frequent, often associated with thundery conditions or a warm front moving in from the W.

The islands are fully exposed to winds from the W and NW, the prevailing direction (see diagram above).

Gales

Gales, which are mostly westerly, can occur at any time of the year but are most frequent between October and January with the lowest incidence between June and August. As a general rule the N part of the area, from Guernsey to latitude 50°N, picks up stronger winds than the S. With comprehensive local forecasting services and a sensitive 'weather nose', it should always be possible to anticipate likely changes and tailor plans accordingly.

If a gale threatens, good shelter with plenty of interest ashore to sustain a weather-bound crew is seldom more than a 4–6 hours' sail away.

St Helier and St Malo are excellent bolt-holes but Alderney (Braye) should be avoided in northeasterlies when it is totally exposed. St Peter Port can be entered in almost all weathers but can be uncomfortable in easterlies. Beaucette Marina should not be approached in strong easterlies.

St Helier's marinas are well sheltered but an approach to the port in a southerly gale could be hazardous.

Gorey (Jersey) is particularly exposed around HW in gales from between SSE and SSW, when taking the ground can be a painful experience.

Sea state

From Alderney southwards the effects of the surrounding coast, other islands and above all strongly tidal waters, will be felt. The longer seas of the English Channel give way to short seas with frequent local changes in shape and direction – the effect of varying depth, shoals, reefs, headlands, gaps and above all the state and run of the tide.

Throughout the area there are several notorious patches where wind against tide conditions can throw up short steep seas. Passage through such areas can range from a barely noticeable sea state to a highly dangerous situation for small craft. Transit through the Alderney Race or the neighbouring Swinge should be carefully timed to coincide with fair weather and slack tide or avoided altogether in bad weather. There are notorious patches around The Race Rocks and further S over Milieu and Banc de la Schôle. Other areas to be wary of are:

Guernsey Big Russel W of Brecqhou
    Little Russel between Platte Fougère lighthouse
    and Roustel beacon tower
Sark East coast
Jersey Pointe Corbière and Noirmont Point

Swell and fetch

Swell is usually developed by deep Atlantic lows. As it enters the strongly tidal waters of the Channel it will become more pronounced, particularly over spring tides.

At such periods many anchorages become untenable around HW. Sark anchorages are notorious in this respect.

CHARACTER OF THE WINDS

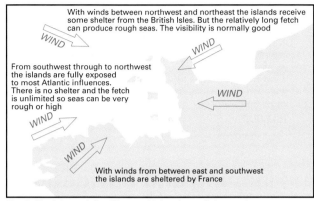

With winds between northwest and northeast the islands receive some shelter from the British Isles. But the relatively long fetch can produce rough seas. The visibility is normally good

WIND

WIND

From southwest through to northwest the islands are fully exposed to most Atlantic influences. There is no shelter and the fetch is unlimited so seas can be very rough or high

WIND

WIND

WIND

With winds from between east and southwest the islands are sheltered by France

Fig 1 Position of the Channel Islands and the main wind/sea effects

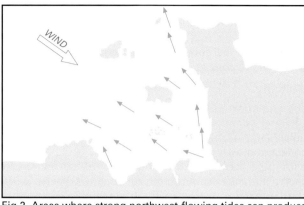

WIND

Fig 2 Areas where strong northwest-flowing tides can produce very rough seas in northwesterly wind situations

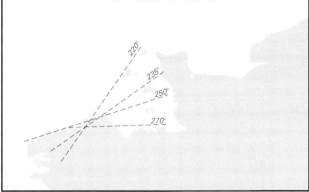

220°
235°
250°
270°

Fig 3 Lines to the south of which there is substantial shelter from Brittany from given wind directions

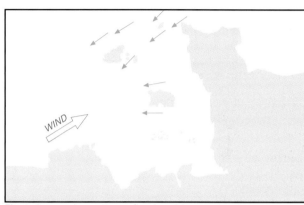

WIND

Fig 4 Areas where strong-flowing tides produce very rough seas in southwesterly wind situations

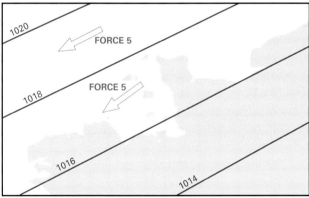

1020

FORCE 5

1018

FORCE 5

1016

1014

Fig 5a Typical isobaric situation and winds with a northeasterly in the early morning

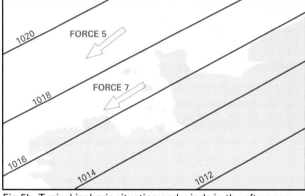

1020

FORCE 5

1018

FORCE 7

1016

1014

1012

Fig 5b Typical isobaric situation and winds in the afternoon after heating over France

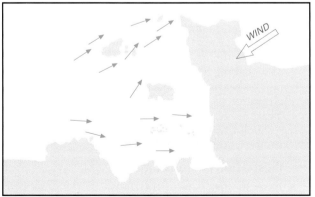

WIND

Fig 6 Areas where strong-flowing tides can produce very rough seas in northeasterly wind situations

Wave height is monitored by wave rider buoys and features in Channel Island weather forecasts and reports. The longer the fetch the higher the waves, so winds from a westerly direction will produce higher waves and longer swell in contrast to easterlies and southerlies where the fetch is short. See Fig 1.

Visibility

Fog and poor visibility is traditionally a major hazard in Channel Island waters, although GPS and radar have taken some of the sting out of it.

Fog is mostly of the advection type, being associated with mild moist air tracking over the cooler seas of spring and early summer. It will usually disperse with a shift in wind direction or the passage of a front. In the summer months, predominantly June and July, radiation fog associated with clear nights in anticyclonic weather tends to generate in the low-lying areas of the Cherbourg peninsula and Brittany. This will often waft towards the islands causing fog that will not lift until late morning when the surface has warmed up.

Fog can also develop suddenly in summer when a very warm southeasterly at the onset of a thundery spell gives way to a cooler westerly flow towards the end of the day. Fog in the islands is rare from mid-August to October.

Sources of weather information

VHF

JERSEY RADIO

Channel Islands Shipping Forecast

Ch 25, 82 at 0545, 0645, 0745, 1245, 1845, 2245 (LT) for area bounded by 50°N, French Coast from Cap de la Hague to Île de Bréhat and 3°W

Gale and strong wind warnings

On receipt and at 0307, 0907, 1507, 2107.

ST HELIER PIERHEADS INFORMATION SERVICE

Ch 18. An automatic broadcast of wind direction and strength at St Helier pierheads. Updated every 2 minutes. Range is about 5 miles.

CROSS JOBOURG

Ch 80 at Jobourg 0715, 1545, 1915 (LT). Granville 0703, 1533, 1903 (LT). For area Cap de la Hague to Pte de Penmarc'h

Gale and strong wind warnings

In French and English on receipt and at H+20 and H+50 (LT) Warnings for coastal areas on receipt and at H+03.

JERSEY METEOROLOGICAL DEPARTMENT SERVICES

The Channel Island Shipping Forecast is also available by telephone, fax and email.

Recorded ☎ 0900 665 00 22 (50p per min)

Fax 0960 100 466 (£1 per min)

Email enquiries@jerseymet.gov.je

Personal Consultation Service ☎ 0905 807 77 77

Internet Services www.jerseymet.gov.je

The above services are also available using a credit card £5 for consultation. £3 for fax back or email. ☎ 01534 745550

BBC RADIO 4 SHIPPING FORECAST (Sea Area Portland)

LW 198kHz. MW 756kHz. FM Channel Islands: 94.8mHz

Times (LT)   0048 LW, MW, FM

0520 LW, MW, FM

1201 LW only

1754 LW, FM (Sat/Sun)

LOCAL RADIO

BBC Radio Jersey

1026kHz, 88.8Mhz

Shipping forecast for local waters Mon–Fri 0635, 1800 LT. Sat/Sun 0735 LT. Sat/Sun at H+00 (0700–1300 after the news) and 0725 LT

BBC Radio Guernsey

93.2Mhz, 1116kHz

Weather bulletins for the waters around Guernsey, Herm & Sark. Mon–Fri 0630, 0730, 0830 LT. Sat/Sun 0730, 0830 LT

INTERNET

Weather websites

www.jerseymet.gov.je

www.met-office.gov.uk

www.rnli.org.uk/weather.asp

www.metbrief.com

TELETEXT

ITV 1 CI's p209

Planning and navigation

Technical information

Nautical miles, cables and metres, bearings

As the metric system is rapidly replacing imperial measures and since vertical heights and soundings are already shown in metres on charts, the practice in this edition will be to give short distances that the navigator is expected to estimate by eye in metres (m).

For these estimated distances, the navigator who normally estimates in cables and yards can, to within 10%, take 200m as 1 cable (in fact 218.7yds) and 30m as 30yds (in fact 32.8yds).

However, since it is normal practice to use the latitude scale on a Mercator chart to measure nautical miles and tenths and although the traditional cable is very close to a tenth of a nautical mile, when referring to a chart and especially when the required track may be plotted on the chart, distances will be given in nautical miles (M) and decimals (e.g. 3.8M, 0.3M).

All bearings are expressed in degrees True. Times are expressed in UTC unless otherwise stated.

Marks

Note that positions are given in the text to the nearest tenth of a minute of latitude and longitude. A large-scale chart should be consulted for a more precise position.

Striking marks and clearing lines

These traditional but effective measures may be used to clear or pinpoint the position of a submerged rock or obstruction. All that is needed is a handbearing compass and an identified mark which will usually be on the shore.

A position line from the mark and crossing the hazard gives the critical bearing at the point where one is likely to strike the hazard. A mark used in this way is known as a striking mark.

The bearing of a mark can also be used to provide safe clearance of a hazard. This position line is known as a clearing line.

Such critical bearings may also be derived from the transit of two marks.

Illustration of transit marks

In many instances of the transit marks described in this book, the front mark obscures the rear. For the sake of

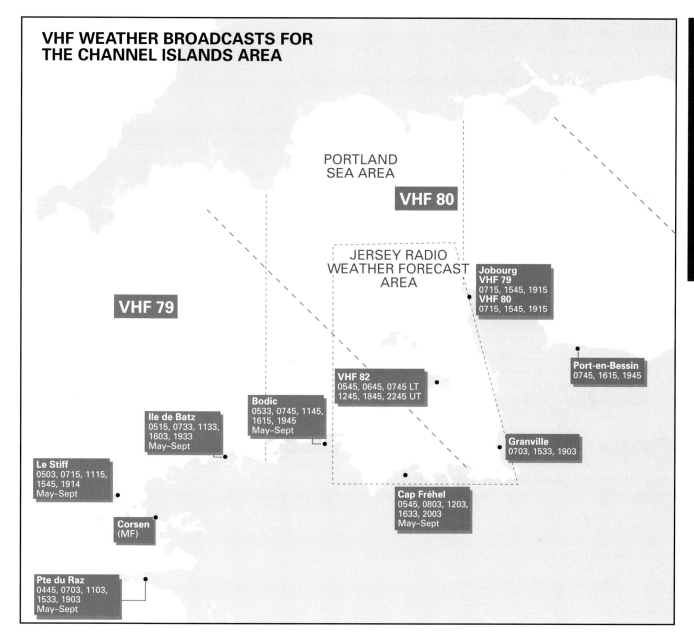

VHF WEATHER BROADCASTS FOR
THE CHANNEL ISLANDS AREA

PORTLAND
SEA AREA

VHF 80

JERSEY RADIO
WEATHER FORECAST
AREA

VHF 79

**Jobourg
VHF 79
0715, 1545, 1915
VHF 80
0715, 1545, 1915**

**Port-en-Bessin
0745, 1615, 1945**

**VHF 82
0545, 0645, 0745 LT
1245, 1845, 2245 UT**

**Bodic
0533, 0745, 1145,
1615, 1945
May–Sept**

**Ile de Batz
0515, 0733, 1133,
1603, 1933
May–Sept**

**Granville
0703, 1533, 1903**

**Le Stiff
0503, 0715, 1115,
1545, 1914
May–Sept**

**Cap Fréhel
0545, 0803, 1203,
1633, 2003
May–Sept**

**Corsen
(MF)**

**Pte du Raz
0445, 0703, 1103,
1533, 1903
May–Sept**

clarity, such marks have been photographed offset (opened). If this slight deviation is permissable, no mention is made in the text.

GPS and chart datum

As of May 2004 editions, all British Admiralty charts covering the Channel Islands are on WGS 84 datum and all positions given in this pilot book are based on this datum.

Caution should be exercised if using pre-metric or old French or private charts which do not show any correction. There may be significant discrepancies between the latitude and longitude on the chart and that shown by GPS set to any datum.

Positions

The latitude and longitude coordinates given under the name of a port or harbour and in some cases an anchorage are not waypoints. They are for the purpose of indicating their general position.

Waypoints

A numbered waypoint is shown in a safe-water position. In most cases this is on an approach line to a port, harbour or anchorage to indicate where pilotage may take over from GPS navigation.

See *Appendix. Waypoint list.*

Safety note

Waypoints and tracks between them must be plotted and checked on an up-to-date chart before being used for navigation.

Tides

All tidal information is based on Standard Port St Helier, unless stated otherwise.

Depths

Depths or drying heights given for passages and channels are based on Chart Datum – the level below which sea level seldom falls.

Understanding the tides

The Channel Islands and its tides are synonymous and the lives of local mariners are governed by them. They should therefore be the first consideration when planning a passage, which whenever possible should be timed to take advantage of favourable streams.

The basic essentials for working the tides are the current *Almanac* for its tide tables and other information, and the *Tidal Stream Atlas*. The Atlas is worth more than any number of words on the subject and should be studied carefully. There are two covering the area:

The Admiralty *Tidal Stream Atlas for The Channel Islands and adjacent coasts of France* (NP 264) *Courants de Marée dans Le Golfe Normand-Breton de Cherbourg a Paimpol* (SHOM 562-UJA). The latter has some excellent large-scale chartlets.

See *Appendix* for large-scale tidal stream diagrams for individual islands. They indicate many of the inshore eddies that do not feature on small-scale diagrams.

An understanding of how the area happens to have one of the world's largest tidal ranges starts with the concept of a tidal wave surging up and down the English Channel every 12 hours. In general, ports to the W will experience HW earlier and ports to the E will be later, so when it is HW at St Helier it will be about 30 minutes after HW at Paimpol and about 1½ hours before HW at Cherbourg. There are, of course, exceptions to this within the area due to the flow around the islands.

Tidal differences based on standard port St Helier

	Times (approx)
Lézardrieux	−0033
Ile de Bréhat	−0025
Paimpol	−0022
St Quay/Portrieux	−0022
Erquy/Dahouet	−0020
St Malo	−0020
Granville	−0015
Chausey	−0014
Carteret	+0010
Diélette	+0020
St Peter Port (Guernsey)	+0005
Braye (Alderney)	+0045
Cherbourg	+0135

A look at the plan for HW Dover +0500 (the equivalent of HW at St Helier −0230) clearly shows the Channel Islands at the confluence of 2 waves of tide. The outgoing wave in the E Channel is turning sharply S through the Alderney Race to bear down on the islands. At the same time the incoming wave is racing in from the W becoming accelerated along the Brittany coast. Both waves converge on the Bay of Mont St Michel SE of Jersey, where the tide is said to run at the speed of a galloping horse and HW rises to a height of nearly 15m (50ft) at spring tides. The outgoing tide is equally savage with the sea retreating up to 7 miles offshore. At nearby St Malo this energy is harnessed to generate electricity. Within this relentless swirl will be found eddies, rotary currents, acceleration zones and bay effects. It can never be said to be boring!

Tidal hints

- Calculate the best time to leave by working back from the deadline for arriving at your destination. This may be influenced by limitations such as a marina sill, tidal conditions or depth in a channel
- Decide the minimum boat speed that needs to be made good and consider using engine if falling behind.
- Mark each page of the *Tidal Atlas* with clock times so you can easily find the set and strength of the stream at any time or place. In the Channel Islands to avoid confusion use St Helier as your Standard Port rather than Dover

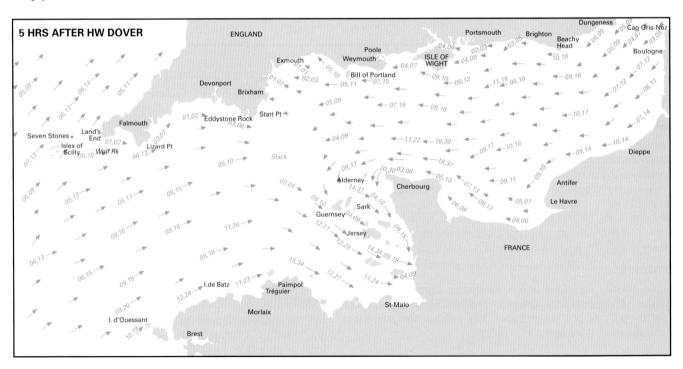

- Add at least 10% to published rates if navigating over Spring Tides and beware of unstable inshore eddies which may not be shown. The first turn of the tide will tend to be felt close inshore, where rates also tend to be stronger
- Try to keep up-tide of the rhumbline and guard against being set onto dangers
- In areas where reference marks are sparse it is easy to become unaware of drift. A useful clue can be provided by GPS cross track error
- Arrange your passage so as to be in strong tidal areas (off headlands, in narrow channels) when the stream is going your way and to be in weak tidal areas when the tide is against you
- The Rule of Twelfths for estimating the height of tide works better in the north of the area where the rise

Channel Islands Tidal Streams

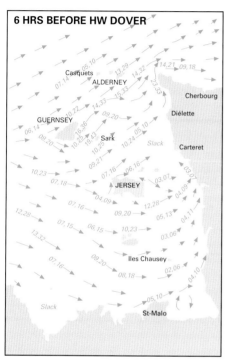

HW St Helier –0100

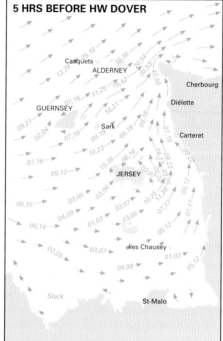

HW St Helier

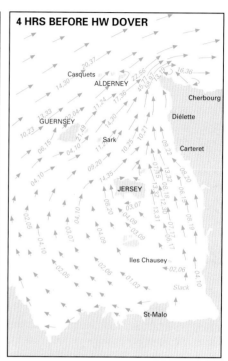

HW St Helier +0100

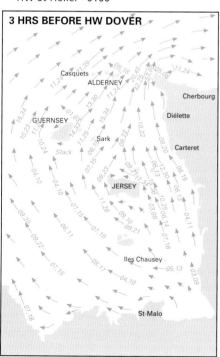

HW St Helier +0200

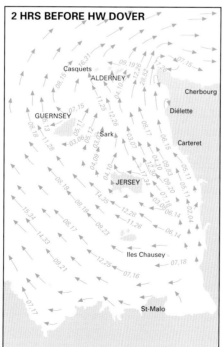

HW St Helier +0300

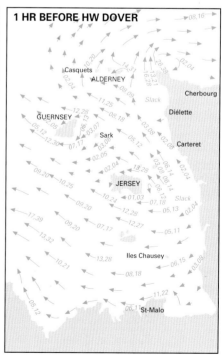

HW St Helier +0400

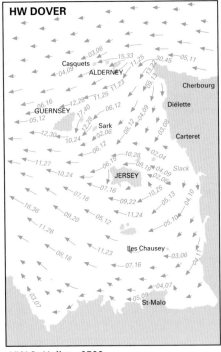

HW St Helier +0500

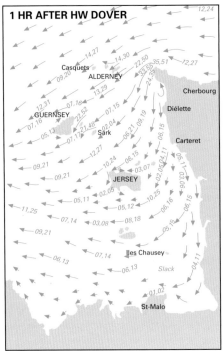

HW St Helier +0600

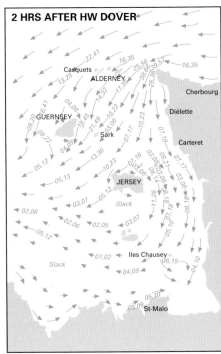

HW St Helier −0530

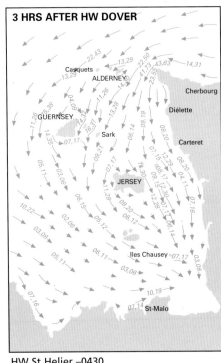

HW St Helier −0430

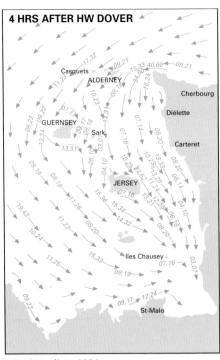

HW St Helier −0330

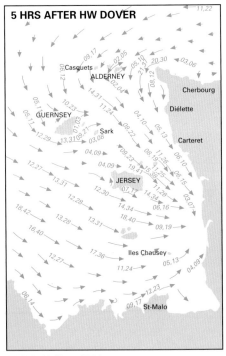

HW St Helier −0230

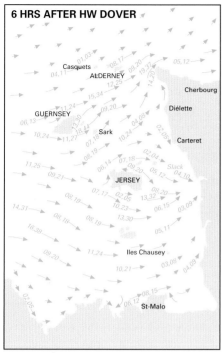

6 HRS AFTER HW DOVER

HW St Helier –0130

and fall total more or less six hours each. In the south, the rise is quicker than the fall, so apply with caution
- Bear in mind that in this area HW at springs occurs morning and evening with LW at noon. At neaps HW occurs at noon and midnight. Spring tides are therefore the best time for planning lunchtime stops in sheltered pools left by the retreating tide.

Planning a visit

A suitable boat

Any well-found yacht capable of making a safe Channel crossing and properly equipped for coastal cruising in these latitudes will meet the demands of Channel Island waters. Special consideration should be given to the auxiliary, which must be reliable and sufficiently powerful to make headway into a foul tide of up to 5 knots or more. With a lee shore never far away the ability to beat out into a fresh breeze with a short sea is essential. Keel type and draught will dictate cruise plans. A draught of more than 2m (6ft) will rule out some of

the best anchorages in the area and limit options particularly at neap tides, when there may be insufficient water. It is worth knowing before a visit if the yacht can be dried out on its keel if necessary. Multihulls, bilge keelers and yachts fitted with beaching legs come into their own as the majority of harbours and anchorages dry: Herm, Creux (Sark), St Aubin and Gorey (Jersey) and Les Minquiers and Les Ecrehous, to mention a few.

Ground tackle should be comprehensive, chain marked and a reliable electric/manual windlass fitted. Visitors unprepared for a large tidal range may find they are short of chain when anchored over high water – particularly in Sark anchorages where depths can be in excess of 17m (55ft) at spring tides (see *A local hazard* below).

Navigational equipment

The yacht should be equipped with VHF radio, GPS and a depth sounder but note that GPS should not be relied upon for pilotage among rocks. With the prevalence of advection and frontal fog in the autumn and winter, and radiation fog in anticyclonic conditions at any time, radar is a useful navigational aid. It can mean less time and tide lost while waiting for visibility to improve and at sea it provides a means of detecting navigational marks and traffic, particularly high-speed inter-island ferries.

Formalities and regulations

Jersey, along with Le Plateau des Minquiers and Les Ecréhous reefs, makes up the Bailiwick of Jersey, while the Bailiwick of Guernsey comprises Alderney, Herm and Sark, the latter being more or less self-governing and a law unto itself. Both Bailiwicks have separate parliaments known as The States and their own customs and immigration services.

Q Flag

This formality is no longer enforced, although some harbour authorities favour use of the Q flag as a means of identifying new arrivals. All vessels are required to complete a customs and immigration form at the port of entry.

Official ports of entry

Alderney: Braye
Guernsey, Herm and **Sark:** St Peter Port, St Sampson (for commercial vessels only) and Beaucette Marina
Jersey: St Helier and Gorey

Prevention of Rabies

The Channel Islands is a rabies-free area and all the islands have legislation that prohibits the landing of animals without a licence. An exception is made if the vessel is arriving from within the Bailiwicks of Guernsey or Jersey, the United Kingdom, the Republic of Ireland or the Isle of Man. A vessel arriving from outside these territories and with an animal on board should first obtain inward clearance from port control and will be directed to an isolated berth. The animal must be securely confined and will not be permitted to land. There are severe penalties for breaking the law.

Marinas and moorings

Marinas

Guernsey: Victoria Marina, QE2 Marina, Beaucette Marina, St Sampsons (locals only)
Jersey: St Helier Marina, Elizabeth Marina, La Collette Yacht Basin

Visitors' moorings

Alderney: Braye Harbour
Guernsey: St Peter Port
Herm: N and W of harbour (drying)
Sark: La Grève de la Ville, Havre Gosselin
Jersey: Gorey (drying)

Yacht clubs

Yacht clubs in the islands welcome visitors:
Alderney Alderney Sailing Club, Braye
☎ 01481 822758/822959/725500
Guernsey Royal Channel Islands Yacht Club, St Peter Port ☎ 01481 723154
Guernsey Yacht Club, St Peter Port
☎ 01481 725342 *Fax 711890*
Jersey Royal Channel Islands Yacht Club, St Aubin,
☎ (01534) 741023/745783 *Fax 490042*
St Helier Yacht Club, St Helier
☎ (01534) 732229/721307 *Fax 720849*

Search and rescue

There is no coastguard as such in the Channel Islands but Marine Search and Rescue operations are coordinated by the Rescue Centres of St Helier Harbour office in Jersey and St Peter Port harbour office in Guernsey, with communications undertaken by Jersey Radio and St Peter Port Radio. Both stations maintain a

Channel Islands Air Search aircraft on service over Les Roches Douvres   *CIAS*

24-hour watch on Ch 16 and Ch 70 on GMDSS. Alderney Radio coordinates its own operations with the backup of St Peter Port. There are 3 RNLI offshore lifeboats and several inshore lifeboats based in the islands.

Channel Islands Air Search

The Channel Islands Air Search charity was founded in 1980 and is funded by voluntary donations. Its main benefactor, the Lions Clubs of Guernsey and Jersey, enabled the acquisition of the PBN 2B Islander *Lions Pride*.

This dedicated search and rescue aircraft, based in Guernsey, is equipped with a heat seeking infrared camera, search radar, night-vision sight, air droppable life-raft (11 man), smoke markers, night strobe markers, marine VHF, VHF/EPIRB homer, loudhailer and searchlight.

CIAS receive some forty callouts a year by Channel Island, French and occasionally UK Rescue Centres.

A local hazard

The fouling of propellers and rudders on fishing pots, traps and nets is the most common cause of calls to rescue services in the Channel Islands. Although local regulations ban the laying of fishing gear in main channels, it is safer to assume that such obstacles may be found anywhere. A sharp lookout for markers should be maintained and always aim to pass downtide of them. It is recommended that a rope cutter be fitted to the propeller shaft and a snorkel, visor and diver's knife kept aboard.

Telecommunications

Mobile telephone service

The whole area is well served by Channel Islands and French networks, and apart from mid Channel there are very few areas where it will not be possible to receive a signal of sufficient strength to make and receive calls.

Mobile phone subscribers to UK and French networks will usually find that their provider has roaming agreements with local networks, but some are limited and it is worth checking before visiting the area. Unless you manually select a new network the handset will automatically connect to the strongest signal. This means that sailing around Jersey, for instance, you could be using a French network off the E coast and a Guernsey network around the NW corner and a Jersey network elsewhere.

Internet services

A service of interest to short-stay visitors is the internet services provided by local telecom companies. A wireless laptop can be used in a wireless internet zone (wi-fi) using broadband technology. All that is required is to buy a voucher, find a signal and log on. Public internet access is readily available, with several internet cafés in all the main islands.

Getting to and from the islands and passages between them

Getting to the islands

The Channel crossing

For the majority of yachtsmen, a visit to the Channel Islands will involve a Channel crossing. This should be achieved within a day but can nevertheless be a challenging hurdle.

Weather

As with any passage, finding a window of settled weather is the first consideration. Follow the trend during the run-up period to your departure and obtain the latest forecast before casting off. Once underway, monitor weather bulletins broadcast by UK coastguards, Cross Jobourg (French coastguards) and Jersey Radio. Should conditions call for a change of plan, there are fewer alternatives in the Channel Islands than on the South Coast and many a

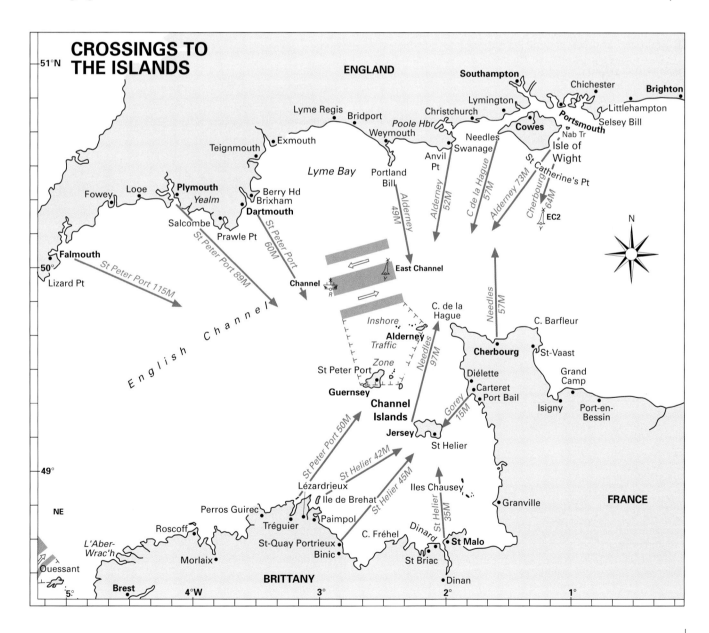

CROSSINGS TO THE ISLANDS

yachtsman has been glad of the shelter provided by the Cherbourg peninsula or the port itself with its ease of access. Barfleur and St Vaast-la-Hougue on the east side are good bolt-holes in westerly weather.

Fog anywhere in the Channel can be unnerving – more so if you are without radar. If this is forecast to affect your route it is better to stay put.

Tidal strategy

For most passages to the islands there is a deadline for arrival at a given point. When this is due to tidal considerations it is known as a 'tidal gate' and will dictate departure time. For instance, on a crossing from the Needles to Jersey via the Alderney Race, the tidal gate is the entry to the Alderney Race at HW Dover (HW St Helier +0500). With an average speed of 6 knots and a distance of 60 miles, departure from the Needles Fairway buoy will need to be 10 hours earlier (2 hours after the previous HW Dover).

With the ebb and flow running E–W in the Channel, the majority of crossings will be across the stream, setting the yacht east and west of track. Since most crossings to the islands can take less than 12 hours under sail, you will not receive equal amounts of ebb and flood. In practice, adjustment will be required to compensate for this imbalance and also the stronger streams on the French side (see diagram below).

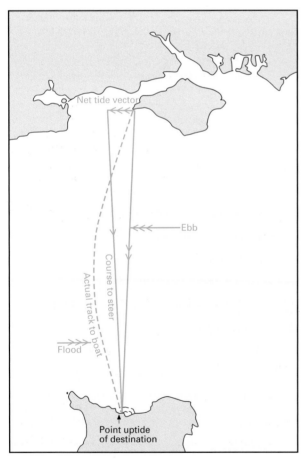

A tidal vector is drawn to calculate the degree of compensation required to offset an imbalance between east and west-going stream. On this cross-Channel passage the sum total of west-going stream exceeded that of the east-going stream, the difference being represented by the length of the tide arrow

Collision avoidance

Every day some 500 ships pass through the English Channel, making it one of the world's busiest shipping routes. With crossing traffic in conflict with the prevailing flow up and down the Channel there is a serious risk of near misses and collisions. When these do occur, small craft come off worst.

A Traffic Separation Scheme (TSS) operates north of the Casquets, which has the effect of concentrating shipping into a small area. Cross-Channel routes followed by yachts will avoid crossing a TSS, where special rules apply, but will pass close to entry and exit points where shipping will be more spread out and movements less predictable. In such areas the normal Regulations for Preventing Collisions at Sea apply and should be followed.

A sharp lookout must be maintained at all times and frequent bearings taken of conflicting vessels, some of which may be little short of a mile long and steaming at 30 knots. It is safer to assume that they are not going to alter course for a sailing vessel.

Too close for comfort

Crossing from the Solent area between Portsmouth and Poole

Departure points Nab Tower, St Catherine's Point, Needles Fairway buoy, Anvil Point

Crossings to Alderney and its Race, or perhaps to Cherbourg, are among the shortest. It is 52M from Anvil Point to The Race.

To Alderney (Braye)

The Alderney landfall from a northeasterly direction when the island is seen end-on can make it elusive. Since it is low-lying compared with the high land of the adjacent Cherbourg peninsula, it is also slower to lift above the horizon.

The approach to Braye Harbour should be carefully controlled to avoid being swept west into The Swinge with its dangerous overfalls or east into The Race. Arrival should coincide with slack water, which is about half tide up or down off Braye (HW St Helier –0215 or +0215).

To Cherbourg

Cherbourg, with its easy landfall and entrance at any time by day or night, makes a good stop over en route to the islands but, in the prevailing westerlies, the 15M haul onwards to The Race can be hard going. See *Alderney Race, Cherbourg to Braye.*

To Guernsey (St Peter Port) and Jersey (St Helier)

If the stream is fair, the logical route is to continue through The Race. This presents no hazard in fair weather when patches of overfalls may be barely noticeable; but if in doubt, avoid The Race Rocks SE of Alderney, the 16m bank off Cap de la Hague, Milieu 4M SSE of Alderney and Banc de la Schôle with only 2.4m at chart datum.

Aim to arrive at a waypoint midway between Cap de la Hague and Quénard Point (⊕1) just before HW Dover (HW St Helier +0500) when the stream is slack. Get it right and it can be a fast passage on the tidal escalator to St Peter Port or all the way to St Helier.

If outbound from Poole for St Peter Port, conditions may favour routeing W of the Casquets. This is described below in *Crossings from the West Country.* Guernsey will usually be approached from the N following a landfall NE of Platte Fougère Lighthouse. An alternative in poor visibility is to route via the Big Russel where there is more sea room and the possibility of diversions via Sark or Herm. Approach to St Peter Port will then be from the Lower Heads S cardinal buoy S of Jethou.

The most direct route to St Helier is via Banc Desormes W cardinal buoy off the NW Corner (⊕28), round Point Corbière and on to the S coast. If routeing via the E coast, approach between the Paternosters and Les Dirouilles. Directions for the NE Corner to St Helier are described under *Approaches to Gorey. From the west (St Helier)* and *From the north.*

Crossing from the west country between Weymouth and Plymouth

Departure Points Portland Bill, Berry Head, River Dart entrance, Prawle Pt, Plymouth Sound.

To Guernsey (St Peter Port)

At just 70 miles from the River Dart, Guernsey is the nearest and most popular arrival point in the islands. Prevailing westerlies and a more favourable slant on the tidal streams can make for a good passage.

If bound for St Peter Port, routeing via Les Hanois Lighthouse at the SW corner and St Martin's Point on the SE corner can be quicker than the N approach, providing the tides are worked intelligently. Care must be taken not to be set onto the W coast of Guernsey, a notorious lee shore. Keep at least 3M off. By contrast, the S coast is well marked and straightforward. Stay just outside the 50m contour and you will be about 1M off all the way along.

The inbound track from Weymouth will pass close to E Channel light buoy at the E end of the Casquets Traffic Separation Scheme. This may involve crossing the lanes, in which case a diversion E to keep clear should be made if it is not possible to comply with the Rules.

The passage close E of the Casquets is the wide Ortac Channel. Overfalls and eddies can be expected anywhere in this area, but providing passage through the channel is

Ortac with Alderney in the distance

made in fair weather and at slack water, HW Dover−0100 (HW St Helier+0400), it presents no hazard. Keep a distance off the lighthouse of at least 1 mile – more if the tidal stream is setting you onto it. With an average speed of 6 knots, departure from Weymouth will have to be some 8 hours earlier (5 hours before the previous HW Dover) in order to meet this tidal gate. This will also ensure a fair stream for the remaining 13M of the passage to Little Russel. Slower boats should consider departing earlier or routeing via an intermediate port if practicable.

To Alderney (Braye)

As with other crossings from the West Country, the prospect of navigating across or around the Casquets Traffic Separation Scheme will need to be considered.

Approaching the island from the NW it is important to guard against being set towards the Casquets and Burhou with its outlying reefs to the N. All will be left safely to the SW if Fort Albert (E of the harbour) is kept open E of the breakwater head on 115°. An alternative clearing line is Quénard Point lighthouse on a bearing of no less than 120°. At night stay in the W sector of Château L'Etoc light (Iso.WR.4s) until the leading lights (both Q) are aligned.

To avoid ending the passage in a tidal battle, aim to arrive well before HW Dover (HW St Helier +0500) when the main English Channel stream turns to run W with a vengeance.

Crossing from the south

North Brittany

Departure Points Tréguier, Lézardrieux, Île de Bréhat, St Quay Portrieux, St Malo

To Guernsey (St Peter Port)

At around 50M these passages are among the longest to the islands from the French coast. As they do not quite fit into one tide some compromise is required. Assuming you want to make the best use of the flood tide when the streams are generally setting ENE, it will be necessary to get underway on the last of the ebb, or earlier if you want to avoid a foul tide in the final approach to St Peter Port.

The initial W-going stream can set like a mill race at spring tides on this corner of the Brittany coast and care should be taken to avoid being set towards Les Roches Douvres and Plateau de Barnouic – an area to be avoided.

A landfall off the S Coast of Guernsey, with its steep cliffs, is among the easiest and the channel up to St Peter Port from St Martin's Point is broad and comparatively clear of dangers.

To Jersey (St Helier)

Inbound from the more southwesterly departure points gives a better slant on the streams. By working the tides it should be possible to make the Passage Rock buoy in St Helier W Passage at HW just before the ebb.

A passage from St Malo will route either E or W about the Plateau des Minquiers depending on wind and tide.

Westabout the Minquiers (40M)

Leave St Malo by the main channel (La Petite Porte) at half ebb (HW St Helier+0300). The turning points are SW Minquiers W cardinal buoy and NW Minquiers W cardinal buoy which will be reached at about LW. The rest of the passage to the Passage Rock N cardinal buoy in the St Helier Western Passage will be made on the first hours of the flood, arriving at about HW St Helier–0300.

Eastabout the Minquiers (36M)

Leave St Malo at HW St Helier–0300 (about 2½ hours before local HW) by La Grande Conchée Channel. Set a course for NE Minquiers E cardinal buoy, at which point alter course for the Demie de Pas light tower. Entry to St Helier will initially be by the South Passage then the Red and Green Passage. A slightly earlier departure from St Malo means that you may make it over St Helier marina sills, which close at half ebb.

Any approach to the island from the SE, particularly from Granville and Iles Chausey, will route close S of the dangers that extend some 8 miles out from the SE corner. On a spring ebb care should be taken to avoid being set N.

The Demie de Pas light tower tends to be inconspicuous, in which case initial approach can be made with the Power Station Chimney (95m) (conspic) on a bearing of 350° (see *Jersey. Electric Passage*).

Returning from the islands

It is easier to leave the Channel Islands for the UK South Coast than to arrive.

Before casting off, one of the main considerations, along with the weather and roueting across or round the Traffic Separation Scheme, will be the powerful streams on the south side of the Channel. Getting a good send-off is all a matter of timing.

Departure from St Peter Port, Guernsey should be timed to ensure a favourable tide for whichever route is chosen. A departure at HW St Helier–0230 or as soon as the marina sill can be cleared will take the first of the N-going stream out of Little Russel and then carry nearly 7 hours fair to the NE. This will mean passing through The Race at its greatest rate and an alternative plan should be made if strong winds from the N or NE are likely. In the Ortac Channel NW of Alderney beware of a strong set to the E towards reefs N of Ortac.

Departure for the N from St Helier is more complicated. A N-going eddy starts at La Corbière at about HW St Helier–0200 (HW Dover+0530), but to

catch it one must stem the tide from St Helier. There are then a good six hours of favourable tide to get up to and through the Alderney Race over 30 miles away – plenty of time at a reasonable speed – but unlike a departure time from St Peter Port there may not be time to carry the tide all the way to Cherbourg. Conditions may favour routeing E-about Jersey, leaving St Helier at HW–0300. At the NE corner, the N-going stream starts just before HW.

At Braye one is best poised for a Channel crossing, just 56M to the Needles, but keep a sharp lookout for shipping leaving the E-going lane of the Casquets Traffic Separation Scheme. The time of departure should be calculated to catch a fair stream through the Needles Channel if bound for the Solent or up to the Nab Tower if bound for Portsmouth.

Some inter-island passages

These passages cover some of the well-trodden tracks around the Channel Islands.

Charts

The charts listed are those editions on which the whole passage may be plotted. Additional large-scale charts will be required to cover departure and approach.

Distance

(M) is in nautical miles by the shortest navigable route.

Time

(h) is based on an average speed of 6 knots through the water. Since most passages will be made on a fair tidal stream, speeds made good will be higher, possibly into double figures at spring tides. Most inter-island passages fall within 30 miles so are achievable on one tidal cycle i.e. 6 hours.

Tides

Passages should be made wherever possible using all of the fair stream. If a part must be taken during a foul stream, dodge out of the worst if possible and use the engine to maintain progress. Punching a strong adverse stream can be a negative experience.

Best time to leave

For most passages there will be a 'gate' to be met and such deadlines dictate the time of departure.

Dangers en route

These include areas of overfalls, banks, shoals and drying rocks, which call for particular vigilance if not a diversion. Navigation and pilotage at LW when many potential dangers are visible is more straightforward than when they are covered.

Tracks and waypoints

Tracks shown on the sketch plans represent typical inter island passages rather than text book routes to be followed. Selected waypoints are those that may be useful for the passage. Navigators should plot any waypoint they intend to use to check that it serves their intended route.

Between Alderney and Guernsey

BRAYE TO ST PETER PORT VIA THE SWINGE

Charts
British Admiraly 3656
Imray C33A
Distance 24M
Time 4h

Tides

The main consideration is safe passage through The Swinge where slack water is around 3 hours after local HW (HW St Helier +0215). Arrival in the Little Russel should also be before the N-going stream starts at HW St Helier –0300 but with a fair stream there should be time in hand to achieve both objectives.

Best time to leave

This is local HW+0345 (HW St Helier+0300).

The top of Little Russel from the southeast. The flood stream is setting hard to the south

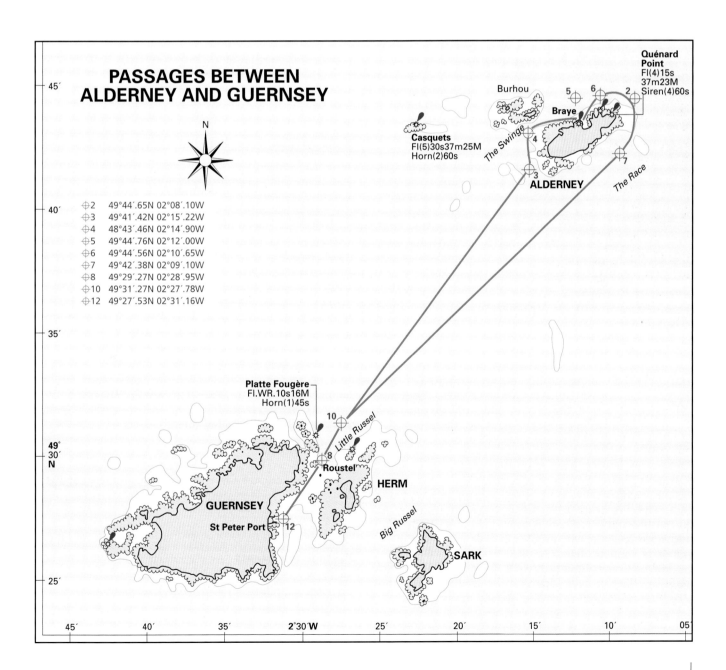

Dangers en route

Submerged end of Braye harbour breakwater – do not turn W until well clear. (See *Alderney. Clearing the submerged breakwater*). The Swinge can throw up dangerous overfalls in wind against tide conditions, when it is prudent to consider the alternate route via The Race. Pierre au Vraic (drying 1.2m) lurks 2 miles WSW of Les Etacs (Garden Rocks).

For clearing marks see *Alderney. Approaches to Braye from the S and SW via The Swinge.*

By night

It is inadvisable to use The Swinge due to lack of suitable lights.

Passage waypoints

⊕ 5, 4, 3, 10, 8, 12
For detailed pilotage information see *Alderney* and *Guernsey* below.

BRAYE TO ST PETER PORT VIA THE RACE

Charts
  BA 3653
  Imray C33A
Distance 25M
Time 4h

Tides

This roundabout route to St Peter Port may be necessary if conditions in The Swinge are unsuitable. Between Braye and Quénard Point at the E end of the island there are only 2 hours of E-going stream (from HW St Helier –0200 to HW St Helier). The Race does not start running to the SW until HW St Helier+0430 so a foul stream round the NE corner of the island must be punched for 2M before getting into the SW-going Race.

Best time to leave

Leave Braye at HW St Helier+0400 and make good speed while the current is comparatively weak.

Dangers en route

Drying rocks extending 0.3M off the N coast. Potentially heavy overfalls along the Brinchetais (Brimtides) Ledge particularly around Blanchard Rock 0.8M E of Quénard Point. Keep 0.5M off the N coast and 1.0M off Quénard Point before altering course SW for Guernsey.

By night

Depart on leading lights (A9 ⊕6) and turn E when Casquets light Fl(5)30s bears 262°(A1 ⊕2). If not visible, an alternative is to turn E when Quénard Point light Fl(4)15s bears 140°. Clear Quénard Point by at least 1.0M and hold Platte Fougère light Fl.W.R.10s N of Little Russel on a bearing of 230° while keeping in W sector of Tautenay light Q(3)6s.

Align Roustel (Q) and Brehon Tower Iso.4s on 198° (G3 ⊕10). This will intercept the leading lights (on 220°) for St Peter Port leaving Roustel to port.

Looking NNE over The Garden Rocks (Les Etacs) off Alderney's west end. It is just after HW springs and the stream is setting N at 6–8 knots

Passage waypoints

⊕ 6, 2, 7, 10, 8, 12
For detailed pilotage information see *Alderney* and *Guernsey* below.

ST PETER PORT TO BRAYE VIA THE SWINGE

Charts
  BA 3653
  Imray C33A
Distance 24M
Time 4h

Tides

In order to carry a favourable stream through to Braye must be taken before HW St Helier+0315 when it turns to run W.

Best time to leave

Bearing in mind your deadline for slack water in The Swinge, it would be prudent to get under way by just before HW St Helier–0230. At this time the N-going stream in the Little Russel is established.

Dangers en route

See *Alderney. The Swinge; Approaches to Alderney from SW via The Swinge Channel;* and also *Braye to St Peter Port via The Swinge* (above).

By night

It is inadvisable to use The Swinge due to lack of lights.

Passage waypoints

⊕ 12, 8, 10, 3, 4, 5
For detailed pilotage information see *Alderney* and *Guernsey* below.

ST PETER PORT TO BRAYE VIA THE RACE

Charts
  BA 3653
Distance 25M
Time 4h

Tides

The 6½ hour slot between HW St Helier–0230 and HW St Helier+0320 is the right time for this passage. The deadline for catching the last of the E-going stream up through The Race is HW St Helier+0400. After this there will be a brief period of slack before the SW-going stream takes over.

Best time to leave

Leave St Peter Port at HW St Helier–0200 when the N-going stream off Guernsey's E coast is established.

Dangers en route

See *Alderney. Alderney Race* (below) and also *Braye to St Peter Port via The Race* (above).

By night

Directions are as for Braye to St Peter Port via The Race, but in reverse order. When abeam Platte Fougère light take up a course to a suitably positioned waypoint S of the area of overfalls within the 30m contour S of Alderney. Keep outside until Quénard Point light, which will have been obscured for most of the passage, bears 310° or less, when course may be altered towards N to pass round Quénard Point, and onto transit A1.

Passage waypoints

⊕ 12, 8, 10, 7, 26
For detailed pilotage information see *Alderney* and *Guernsey* below.

Between Guernsey and Sark

ST PETER PORT TO LA GRÈVE DE LA VILLE ANCHORAGE VIA HERM, ROUTEING BY ALLIGANDE PASSAGE, PERCÉE PASSAGE AND BEC DU NEZ

Charts BA 808
Distance 7.5M
Time 1–2h

Tides

The best time to cross the Big Russel is over the half tide period when streams here and all round Sark are comparatively weak. At this time there will also be a least depth of about 4m in the Alligande Passage.

Best time to leave

HW St Helier–0300

Dangers en route

Most of this passage involves pilotage among rocks so visibility of at least 3.5M is required to sight marks. The marks in the Alligande and Percée Passages must be held accurately until Meulettes (drying 1.7m) are cleared (see plan page 72). On the E side of Sark the inshore channel between Bec du Nez and Pécheresse (drying 8.9m) has a least width of 200m (see *Sark. East Coast. Approaches from the N*).

By night

Pilotage round Sark is not possible after dark.

Passage waypoints

⊕ 12, 19, 20, 21
For detailed pilotage information see *Guernsey* and *Sark* below.

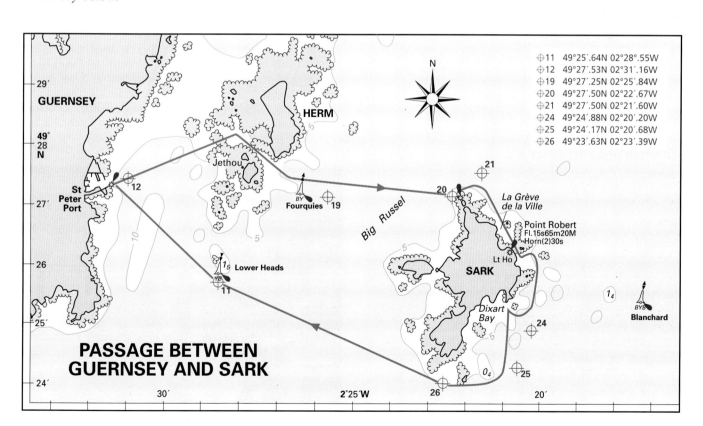

⊕11	49°25´.64N 02°28°.55W
⊕12	49°27´.53N 02°31´.16W
⊕19	49°27´.25N 02°25´.84W
⊕20	49°27´.50N 02°22´.67W
⊕21	49°27´.50N 02°21´.60W
⊕24	49°24´.88N 02°20´.20W
⊕25	49°24´.17N 02°20´.68W
⊕26	49°23´.63N 02°23´.39W

PASSAGE BETWEEN GUERNSEY AND SARK

DIXCART BAY ANCHORAGE TO ST PETER PORT SOUTHABOUT

Charts BA 808
Distance 9M
Time 2h

Tides

The decision whether to go N or S of Sark will depend on wind and tide. If leaving for St Peter Port at about half tide on a rising tide (HW St Helier–0300) and just before HW, it is better to go S of Sark. Initially the stream will be unhelpful but once L'Etac has been rounded and the course altered for the Lower Heads buoy, there will be a NE-going stream till about HW St Helier+0230.

Best time to leave

HW St Helier–0300.

Note An alternative return N of Sark will make use of the S-going eddy in Banquette Bay (W coast) which runs from just before HW St Helier to HW St Helier+0300, while the stream in the Big Russel is running NE. It may be practical to take the Percée Passage and Alligande Passage, or with caution one of the passages S of Jethou.

Best time to leave

HW+0200

Dangers en route

When rounding the S of Sark take care not to be swept towards Balmée which may be covered, Les Vingt Clos and dangers S of Sercul.

By night

If bad weather is forecast, leave before nightfall, as pilotage round the island is not possible after dark.

Passage waypoints

⊕ 24, 25, 26, 11, 12
For detailed pilotage information see *Sark* and *Guernsey* below.

Between Guernsey and Jersey

ST PETER PORT TO ST HELIER

Charts
  BA 2669
  Imray C33A
Distance 26M
Time 4h

Tides

Fair from HW St Helier+0420 at the earliest to just before HW St Helier. The best hours are from HW St Helier–0500 to HW St Helier–0030. For much of the passage the stream is square on the port beam, so expect to be set S of track. This is not a bad thing as you will want to pass clear of Point Corbière.

Dangers en route

To clear reefs off Point Corbière, known as the Jailers, keep a distance of at least 1 mile off the lighthouse. In wind against tide conditions, more particularly around HW springs, overfalls can extend up to 2M off the Point.

By night

Soon after passing Lower Heads S cardinal buoy it should be possible to identify Grosnez Point light Fl(2) and Corbière Point light Iso.10s on Jersey. Keep in the W sector of both. Use ⊕37 to clear dangers W of Point Corbière and approach St Helier by the Northwest Passage (J2) or Western Passage (J6) ⊕36.

Passage waypoints

⊕ 12, 11, 37
For detailed pilotage information see *Guernsey* and *Jersey* below.

ST HELIER TO ST PETER PORT

Charts
  BA 2669
  Imray C33A
Distance 27M
Time 4h

Tides

Fair from HW St Helier–0100 to HW St Helier+0320.

  Inshore streams turn to the N on the W coast of Jersey at HW St Helier–0300 but only turn fair to the W along the S coast of the island at HW–0100. The later the departure after HW the greater the likelihood of overfalls off La Corbière. A compromise is to leave at HW St Helier–0100 which should carry a fair stream between the islands and, if good speed is maintained, the last of the N-going up the Little Russel.

Best time to leave

HW St Helier –0100

Dangers en route

Lobster pot markers off Point Corbière and into St Ouen's Bay.

By night

Leave on Red and Green Passage (J11) then take up W Passage (J6). Pass midway between Noirmont Point light Fl(4)12s and Les Fours N cardinal buoy. Take up a westerly heading into the W sector of La Corbière light Iso. Keep at least 1.0M off as you round Point Corbière. ⊕37 is aligned with the turning point which is the FR on

Victoria Marina, St Peter Port   *Visit Guernsey*

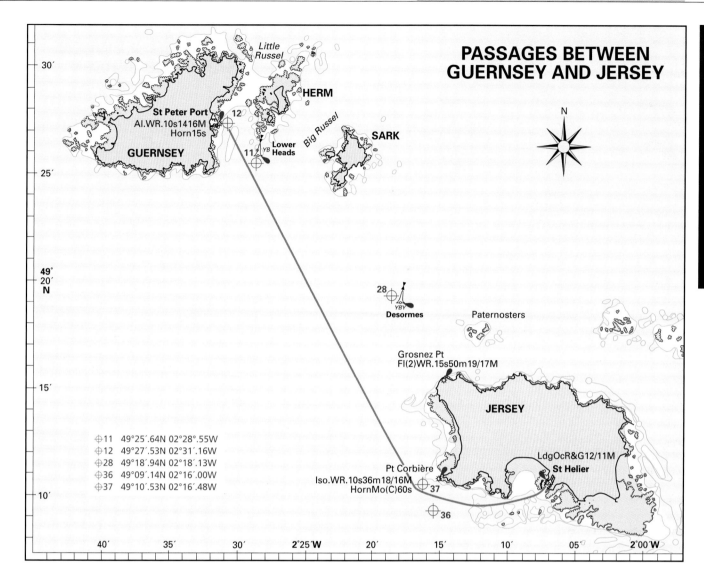

PASSAGES BETWEEN
GUERNSEY AND JERSEY

⊕11   49°25′.64N 02°28′.55W
⊕12   49°27′.53N 02°31′.16W
⊕28   49°18′.94N 02°18′.13W
⊕36   49°09′.14N 02°16′.00W
⊕37   49°10′.53N 02°16′.48W

the shore on with La Corbière light. Set course for Lower Heads S cardinal buoy (⊕11) and then directly to Castle Cornet breakwater light Al.WR.

Passage waypoints
⊕ 37, 11, 12
For detailed pilotage information see *Guernsey* and *Jersey* below.

Between Sark and Jersey

DIXCART BAY ANCHORAGE TO GOREY
Charts
BA 808, 2669
Imray C33A
Distance 20M
Time 3h

Tides
The most favourable period is from HW St Helier–0500 to HW St Helier, a total of 5 hours. The strongest stream is close inshore off the NE corner of Jersey, up to 6 knots at springs, a tidal 'gate' to be met before the turn of the tide at just before HW.

Best time to leave
HW St Helier–0500.

Dangers en route
With the stream on the port beam for most of the passage, take care not to be set S onto the Paternosters Reef.

By night
Departure should be made before darkness. The route from Banc Desormes W cardinal buoy ⊕28 along the N coast of Jersey to Gorey is not easy by night, due to the Paternosters reef and few lights.

Approach in the W sector of Sorel Point light LFl.7.5s and keep no less than 1.0M off the coast until established on Gorey leading lights.

Conditions may favour a more direct route N of the Paternosters with ⊕29 as shown.

Passage waypoints
⊕ 25, 29, 30, 31, 32
For detailed pilotage information see *Sark* and *Jersey* below.

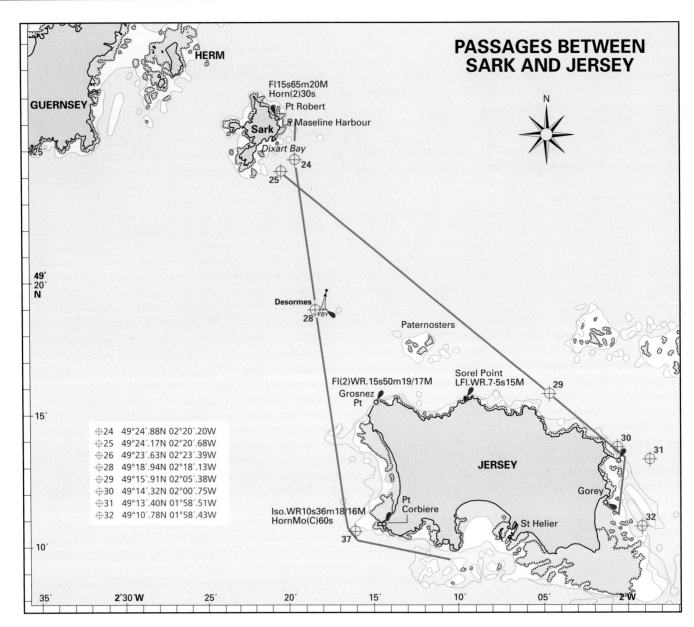

PASSAGES BETWEEN SARK AND JERSEY

(map labels)

HERM

GUERNSEY

Fl15s65m20M
Horn(2)30s
Pt Robert
La Maseline Harbour
Sark
Dixart Bay
⊕24
25

N

49° 20' N

Desormes
28 YBY

Paternosters

Fl(2)WR.15s50m19/17M
Grosnez Pt

Sorel Point
LFl.WR.7·5s15M
⊕29

15'

⊕24 49°24'.88N 02°20'.20W
⊕25 49°24'.17N 02°20'.68W
⊕26 49°23'.63N 02°23'.39W
⊕28 49°18'.94N 02°18'.13W
⊕29 49°15'.91N 02°05'.38W
⊕30 49°14'.32N 02°00'.75W
⊕31 49°13'.40N 01°58'.51W
⊕32 49°10'.78N 01°58'.43W

JERSEY

⊕30
⊕31
Gorey
⊕32

Iso.WR10s36m18/16M
HornMo(C)60s
37

Pt Corbiere
St Helier

10'

35' 2°30'W 25' 20' 15' 10' 05' 2°W

ST HELIER TO LA MASELINE HARBOUR

Charts
BA 2669
Imray C33A
Distance 21M
Time 3h

Tides

The most favourable period is from just before HW St Helier to St Helier HW+0320, after which the first of the flood tide swoops in from the Alderney Race with increasing strength. Either keep the speed up or leave earlier.

Best time to leave

HW St Helier–0100

Dangers en route

See *St Helier to St Peter Port.*

By night

Approach to La Maseline Harbour is not possible after dark.

Castle Cornet lighthouse, St Peter Port

Passage waypoints

⊕ 37, 28, 24
For detailed pilotage information see *Jersey* and *Sark* below.

Alderney

Local Information

STD code: 01481

TRAVEL

Air
Direct flights from Southampton, Bournemouth, Brighton and inter-Island
Aurigny Air Services ☎ 822886
Blue Islands ☎ 824567

Sea
Connections with Diélette and St Peter Port
Manche Iles Express ☎ 822881

Charter boats
Lady Maris ☎ 823666
Voyager ☎ 823532

PORTS OF ENTRY
The official Ports of Entry into the Bailiwick of Guernsey are Braye in Alderney and Beaucette Marina, St Sampson (for commercial vessels only) and St Peter Port in Guernsey. At St Peter Port, all visiting yachts must clear in at the main harbour irrespective of which marina they moor in.

CHARTS
British Admiralty (WGS 84)
2845 Alderney Harbour (Braye)
60 Alderney and the Casquets
3653 Guernsey to Alderney and adjacent coast of France
2669 Channel Islands and adjacent coast of France
Leisure Folio 5604
7 Alderney
8 Alderney Harbour
11(c) Casquets

Imray C charts
C33A Channel Islands plan: Alderney Harbour
Imray 2500 Chart pack

Stanfords Allweather
7 Central Channel
16 The Channel Islands
26 Chart Pack – Channel Island Harbours (Alderney and The Swinge)

French SHOM
6934 Aurigny et Les Casquets
7158 Du Cap de Carteret au Cap de la Hague-Raz Blanchard

RADIO FACILITIES
Alderney Radio
Location Harbourmaster's office
☎ 822620
Fax 823699
www.alderney.net
Hours of operation
October–April Mon–Fri 0800–1700. May 0800–1800
June–September 0800–2000. 7 days a week

Outside these hours call Jersey Radio, St Peter Port Radio or Crossma (French coastguard) who can activate Alderney Radio within minutes in an emergency.

VHF
Call *Alderney Radio* on VHF Ch 16, 74. The harbour launch, operated by the harbour officials, also listens on Ch 74, call *Harbour Launch*

NAVIGATIONAL AIDS
Radiobeacon (Aeronautical NDB)
Ident: ALD Position: 49°42′.6N 02°11′.9W. Freq 383kHz. Range 50M

Radar VTS and RDF service available on request

USEFUL TELEPHONE NUMBERS
Harbourmaster, Customs, Coastguard, Lifeboat ☎ 822620
Alderney Tourist Information Centre ☎ 822811
Alderney Sailing Club ☎ 822758/822959
Doctor: Eagle Medical Practice ☎ 822494

SUPPLIES AND SERVICES

Mainbrayce Chandlers in Little Crabby Harbour provide water, diesel (duty free), bottled gas, spares and mechanical assistance. A tide gauge at the entrance indicates depth of water alongside. Access to yachts is approximately 2 hours either side of local HW. Mainbrayce is open 0830–1800 7 days a week in the summer.
☎ 822772 *Fax* 823 683 *Mobile* 07781 415420
Email mainbrayce.alderney@virgin.net VHF Ch 80.

Water taxi: call Mainbrayce Taxi on VHF Ch 37 (M) or the chandlery on Ch 80. Hours of operation are the same as the chandlery but can extend well into the evening during the season. The fare is £2 for delivery to the shore and £1 for return to the yacht (2006).

Alderney Sailing Club next to the harbourmaster's office welcomes visiting yachtsmen.

Restaurants, bars and shopping: there is a good selection in harbour area.
The First and Last Restaurant ☎ 823162

Alderney Duty Free Consortium on the harbour quay (☎ 823414 Mobile 07781 112309) goods will be delivered to your boat. Le Riches Supermarket, Braye Street; is one of several duty free outlets in the island. Goods will be delivered to your boat on departure – but don't forget to supply your buoy number.

Car and bike hire: Braye Hire, Braye Street ☎ 823352
Top gear ☎ 822000.

Bike hire Top Gear ☎ 822000

Alderney Fuel Services (Total Garage) ☎ 823352

Taxis
A.B.C Taxis ☎ 823760, Island Taxis ☎ 823823,
J S Taxis ☎ 07781 100830

Alderney from the east

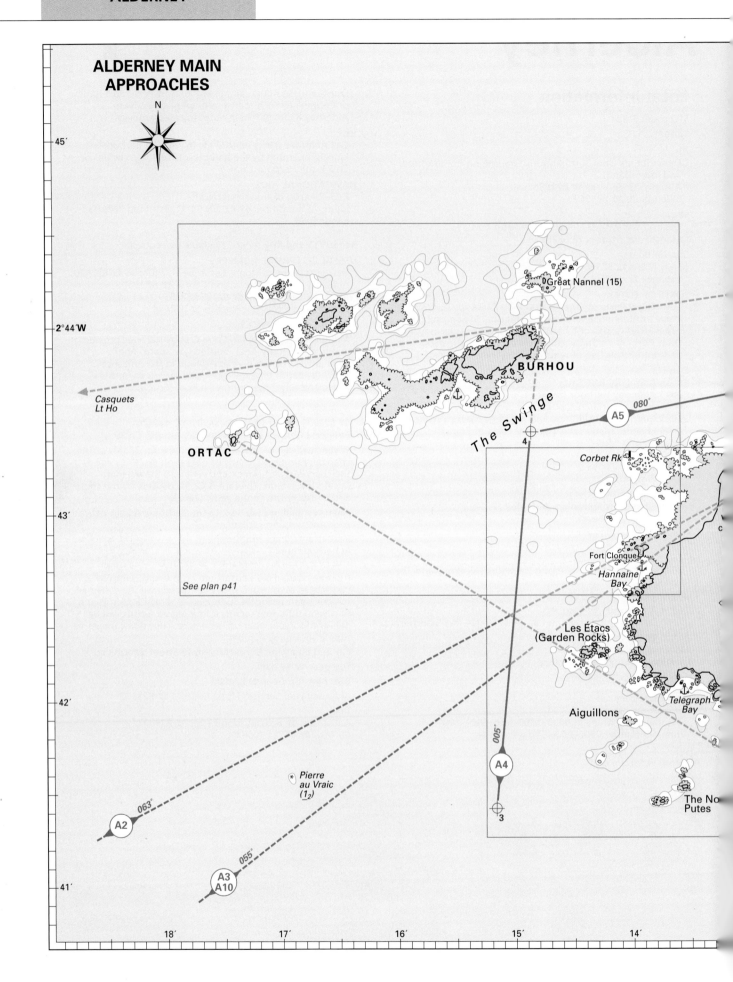

ALDERNEY MAIN
APPROACHES

N

45´

2°44´W

Great Nannel (15)

BURHOU

Casquets
Lt Ho

The Swinge

A5   080°

ORTAC

Corbet Rk

43´

See plan p41

Fort Clonque

Hannaine
Bay

Les Étacs
(Garden Rocks)

42´

Telegraph
Bay

Aiguillons

005°

A4

Pierre
au Vraic
(1₂)

The No
Putes

063°

A2

3

055°

A3
A10

41´

18´   17´   16´   15´   14´

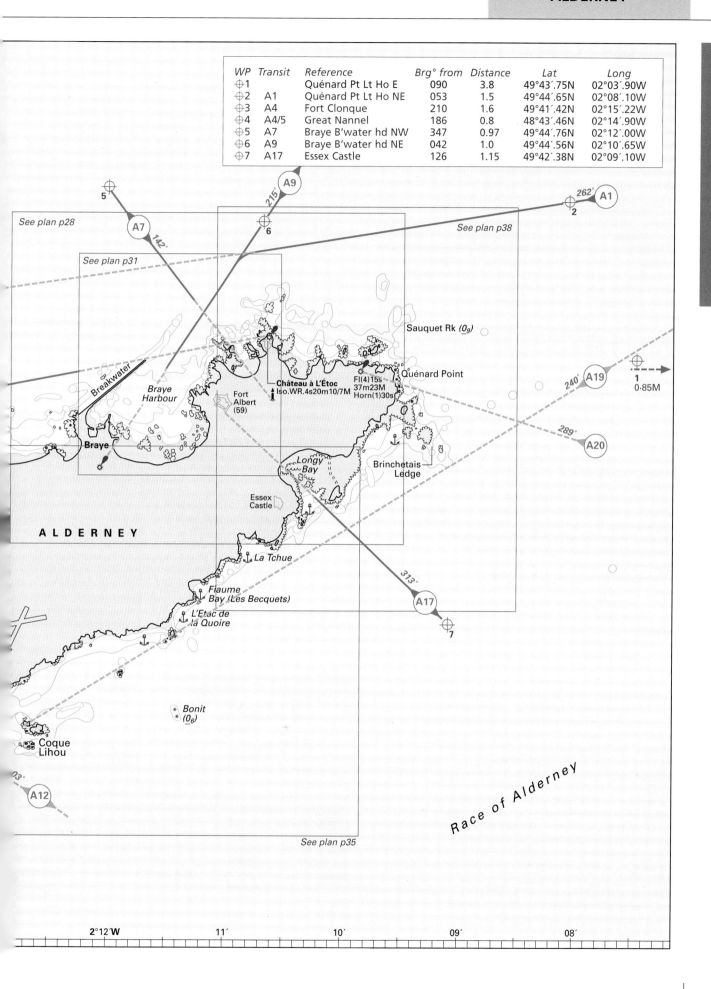

WP	Transit	Reference	Brg° from	Distance	Lat	Long
⊕1		Quénard Pt Lt Ho E	090	3.8	49°43′.75N	02°03′.90W
⊕2	A1	Quénard Pt Lt Ho NE	053	1.5	49°44′.65N	02°08′.10W
⊕3	A4	Fort Clonque	210	1.6	49°41′.42N	02°15′.22W
⊕4	A4/5	Great Nannel	186	0.8	48°43′.46N	02°14′.90W
⊕5	A7	Braye B'water hd NW	347	0.97	49°44′.76N	02°12′.00W
⊕6	A9	Braye B'water hd NE	042	1.0	49°44′.56N	02°10′.65W
⊕7	A17	Essex Castle	126	1.15	49°42′.38N	02°09′.10W

See plan p28

See plan p31

See plan p38

Sauquet Rk (0₉)

Breakwater

Braye
Harbour

Fort
Albert
(59)

Château à L'Étoc
Iso.WR.4s20m10/7M

Fl(4)15s
37m23M
Horn(1)30s

Quénard Point

Braye

Longy
Bay

Brinchetais
Ledge

A19
240°

1
0·85M

A20
289°

Essex
Castle

ALDERNEY

La Tchue

313°

A17

7

Fiaume
Bay (Les Becquets)

L'Etac de
la Quoire

Bonit
(0₆)

Coque
Lihou

A12

Race of Alderney

See plan p35

2°12′W   11′   10′   09′   08′

Introduction

For many, the first glimpse of this small northern outrider of the Channel islands will be seen towards the end of a crossing from the UK south coast. The trail of shipping lies behind and as the island comes into view, concentration is very much focused on tidal streams that are amongst the fiercest in Europe. The area between the Casquets and Alderney Race has something of a reputation as a ship's graveyard and should be approached with respect and caution.

Once safely moored in Braye Harbour, visitors will discover a peaceful, unpretentious island with a friendly and relaxed atmosphere. Although only 8M from the Normandy coast, the feel is more English than French – the legacy of 160 years of occupancy by English garrison troops and a total evacuation during the last war.

To the Romans, Alderney was Vecta Riduna and its natives Ridunians. They established a station at Longis (Longy) Bay, which became the island's first port until it silted up in the Middle Ages.

The era of privateering brought wealth to the island and led to the building of the Old Jetty at Braye in 1736.

The Great Admiralty Breakwater was constructed in response to the threat from France in the 19th century. Like St Catherine Bay in Jersey, it was intended to enclose a large harbour to shelter the British Fleet. The plan was abandoned but the breakwater was completed to a length of 4,800 feet in 1864. By 1900, Atlantic rollers had undermined most of it and the outer 600m (2,000ft) was abandoned. Maintenance and reinforcement of the remaining 900m (3,000ft) has been a constant and expensive battle against the elements ever since. The cost is covered by the States of Guernsey as the Bailiwick's contribution to Britain's defence of the islands.

Alderney is famous for its seabirds, especially the gannet. About 5,000 pairs nest on the Channel Islands' two gannetries, Ortac and Les Etacs (Garden Rocks) both W of Alderney.

Ashore

With over forty miles of walks and paths the best way to discover Alderney is on foot or by bike.

The Alderney Visitor and Wildlife Information Centre (☎ 823737) in Victoria Street, St Anne, provides advice and leaflets on recommended walks and bird watching tours. There are several historical sites worth visiting including the Victorian forts and more recent German fortifications and bunkers.

The less energetic can hire a car or use the seasonal bus service that calls at the harbour. Alderney has the only working railway in the Channel Islands. This runs at weekends in Summer between Braye harbour station and the northeast coast. From the station at Mannez you can take a short walk to visit Quénard Point lighthouse.

Beaches

The most accessible from the harbour are Braye bay and further east Saye (pronounced 'soy'), Arch and Corblets. On the south coast Longy Bay is reputed to be the best in the island.

Tidal information

Braye 49°43′.60N 2°11′.70W

MHWS	MHWN	MLWN	MLWS	MTL
6.3m	4.7m	2.6m	0.8m	3.6m

Tidal Differences based on HW Braye

Dover	–0400
St Helier, Jersey	–0045
Cherbourg	+0052
Carteret	–0036
Diélette	–0030
St Peter Port, Guernsey	–0040

Tidal streams

The Admiralty *Tidal Stream Atlas* for the Channel Islands and adjacent coasts of France (NP 264) includes large-scale plans of Alderney and the Casquets. Additional information on inshore directions and rates may also be found in the tidal section of the *Appendix*.

Inshore eddies

Like a boulder in the rapids, Alderney lies in the main NE–SW English Channel stream and the associated stream that scurries up and down the Normandy coast. Directions and rates are modified round the coast, particularly in the tide shadow at either end. There are numerous and complex eddies which may be used to advantage. Some will not be indicated in the *Tidal Atlas* and in the absence of local knowledge, the navigator should be on the lookout for changes in set and act accordingly.

Main eddies around Alderney

Northeast corner Here the NE stream turns to follow the coast W towards The Swinge from just after HW St Helier to HW St Helier–0220 attaining over 3 knots.

South Coast Along the S coast from off Houmet Herbé Fort on the NE corner to Coupé Rock on the SW corner, there is a narrow eddy close inshore. The stream sets E and NE for 9 hours out of 12, only running W from about HW St Helier+0300 to HW St Helier+0530.

TIDAL RACES AND OVERFALLS

Caution

Where the streams are accelerated through gaps, tidal races occur. Passing over shoals, ledges or uneven seabed, overfalls will form in all but calm weather. The main tidal races off Alderney are The Alderney Race to the east and The Swinge to the northwest. See below.

St Anne, with an adequate selection of shops, pubs and restaurants, is a twenty-minute walk up from the harbour
Alderney Tourism

Alderney Race

This 8-mile gap between Cap de La Hague on the Normandy coast and the E end of Alderney is the commonly used gateway to and from the Channel Islands. With spring rates in the order of 10–12 knots and dangerous overfalls, yachtsmen justifiably approach The Race with some trepidation. Even in the lightest conditions skippers would be wise to re-check stowage, hatches and harnesses well before reaching The Race. The secret lies in timing and avoiding areas of overfalls.

OVERFALLS

West side When overfalls are active and at night, the Brinchetais (pronounced Brimtides) Ledge should be given a clearance of at least 1M. The area around Race Rock (5.5m) and Inner Race Rock (5.5m) and Blanchard Rock (3.7m) SE of Quénard Point should be treated with caution and avoided in wind against tide conditions.

Middle There is a clear fairway 2.5m wide undisturbed by rocks and shoals between Race Rocks and the 16m bank with heavy overfalls which lie 4M WSW from Cap de la Hague; this passage should be used whenever possible.

East side To the E of the 16m bank referred to above is another 17m bank which does not break so heavily but should be avoided in wind over tide conditions. Between the 17m bank and La Foraine beacon off Cap de la Hague is a 1.5M passage which, although situated in the fiercest streams, may be used if rounding the Cap to or from Cherbourg in suitable conditions (see BA Chart 60).

South of Alderney While clear of the fierce streams of The Race there are three banks where overfalls may occur. From N to S these are:

South Banks (11m) 1M SSE of Alderney
Milieu (14m) 4M SSE of Alderney
Banc de la Schôle (2.4m) 8M S of Alderney. This bank is constantly shifting and depths may be less than charted. There is now a wreck 1M N of the bank with 3.2m over it and marked by a N cardinal buoy. See diagrams of overfalls in *Alderney Race* and *The Swinge*.

Tidal strategy

Southbound Aim to be at least 2M NW of Cap de la Hague at HW Dover–0040 (HW St Helier+0410). ⊕1 (see plan on pages 22-3) is a recommended safe-water waypoint 3.8M due E of Quénard Point lighthouse. This will ensure that your passage through The Race is made at dead slack, following which the stream will turn in your favour. The initial push in a SW direction will gradually swing to a southerly direction and strengthen. You could carry a fair stream all the way to St Helier.

Northbound Departing from St Helier or St Peter Port, there is always the risk of running out of fair stream just short of The Race. The deadline is about HW St Helier+0430 or earlier if proceeding to Cherbourg. It may be better to leave early and maintain the best possible speed.

Cherbourg to Braye The main concern is to avoid rough conditions off Cap de la Hague and make a smooth passage across the top of The Race without getting sucked into it. The answer is to cross at about HW St Helier+0400. Keep a good 2M off the Cap and aim to stay N of the rhumbline.

The Swinge

This channel lies between the NW of Alderney and the islets between the Nannels and Ortac to the N. It is the quickest passage between Alderney and Guernsey.

OVERFALLS

Caution

BA chart 60 warns, 'Dangerous overfalls form in the main Swinge Channel. Their position varying with the tidal stream.' They cover a smaller area than those in the Race but are less easy to avoid. Seas can be short and steep when wind and tide are opposed. As with the Race, timing is of the essence and in general the channel should be taken near slack water at neap tides. The calmest area is often on the S side near Corbet (pronounced Kerby) Rock (0.5m) (see *Approaches to Braye from the S and SW* on page 29).

Tidal strategy

Northeast bound There is a brief window of slack water in The Swinge at HW St Helier–0210 following which the NE-going stream sets in until HW St Helier+0300. Slack water returns at HW St Helier +0200. There is also a brief period of slack at HW St Helier+0515 (local LW).

Southwest bound The SW-going stream starts inshore just after HW St Helier+0300 and ends at about HW St Helier–0300 (local HW–0345).

Ortac

AREAS OF OVERFALLS ≋ **ALDERNEY RACE AND THE SWINGE**

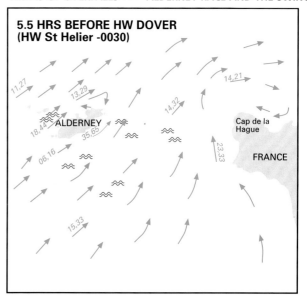

5.5 HRS BEFORE HW DOVER
(HW St Helier -0030)

AREAS OF OVERFALLS ≈ **ALDERNEY RACE AND THE SWINGE**

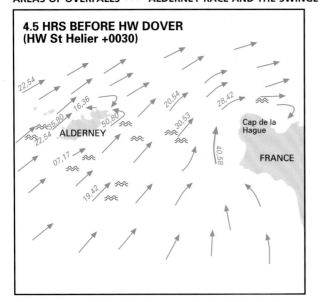

4.5 HRS BEFORE HW DOVER
(HW St Helier +0030)

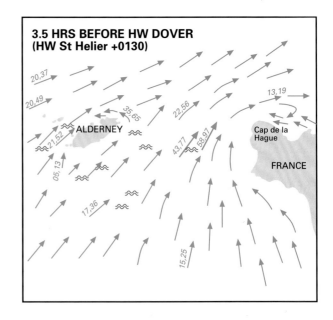

3.5 HRS BEFORE HW DOVER
(HW St Helier +0130)

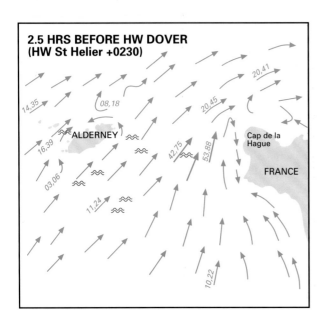

2.5 HRS BEFORE HW DOVER
(HW St Helier +0230)

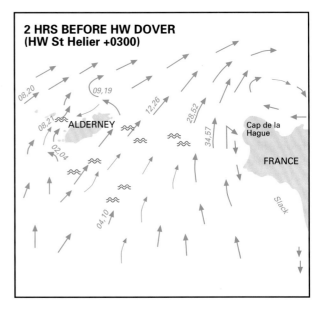

2 HRS BEFORE HW DOVER
(HW St Helier +0300)

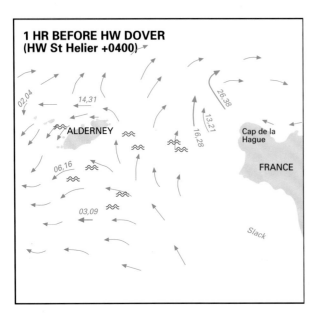

1 HR BEFORE HW DOVER
(HW St Helier +0400)

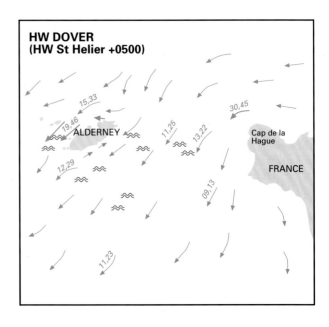

HW DOVER
(HW St Helier +0500)

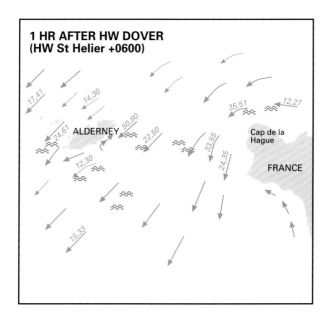

1 HR AFTER HW DOVER
(HW St Helier +0600)

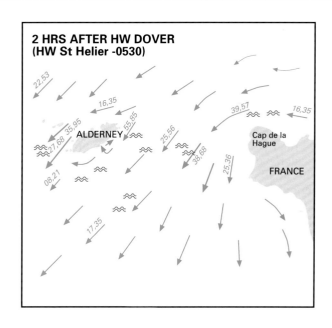

2 HRS AFTER HW DOVER
(HW St Helier -0530)

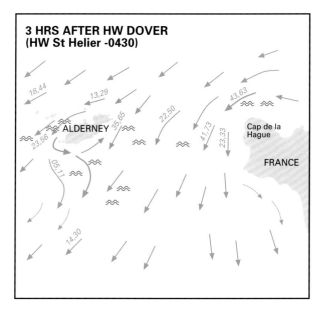

3 HRS AFTER HW DOVER
(HW St Helier -0430)

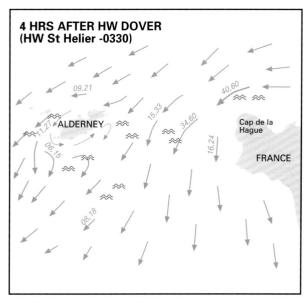

4 HRS AFTER HW DOVER
(HW St Helier -0330)

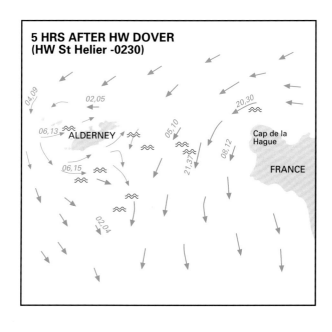

5 HRS AFTER HW DOVER
(HW St Helier -0230)

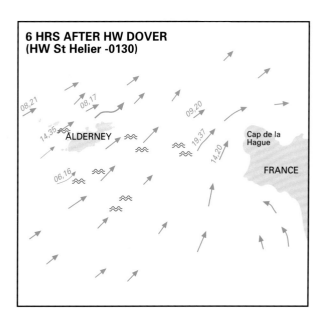

6 HRS AFTER HW DOVER
(HW St Helier -0130)

Approaches to Alderney

All directions given here are focused on Braye Harbour. Approaches are straightforward providing key marks are identified and the yacht's position confirmed as early as possible. Compensation can then be made for any cross-set which can be powerful. Strategically it is best to arrive at slack water, but if late and being carried SW down the Race, it may be necessary to give up the fight, particularly at spring tides, and change plans.

The final stage of an approach to Braye from any direction, apart from NE, involves clearing the hazardous remains of the submerged breakwater. For directions see *Entry to Braye Harbour: clearing the submerged breakwater*, page 30.

FROM THE EAST OR NORTHEAST
(See plan page 23)

A1 Until the breakwater and leading marks are identified it should only be necessary to keep 0.5M offshore. The transit for this, which is aligned with ⊕2, is as shown on the photo.

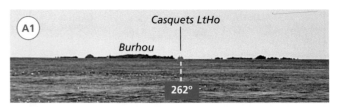

A1 262° (⊕2) Casquets LtHo open to N of Burhou will clear the Grois Rocks (drying 5.5m) to N of the island

By night

Keep Casquets (Fl(5)30s37m24M) bearing no more than 260° until leading lights are aligned.

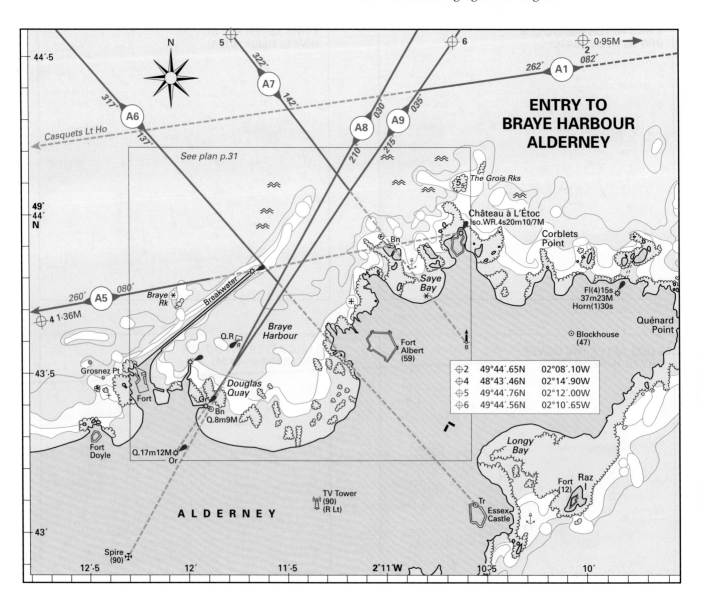

ENTRY TO
BRAYE HARBOUR
ALDERNEY

⊕2	49°44´.65N	02°08´.10W
⊕4	48°43´.46N	02°14´.90W
⊕5	49°44´.76N	02°12´.00W
⊕6	49°44´.56N	02°10´.65W

Features on the northeast coast of Alderney

FROM THE NORTHWEST

(See plan page 28)

The aim is to avoid being set SW towards Casquets and Burhou with its surrounding reefs

Approach with Quénard Point lighthouse Fl(4)15s 37m23M Horn(1)30s bearing no less than 120°. This is a powerful light that flashes by day and night.

A useful transit is:

115° Fort Albert (E of the harbour) kept open E of the breakwater head

There are marks to clear the outer end of the submerged breakwater by day. See *Clearing the submerged breakwater* below.

When the harbour opens up, turn onto Transit A8 or A9 ⊕6 to enter as described under *Braye Harbour. Entry Marks.*

By night

Stay in the W sector of Château à L'Etoc light (Iso.WR.4s20m10/7M) until leading lights are aligned on A9 ⊕6. (See *Braye Harbour. Entry.*)

FROM THE SOUTH AND SOUTHWEST VIA THE SWINGE

(Plan page 22)

The SW approach to The Swinge would be straightforward were it not for the Pierre au Vraic (49°41'.60N 02°16'.92W) (drying 1.2m) 2M WSW of Les Etacs (Garden Rocks). The key to clearance is the use of transits using Fort Clonque (20m) on the island's W end.

Clearing North of Pierre au Vraic

A2 063° A white pyramid S of Roque Tourgis Fort to the N of Fort Clonque

Clearing South of Pierre au Vraic

A3 055°. The same pyramid to S of Fort Clonque

Note This transit is also used for approach to Hannaine Bay (**A10**) (see *Round the island westabout*).

Entry to The Swinge is made on a northerly course using transit:

A4 005° ⊕3, 4 Great Nannel open E of Burhou Isand

This will leave Les Etacs (Garden Rocks) with their colony of gannets about 0.5M to the E and lead well into The Swinge. There are offlying reefs on this corner and all the way up to Braye Harbour breakwater. Corbet Rock (0.5m) (its beacon was destroyed in 1993) lying 0.5M from the shore, is the main consideration in The Swinge. It reduces its width to 0.5M between Burhou and Corbet.

Continue N until:

A5 080° N side of Château à L'Etoc in line with N end of breakwater. Follow this transit up to the breakwater head giving due clearance to Braye Rock and The Follets (dry 4.3m)

VIA ALDERNEY RACE

(See page 25 and plans pages, 23, 38)

Yachts from Jersey and ports on its adjacent coasts will usually approach Braye via the Race. This offers more sea room and fewer navigational obstacles but, as with the Swinge, it is a question of weather and timing the tide.

The passage northbound through the Race is covered under Alderney Race above. The pilotage round the E end of the island and into Braye is covered under *Round the island westabout: Longy Bay to Braye*, page 40.

Entry to Braye Harbour: clearing the submerged breakwater (by day only)

(See plan page 28)

Pieces of the old wall lying on their side on top of the original foundation are a hazard for vessels approaching the harbour from between SW and N. The least charted depth is 1.2m but there is a crossing over a relatively flat area with a minimum of 2.3m 50m (160ft) off the breakwater head (BA chart 2845). The harbour may be entered over this 2.3m section of the submerged breakwater with caution not less than 3 hours either side of local LW (LW St Helier–0430) when there is no ground swell. The transit is as shown below.

A6 137° Turret (known as 'Pepper Pot') on Essex Castle, over gap in slope below Fort Albert. A bush has recently grown beside the turret, as shown on the inset

Outside this period, in less than ideal conditions or if in any doubt, it is safer to pass well N of the submerged breakwater using Transit **A7** ⊕5:

A7 142° ⊕5 *The beacon on the foreshore (the 'Ball') in line with beacon with triangle 0.25M E of Fort Albert*

Note *Both these marks are inconspicuous, particularly when viewed into the sun*

Braye Harbour

49°43′.83N 02°11′.45W (0.15M E of breakwater head)

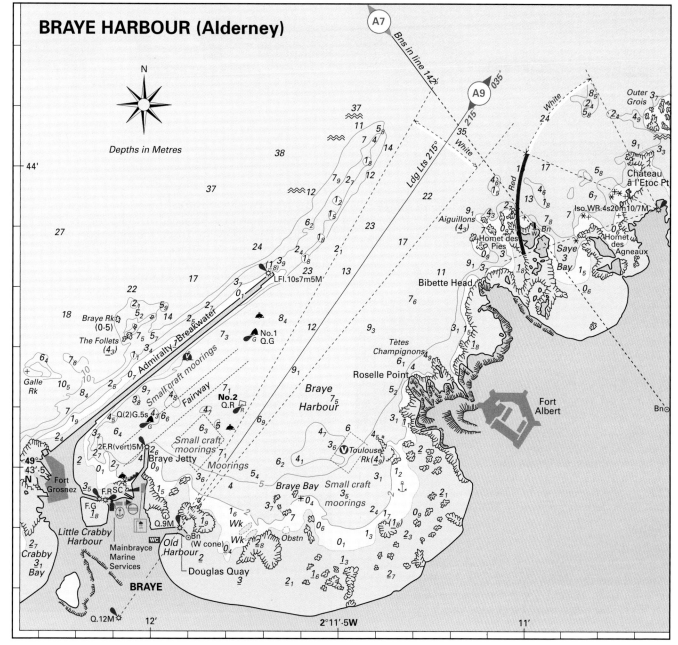

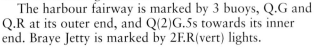

210°

Entry marks

A8 210° White pyramid on Douglas Quay in transit with St Anne's church spire

This should be held accurately as the line passes within 200m of the submerged remains off the breakwater head.

By night

(See plan page 28)

A9 215° ⊕6

The new (2004) leading lights (front Q.8m9M, rear Q.17m12M) serve well as day marks now that they are mounted on conspicuous dayglo orange triangles

Entering on these marks gives about 200m more clearance from the submerged breakwater.

Rear leading light/mark

The harbour fairway is marked by 3 buoys, Q.G and Q.R at its outer end, and Q(2)G.5s towards its inner end. Braye Jetty is marked by 2F.R(vert) lights.

Shelter

Caution

Good in all but N–NE winds, when the harbour is totally exposed and should be avoided in winds above Force 4. In gales from W and SW a heavy swell can enter the harbour and seas may break spectacularly over the breakwater.

Moorings

There are 64 yellow visitors' buoys and it is possible to raft up on these in calm weather. With the exception of the first five rows in from the entrance which are intended for use by larger vessels, all moorings are suitable for vessels up to 40ft.

Some moorings are located SW of Toulouse Rock on the E side of the bay, which may offer some shelter from northeasterlies, if not the swell. Here there is a minimum depth of between 3.5m and 5.5m at Chart Datum. It is not permitted to dry out in Braye or Saye bays unless in an emergency and with authorisation from the harbourmaster.

Moorings in Toulouse Bay

St Anne

Douglas Quay

Braye Jetty

Dinghy pontoon

Fuel Water

Little Crabby harbour

Moorings

Harbourmaster's office

Facilities block

Alderney Sailing Club

Braye

Harbourmaster's office

Mainbrayce

Fuel Water

Little Crabby Harbour

Little Crabby inner harbour is reserved for local craft but may be entered for fuel and water. See *Harbour Facilities* below.

Anchoring

The anchorage in the middle of Braye Bay has good holding in sand, but there are areas of rock and weed. Towards the entrance of the harbour, the bottom is generally more rocky. Due to the tidal range at springs (up to 6.9m) a good scope should be put out especially if anchoring in shoal areas. It is not permitted to anchor in the fairway or close to Braye Jetty.

Entry formalities

Vessels entering from outside the Bailiwick of Guernsey must complete a customs form at the harbourmaster's office. Channel Islands Regulations concerning the prevention of rabies apply. There is a 4-knot speed limit in the harbour.

The harbourmaster's office is located at the SW end of the harbour and fulfils the function of customs, coastguard, Alderney Radio Station and lifeboat. Excellent weather forecasts are available. Hours are as for Alderney Radio (see *Radio Facilities* above).

Harbour facilities

Dinghy pontoon, slipway, showers, toilets, launderette, telephones, chandlers and rubbish skip are all located near the harbourmaster's office.

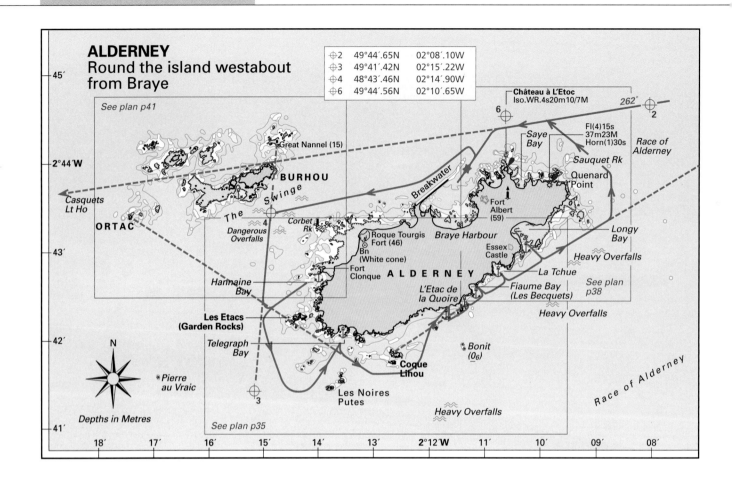

ALDERNEY
Round the island westabout
from Braye

⊕2	49°44'.65N	02°08'.10W
⊕3	49°41'.42N	02°15'.22W
⊕4	48°43'.46N	02°14'.90W
⊕6	49°44'.56N	02°10'.65W

Alderney from the west

Round the island westabout from Braye

There is a 9-hour tidal envelope in which to make a circumnavigation to include a few anchorages. Choose settled weather and avoid large spring tides. These directions assume an average boat speed of 6 knots.

A visit to Burhou Island is not included in this trip but described separately at the end of this section.

CHART
BA 60 Alderney and the Casquets
DISTANCE
Approximately 11M (Outside Garden Rocks)

TIDAL STRATEGY
The aim is to carry a fair tide as much as possible and catch The Swinge and the Race near slack water. The period around local LW (HW St Helier+0515) is the time to visit S coast anchorages. Return to Braye just before local HW (HW St Helier+0045).

Leaving at local HW+0415 (HW St Helier+0330) will give a fairly slack W-going stream through The Swinge. From HW St Helier+0430 and over the LW period up to HW St Helier–0400, the S coast is in the grip of a SW-going stream. This gives way to a NE-going stream for the best part of 6 hours. The Race is best taken around HW St Helier–0230 when there is slack water N of the island.

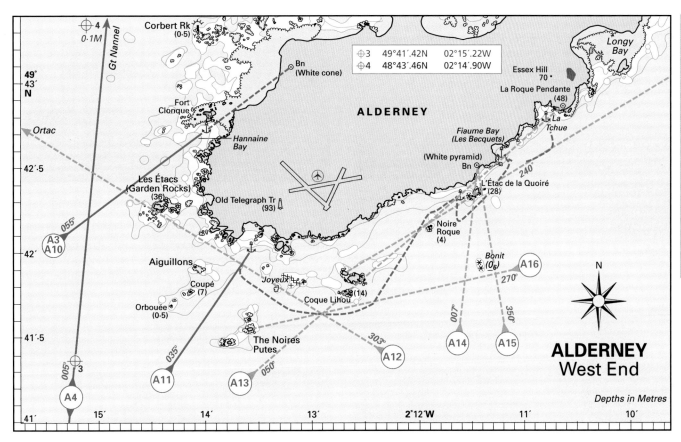

⊕3	49°41′.42N 02°15′.22W
⊕4	48°43′.46N 02°14′.90W

ALDERNEY

ALDERNEY West End

Depths in Metres

ALDERNEY

Braye to Longy Bay

(See plan pages 22–3 and 28)

Depart from Braye on the leading marks (A8 or A9 ⊕6) then A7 ⊕5 to clear the submerged breakwater or A6 subject to depth. When clear, take up A5 ⊕4 to enter The Swinge. Continue until Great Nannel (15m) bears 005° then come S onto Transit A4 ⊕3. Avoid cutting the corner.

Hannaine Bay

49°42′.73N 02°14′.02W
(See plan above)

A10 This anchorage S of Fort Clonque provides excellent protection in NE–E winds and can be useful to yachts approaching from the SW that need to wait for a fair tide up through The Swinge. Entry from Transit A4 is not easy, particularly if there is a strong current across the 200m wide entrance between rocks. Marks must therefore be held accurately. These are shown below.

A10 *055° White pyramid beacon S of Roque Tourgis Fort open to S of Fort Clonque and midway between Fort Clonque and white gable*

Hannaine Bay

Note This is the same transit as A3, the southerly clearing line for Pierre au Vraic (drying 1.2m) (see plan page 22 and *Approaches to Braye from the S and SW*). Anchor in 3m (sand) 100m or more S of Fort Clonque. Depart using same marks to rejoin A4.

Caution

The coast between Les Etacs (Garden Rocks) and Noire Roque is peppered with rocks. Short cuts close inshore are not advised without local knowledge aboard (see plan page 35).

Alderney west end looking northwest

Leave Garden Rocks 0.3M to port and steer 160° to leave Orbouée (0.5m) and Coupé (7m) NE of it 0.3M to port.

Alderney west end looking northeast

Telegraph Bay

49°42′.04N 02°13′.55W
(See plan page 35)

Approach between Coupé (7m) and Les Noires Putes (19m, 12m and 6m) with clearing line A11. The tower is on the skyline, so will not be visible close in. Holding is good but the bay is encumbered with rocks, so consult the chart carefully.

A11 035° The Old Telegraph tower (85m) on a bearing of 035°

Depart on 215° and hold until:

A12 303° Ortac is open S of the Les Etacs (Garden Rocks) and midway between them and Aiguillons (5m)

If Ortac is not visible keep the S edge of the Garden Rocks on 310°. Steer out on 130° with attention to tidal stream, leaving Joyeux (dries 5.4m) to port and the Noires Putes to starboard. When the tallest of the Noires Putes (19m) is abeam identify:

A13 050° La Rocque Pendante (48m) is just touching the left (E) edge of L'Étac de la Quoiré

Then turn E. Leave Coque Lihou (14m) 200m to port and steer in to pass either side of Noire Roque (4m) but well inside the isolated rock Bonit (dries 0.6m) (see *Clearing Bonit* below).

Note Noire Rocque should be given a wide berth to the NW and N, particularly at low water, as reefs run off the main rock.

Tidal disturbance marks the position of Bonit 0.5M SSE of the ruined pier at Cachelière

Clearing Bonit

(See plan page 35)

The marks for clearing this danger are:

To the west A14 *007° White pyramid open left (W) of L'Etac de la Quoiré*

To the east A15 *350° White pyramid open right (E) of L'Etac de la Quoiré*

To the south A16 *258° All the Noires Putes are open S of Coque Lihou Rocks*

Les Becquets (Vaulto)

49°42′.65N 02°11′.13W

(See plan page 35)

When entering this obscure bay (locally known as Vaulto) from the SW, beware of drying rock (dries 4.3m) off the S point. When the whole of the old pier at Cachalière is visible between L'Etac and the cliff, it is clear to enter with the centre of the bay on a bearing of 307°.

La Tchué

(See plan page 38)

49°42′.87N 02°10′.71W

This bay affords the next more attractive anchorage. Approach with the middle of the bay on 330°. The spectacular Rocque Pendante (48m) may be seen hanging out of the cliff to the E. The bottom is generally sand and the holding good.

Longy Bay

49°43′.12N 02°10′.21W

(See plan page 38)

This is the island's most popular anchorage and has a fine beach. It provides a good bolt-hole when Braye is suffering from northeasterlies or while waiting for the tide up through the Race.

Approach on

A17 *313° ⊕7. The W wall of Fort Albert in line with the Nunnery (the E end of Château de Longy)*

This transit will leave Queslingue (10m) 250m to port and a drying rock (dries 0.5m) in the middle of the bay 80m to port.

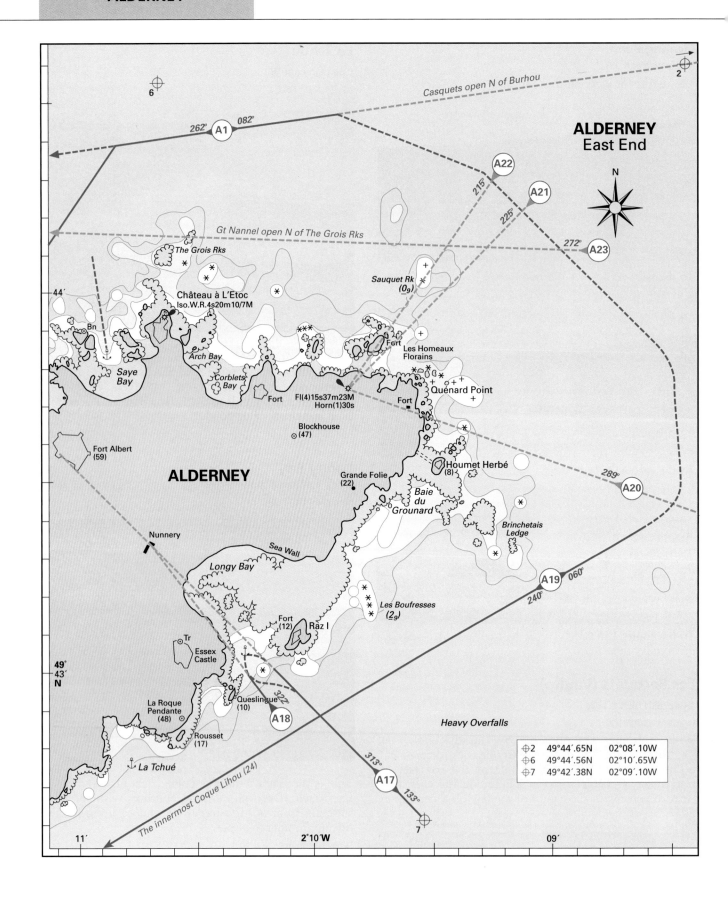

ALDERNEY
East End

Casquets open N of Burhou

262° 082° A1

6

2

A22

215°

A21

225°

Gt Nannel open N of The Grois Rks

272° A23

The Grois Rks

Sauquet Rk
(0₉)

44′

Château à L'Etoc
Iso.W.R.4s20m10/7M

Bn

Arch Bay

Saye
Bay

Corblets
Bay

Fort

Les Homeaux
Florains

Quénard Point

Fort

Fl(4)15s37m23M
Horn(1)30s

Fort

Blockhouse
⊙ (47)

Houmet Herbé
(8)

289° A20

Fort Albert
(59)

ALDERNEY

Grande Folie
(22)

Baie
du
Grounard

Brinchetais
Ledge

Nunnery

Sea Wall

Longy Bay

A19 060°

240°

Les Boufresses
(2₉)

Fort
(12)

Raz I

Tr

Essex
Castle

49°
43′
N

La Roque
Pendante
(48)

Queslingue
(10)

A18

Rousset
(17)

La Tchué

313° A17 133°

Heavy Overfalls

The innermost Coque Lihou (24)

⊕2	49°44′.65N	02°08′.10W
⊕6	49°44′.56N	02°10′.65W
⊕7	49°42′.38N	02°09′.10W

7

11′

2°10′W

09′

Fort Albert   The Nunnery   Fort Raz

Queslingue

313°

Anchorage

The preferred anchorage, offering more room and better holding, is to the W of this drying rock, therefore when Queslingue bears W, come to port, west of your approach line, and transfer to:

Sound in carefully, the bottom is sand with rocky patches. Anchor when:

Nunnery

322°

A18 *322° The Nunnery is just open of the W side of the bay*

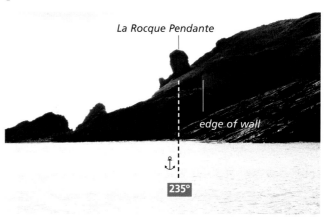

La Rocque Pendante

edge of wall

235°

La Rocque Pendante is open of the end of the wall on 235°

Longy Bay to Braye

(See plan page 38)

Leaving Longy Bay steer SE until Brinchetais Ledge can be cleared. The clearing marks are as shown below.

A19
Cocque Lihou   L'Étac de la Quoiré   Cachelière
240°

A19 240° The innermost Coque Lihou open E of L'Etac de la Quoiré

Steer NE until the turning point:

A20
289°

A20 289° Quénard Point LtHo is over a small yellow house with black roof and a chimney at each end

Then steer N taking care to avoid the overfalls round Blanchard Rock (3.7m).

Clearing Sauquet rock (dries 0.9m)
49°44′.02N 02°09′.56W

The final hazard is the much-hit Sauquet Rock and its reef.
E clearance is:

A21
Bunker
225°

A21 225° Quénard Point LtHo open to S of the bunker on Fort Homeaux Florains

Striking marks

A22
Fort Homeaux Florains
215°

A22 215° Quénard Point LtHo in line with Fort Homeaux Florains

With these marks on, locals use the horizontal WBW stripes to estimate distance off. If all of the black stripe is visible you are outside Sauquet. If none of the black stripe is visible you are passing inside it. **N clearance is:**

A23
The Grois Rocks   Gt Nannel
272°

A23 272° Gt Nannel open N of all the Grois Rocks (dry 5.5m)

Come round to the NW and leaving Sauquet Rock to port regain Transit A1, then A9 ⊕6 for entry to Braye Harbour.

Saye Bay
49°43′.85N 02°10′.87W
(See plan page 38)

Just 0.5M short of the breakwater, this cove offers one final diversion in settled weather. There is a safe sandy beach for bathing and good holding. Enter between the high heads on either side and anchor with reference to the chart. *Note* Saye is pronounced 'soy'.

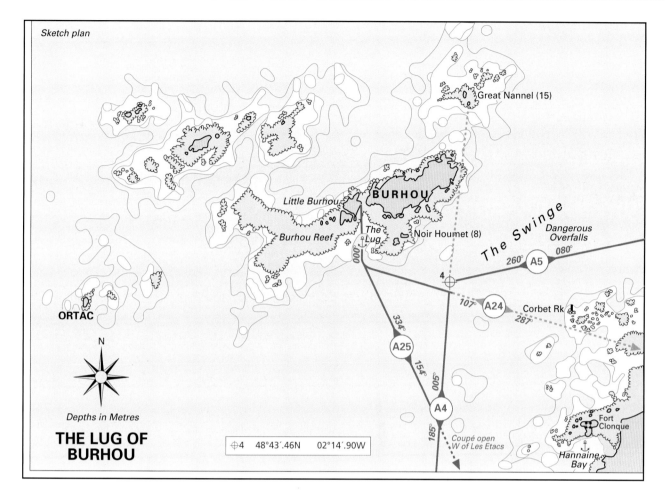

Sketch plan

Great Nannel (15)

Little Burhou

BURHOU

Burhou Reef

The Lug

Noir Houmet (8)

The Swinge

Dangerous Overfalls

260° A5 080°

107° A24

Corbet Rk

287°

334°

154°

A25

500°

A4

185°

Coupé open W of Les Etacs

Fort Clonque

Hannaine Bay

ORTAC

N

Depths in Metres

THE LUG OF BURHOU

⊕4 48°43′.46N   02°14′.90W

Burhou from the east

Burhou Island

49°43′.64N 02°15′.49W

This island 2M WNW of Braye has the distinction of being home to the largest colony of puffins in the Channel Islands. For this reason landing is prohibited in their breeding season (15 March–21 July).

In settled weather and preferably at LW neaps when the reefs afford some protection, there is an anchorage known as The Lug (La Logue in local patois), between Burhou Island and Burhou Reef. As with Hannaine Bay this is a useful LW anchorage in which to await slack water if a yacht fails to make Braye before the tide turns. It can be dangerous approaching at HW springs when the NW-going flood stream courses through the anchorage.

There is a refuge hut on the island, maintained by the States of Alderney.

Caution

The Lug should only be used towards LW and on the ebb. It should be left before the easterly flood stream sets in or if there is any likelihood of the anchorage becoming exposed to the weather. Approaching from the S or E, allowance must be made for a westerly set which can be strong.

The Lug viewed from WNW at low water springs

Refuge hut

Burhou

Little Burhou

Approach from Braye

(See plan page 41)

Hold stern Transit A5 080° ⊕4 down The Swinge until Gt Nannel bears N then transfer to stern transit:

A24 107°

A24 107° St Anne's church spire on the right (S) edge of Rocque Tourgis fort (white pyramid). This line will clear the rocky shoreline E of the anchorage by 100m

Approach from SW

(See plan page 22)

Make initial approach on A4 005° ⊕4 then transfer to stern transit A25 (154°) for entry.

A25

Les Etacs (Garden Rocks)   Coupé   Orbouée

154°

A25 154° Coupé Rock open to the W of Les Etacs (Garden Rocks)

Avoid any overfalls in The Swinge and keep a check on any cross set.

Anchorage

When the broad anchorage opens up, enter from the S. The anchorage is deep, gradually shelving around the edge. The bottom is sand with rocky patches and the holding is good. The scenery is starkly beautiful.

Entering the Lug from the south

Guernsey

Local Information

STD code: 01481

TRAVEL INFORMATION
The island is well served by air and ferry routes. Regular flights operate from Southampton, Exeter, Gatwick and elsewhere. Condor high-speed ferries cross the Channel from Weymouth or Poole in less than three hours and the terminal is a short walk away from the marinas. They also operate the St-Malo route via Jersey. Inter-island ferries regularly ply the short distance between St Peter Port, Herm and Sark.

Air
Direct flights from Gatwick, Southampton, Stansted and many regional airports
Flybe (British European) ☎ 0871 7000123
Inter-Island and several UK airports. Dinard (France):
Aurigny Air Services ☎ 882888
Blue Islands ☎ 824567

Sea
Jersey, St Malo, Weymouth, Poole:
Condor Ferries ☎ 0845 3452000
Jersey, Alderney Diélette: Granville, Sark:
Manche Iles Express ☎ 01534 766566

PORTS OF ENTRY
The official Ports of Entry into the Bailiwick of Guernsey are Braye in Alderney and Beaucette Marina, St Sampson (for commercial vessels only) and St Peter Port in Guernsey. At St Peter Port, all visiting yachts must clear in at the main harbour irrespective of which marina they moor in.

CHARTS
British Admiralty WGS 84
807 Guernsey and Herm. Beaucette Marina
808 E Guernsey Herm and Sark. Beaucette Marina
2669 Channel Islands and Adjacent Coast of France
3140 St Peter Port
3653 Guernsey to Alderney and Adjacent Coast of France
3654 Guernsey Herm and Sark
Leisure Folio 5604
1   Isle of Wight to Guernsey
2   Plymouth to Guernsey
3   Cherbourg to Guernsey
4   Guernsey to Jersey
9   Guernsey Herm and Sark
10   Approaches to St Peter Port
11   Plan A St Peter Port. Plan B Beaucette Marina
Imray
C33A Channel Islands (North) Plans of St Peter Port, Beaucette Marina
Imray 2500 Channel Islands Chart Pack
Stanfords Allweather
16   The Channel Islands
26   Channel Islands Harbours. Plans Guernsey and the Russel Channels

French SHOM
6903 Guernsey et Herm. Marina Beaucette
6904 Guernsey Est, Herm et Sark. Marina Beaucette

RADIO FACILITIES
St Peter Port Radio
☎ 720672
☎ 710277 for shore to ship calls
Fax 723394
Email guernsey.harbour@gov.gg
MMSI: 00 232 00 64
Hours of Watch 24
VHF Ch16, 20 (direct calling), 62 (link calls), 70 (DSC)
Traffic Lists Vessels are initially called on Ch 16. Lists are broadcast on Ch 20 after navigation warnings at 0133, 0533, 0933, 1333, 1733, 2133 UT
VHF Direction-finding Bearings can be provided on Ch 16 or 67. Note the aerial position for D/F purposes is 49°26′.27N 02°35′.77W (Guernsey Airport)
Port Control Ch 12 This channel should be monitored entering/exiting St Peter Port but is not to be used for berthing information and general enquiries
Water taxi Summer months only 0700–2200. Ch 10

NAVIGATIONAL AIDS
Racons (radar beacons):
Platte Fougère LtHo 49°30′.88N 02°97′.05W (P)
RDF beacon
S breakwater 49°27′.37N 02°31′.37W 304.5kHz (GY)

USEFUL TELEPHONE NUMBERS
Harbourmaster's office ☎ 720229
Duty dockmaster ☎ 712422
Customs 741700
Victoria Marina office (dockmaster) ☎ 725987
Visitor Information Centre ☎ 723552
Guernsey Yacht Club ☎ 722838 Bar ☎ 725342
Royal Channel Islands Yacht Club ☎ 723154/725500
White Rock Signal Station ☎ 720672
St Sampson (Dockmaster) ☎ 720229
Beaucette Marina Office ☎ 245000

SUPPLIES AND SERVICES
St Peter Port
Chandlery, fuel, bottled gas: Boatworks+
☎ 726071
Engine servicing and repairs: Herm Seaway Marine
☎ 726829
Sailmaker: Katy Barrett ☎ 246741
St Sampson
Marine and General Boatyard ☎ 243048
Fuel ☎ 200800
Quayside Chandlery ☎ 245881

Introduction

Guernsey is the second largest of the Channel Islands and 'big sister' to the group of dependent isles that make up the Bailiwick – Alderney, Sark, Herm and Jethou. Despite sharing common roots, Guernsey has managed to retain a more leisurely pace of life that is threatened by commercialism elsewhere.

One of the island's greatest assets is St Peter Port harbour and the sheltered waters of the roadstead outside, which together provide the safest haven in the Channel Islands, accessible at any state of tide and in almost any weather. This has been exploited throughout the centuries, establishing Guernsey as a vital staging post on lucrative trading routes. Evidence of this goes back to Roman times, by the discovery in 1984 of the remains of a flat-bottomed Gallo-Roman vessel in the harbour entrance. Its cargo of tiles and pottery confirms that it is the oldest wreck to be discovered in the British Isles.

The harbour is dominated by Castle Cornet which was an important stronghold up to Napoleonic times. Apart from being captured by the French on three occasions, it was a Royalist stronghold during the Civil War – the last in the British Isles to be overcome. It is now a museum.

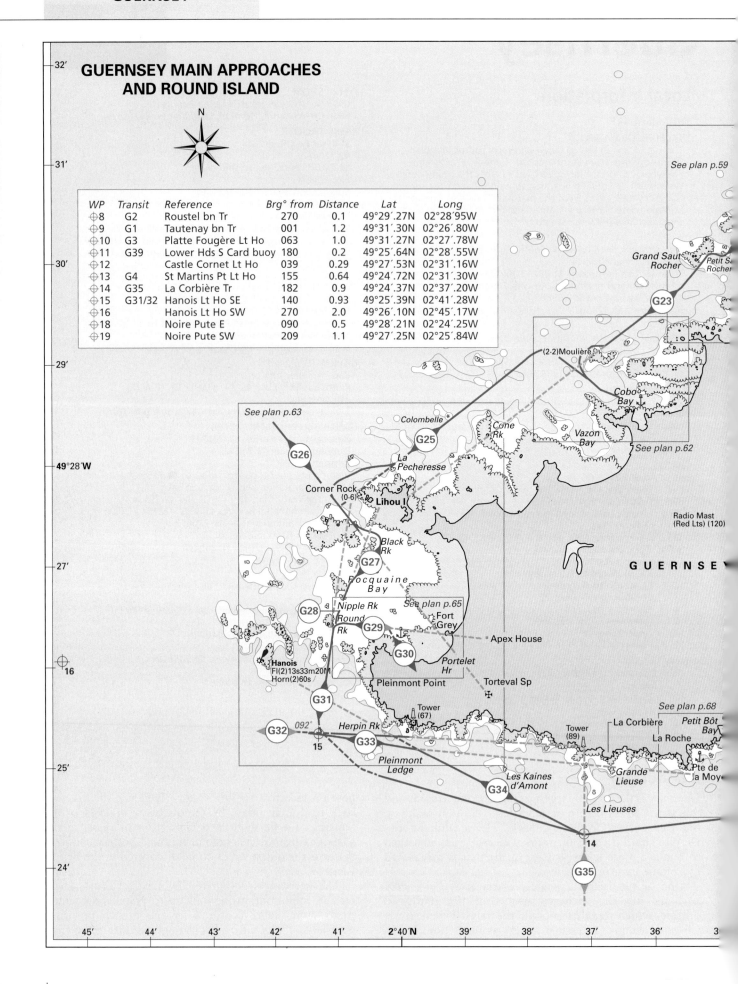

GUERNSEY MAIN APPROACHES AND ROUND ISLAND

WP	Transit	Reference	Brg° from	Distance	Lat	Long
⊕8	G2	Roustel bn Tr	270	0.1	49°29′.27N	02°28′.95W
⊕9	G1	Tautenay bn Tr	001	1.2	49°31′.30N	02°26′.80W
⊕10	G3	Platte Fougère Lt Ho	063	1.0	49°31′.27N	02°27′.78W
⊕11	G39	Lower Hds S Card buoy	180	0.2	49°25′.64N	02°28′.55W
⊕12		Castle Cornet Lt Ho	039	0.29	49°27′.53N	02°31′.16W
⊕13	G4	St Martins Pt Lt Ho	155	0.64	49°24′.72N	02°31′.30W
⊕14	G35	La Corbière Tr	182	0.9	49°24′.37N	02°37′.20W
⊕15	G31/32	Hanois Lt Ho SE	140	0.93	49°25′.39N	02°41′.28W
⊕16		Hanois Lt Ho SW	270	2.0	49°26′.10N	02°45′.17W
⊕18		Noire Pute E	090	0.5	49°28′.21N	02°24′.25W
⊕19		Noire Pute SW	209	1.1	49°27′.25N	02°25′.84W

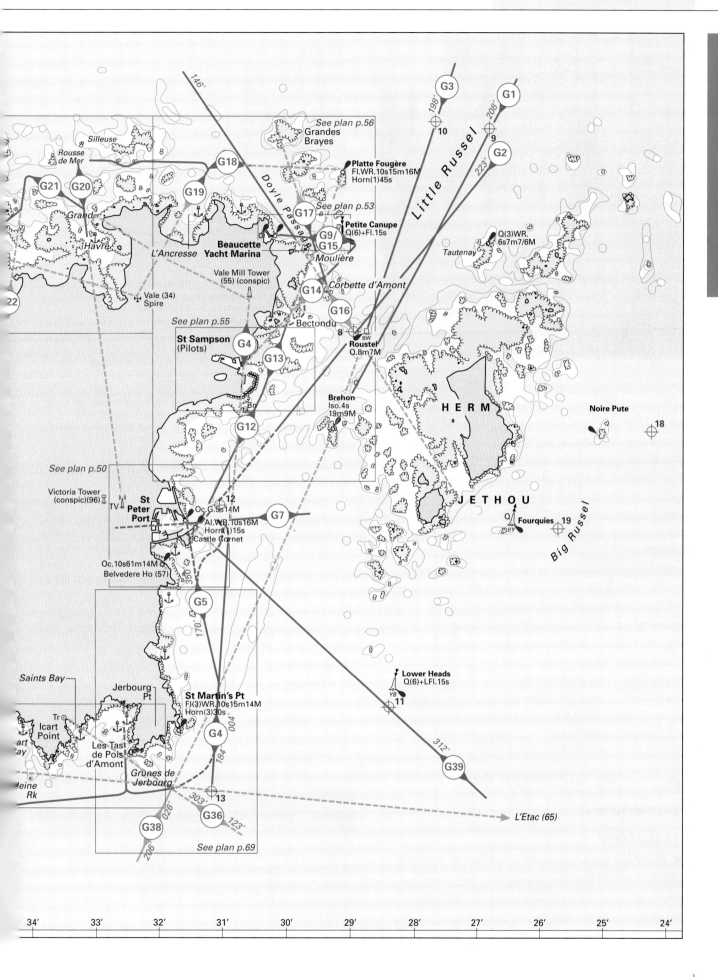

Ashore in St Peter Port

Today it is yacht crews that throng the waterfront and in high season the harbour can brim with pleasure craft of all flags. Somehow the friendly marina staff can always find room for one more. For the cruising fraternity, St Peter Port is a popular stopover en route to N Brittany, while others find that the excellent facilities and close proximity of Sark and Herm make it an ideal holiday base for day sailing.

Ashore

There is a comprehensive selection of shops, restaurants and bars close to St Peter Port Marinas. Saltwater Restaurant and Bar on Albert Quay (720823) specialising in local sea food is recommended. Castle Cornet Fortress overlooking the harbour has a fascinating Maritime Museum.

Before venturing out of town, the Visitor Information Centre on the Esplanade can advise on the numerous environmental and historical sites in the island. You will need to rent a car or take the bus for a visit to the west coast and Lihou Island with its bird sanctuary.

Beau Sejour Leisure Centre on the outskirts of St Peter Port is a sports centre with a gym and 25m pool.

Approaches to St Peter Port

FROM THE NORTH

Via Little Russel

The gateway to this well-worn route lies between Platte Fougère lighthouse off the island's NE corner and Tautenay beacon tower a mile N of Herm.

The key to a successful approach is positive and early identification of the main marks.

Make the initial approach with Platte Fougère LtHo

Tidal information

(Tidal levels referred to chart datum)
St Peter Port 49°27′N 2°31′W

MHWS	MHWN	MLWN	MLWS	MTL
9.3m	7.0m	3.6m	1.5m	5.3m

St Peter Port is a Standard Port with its own predictions. The mean difference on St Helier is +0005 to 0010.

Guernsey is positioned in the main tidal flow as much as Alderney, with the N-going stream running from about local HW–0300 to +0300, and the S-going from local LW–0300 to +0300.

Streams are generally not as strong as around Alderney but the island's triangular shape and the close proximity of its neighbours create complexities and locally accelerated rates up to 6 knots. Overfalls, severe at spring tides, can be expected in wind against tide conditions. Areas to be wary of are:

Little Russel
At the northern end off Beaucette and Roustel beacon tower. Overfalls around Roustel are notorious and on the flood with fresh northeasterlies can be vicious

SW of Brehon Tower smaller overfalls may occur on the ebb in southwesterlies

Off St Martin's Point
The stream is strongest just after HW and LW and should be given a good clearance when wind is against tide

Big Russel
Numerous overfalls can be expected on a line between Brecqou and the Lower Heads S of Jethou. Upwind and uptide it can be comparatively smooth but downwind expect areas of confused sea in anything over Force 5.

on a bearing of 220° until other marks have been identified. A suitable arrival waypoint would be ⊕9 or ⊕10 both about 1M ENE of the lighthouse. Off Roustel beacon tower the channel narrows to little more than 1M wide before opening out to the broad roads off St Peter Port.

There are several options for approach which may be used in conjunction with each other. Selection will depend on the range of visibility.

Good visibility
By day only

G1 208°⊕9 *St Martin's Point open of Brehon Tower*

This transit if held will pass close E of Roustel beacon tower. While there may be reasons for taking this route it is more usual to pass W of this beacon (⊕8) to intercept the leading marks (G2). Note rock (dries 0.6m) close NE of the beacon and Cavale (dries 1.2m) 0.3M E of it.

SSW

Brehon Tower   St Martin's Pt Castle Cornet

Platte Fougère

Brehon Tower

Looking SW into Little Russel

Moderate visibility

G2

Belvedere House Belvedere Lt

223°

G2 223° ⊕8 Belvedere House in line with Castle Cornet white mark

This is the main approach line through Little Russel to St Peter Port. Belvedere House is the most northerly and prominent of a group of white houses SW of Castle Cornet. Note that Belvedere light is NW of the House.

By night

Align rear light (Belvedere Oc.10s61m14M) and front light (Castle Breakwater Al.WR.10s14m16M) on 220°. This transit is easier to see by night than by day, but as it passes over Boue Agenor (2.1m) which is guarded by the red sector of Platte beacon (Fl.WR.3s) it is necessary for deep draught vessels to borrow 100m to port when abreast of Brehon tower.

Poor visibility

This option requires visibility of at least 2M. If the weather is, or seems likely to become foggy, it is better to approach St Peter Port by Big Russel.

G3

St Martin's Point

198°

G3 198° ⊕10 Roustel beacon tower in line with Brehon tower

Leave Roustel and Brehon to port and then transfer to the main approach line (see *Moderate visibility* (by day) above).

By night

Align Roustel (Q.8m7M) with Brehon (Iso.4s19m9M).

Roustel

Via Big Russel

(See plans pages 45, 75 and 76)

When beating down to St Peter Port by day from the NE against a southwester, Big Russel provides a channel seldom less than 2.5M wide between Herm and Sark which is largely free of traffic.

Apart from overfalls in the S there are only two offlying dangers: Noire Pute (2m) is marked by a lit beacon (Fl(2)WR.15s) and Fourquies (dry 2.3m) marked by a lit N cardinal buoy (Q). The buoy should be given a good clearance as it tends to drift around in this area of powerful streams. Once round the Lower Heads S cardinal buoy (⊕11) you can head up to St Peter Port (see *St Peter Port from the East* below).

FROM THE NORTHWEST

(See plans pages 45 and 56)

The marks to clear NE of the Brayes reefs are as shown on BA chart 807:

149° SW extremity of Little Sark on the (low) NE point of Herm

This will leave Platte Fougère lighthouse 0.3M to the W. Proceed as for *Approach from the north via Little Russel,* above.

Doyle Passage (by day only)

(See plan page 56)

This approach from the NW provides a useful cut inside Platte Fougère to join Beaucette Marina channel and Little Russel approaches to St Peter Port. It calls for fair weather and good visibility. The streams are strong on this corner and this passage should only be attempted on the flood when the stream is setting E. HW–0300 is a good time.

There is one mark which should be held accurately:

G16 146° Corbette d'Amont beacon tower midway between Herm and Jethou

For view and details for entry to this passage from the S see *Round the island northabout from St Peter Port. St Peter Port north to Fort Doyle,* below.

FROM THE EAST

(See plans pages 45, 75 and 76)

Getting around Sark, Herm and Jethou and into Little Russel offers interesting pilotage. From N of Sark one option is to cross Big Russel into Percée Passage between Herm and Jethou and then, subject to enough water, to join Alligande Passage across to St Peter Port (see *Herm. Passages N of Jethou.*)

From S of Sark, route via Lower Heads S cardinal buoy (⊕11) and then make good a NNW track to St Peter Port pier heads with:

G39 312° ⊕11 White Rock LtHo open S of Castle cornet breakwater LtHo (no view)

By day and in good visibility a more direct route is possible via the Musé Passage (see *Herm. Passages S of Jethou*).

By night

Sark waters are not an option and the Percée Passage and Alligande Passage should not be used without local knowledge (see *St Peter Port from the South* below).

FROM THE SOUTH

(See plans pages 45 and 69)

Via Little Russel

Enter Little Russel anywhere between Lower Heads S cardinal buoy (⊕11) and a point 800m E of St Martin's Point. The only dangers are those on Guernsey's E coast between St Peter Port and St Martin's Point (See *Round the Island. St Martin's Point to St Peter Port*).

Good visibility

G4 004° ⊕13 Vale Mill over the middle shed of a group of three (green) at St Sampson

Poor visibility

G5 350° White Rock LtHo open to the E of Castle Cornet clears dangers off the coast as far as Oyster beacon (O)

200m NE of Oyster lies Ferico (0.9m). To clear both steer out into Little Russel after passing Moulinet beacon (M) until the pier heads are open:

G6 298° St Peter Port pier heads open will clear Ferico

By night

Approaching off St Martin's Point you will be clear of all dangers off the S coast, providing Hanois (Fl(2)13s33m20M) is visible. The red sector of St Martin's Pt (Fl(3)WR.10s15m14M) guards the rocks off the point but note this does not include Longue Pierre (LP) beacon (unlit) and its reef, which extends 400m NE of the point. Aim to keep at least 0.75M off the point and steer E until Castle Breakwater (Al.WR.10s16M) is on a safe bearing of between 312° and 345°. This will put White Rock (Oc.G.5s) open W of Castle Breakwater (Al.WR.10s) and open E of Castle Cornet. The E side of the approach is marked by The Lower Heads S cardinal lit buoy. Approaching the breakwater, come E until White Rock light is just open E of Castle Breakwater light in order to open up the entrance.

See also *Round the island northabout from St Peter Port. St Martin's Point to St Peter Port*, below.

St Peter Port

St Peter Port

49°27'.44N 02°31'.60W White Rock port control

Entry

Port Control Signal Station

Entry signals

These are displayed from Port Control Signal Station on White Rock Pier.

Red: Large vessels are under way. Entry and exit of other vessels prohibited except small boats of 15m or less under power, which may proceed keeping well clear. See *Local information. Radio Facilities*, page 43.

Speed limit

4kn in the inner harbour to 6kn in the outer harbour.

Entry is midway between the pier heads:

G7 265° Green church spire over Victoria Marina Lt Tr

By night

265° Lights in line
Front (on light tower) Oc.R.5s.10m14m,
Rear (on building behind) Iso.R.2s22m3M

This transit will give a good indication of the cross set outside the entrance. Contrary to the usual convention yachts entering must keep to the port and S side where the yacht approach channel is marked by a green conical buoy (Q.G) and three red can buoys (Fl.R). When the last port-hand buoy is reached and just past the fuel jetty, turn hard to starboard towards the waiting and visitors' pontoons.

THE CHANNEL ISLANDS **49**

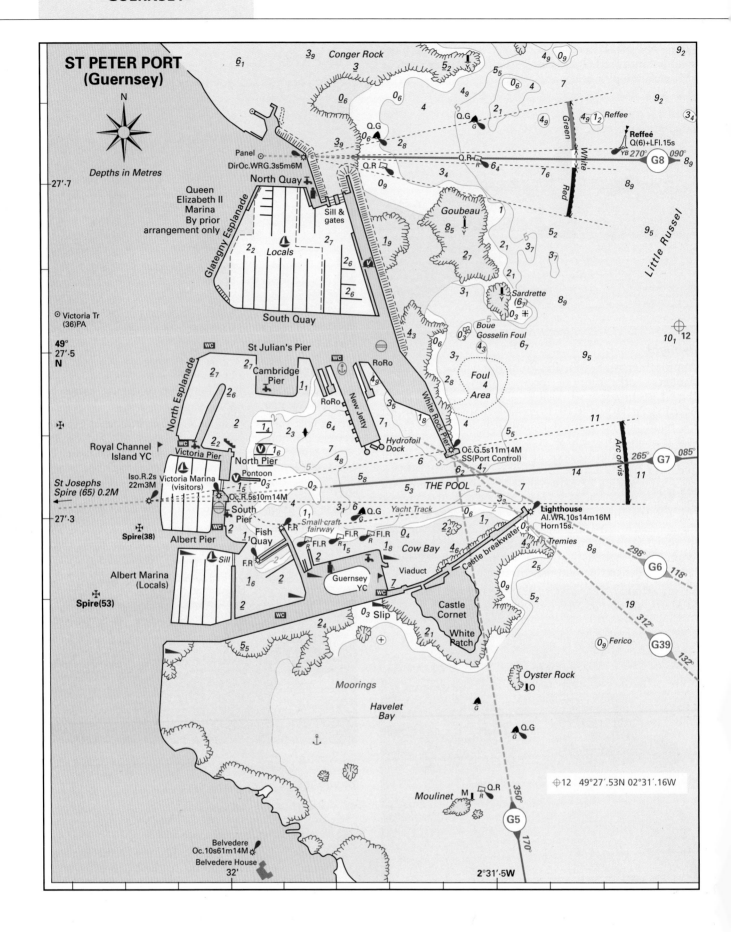

ST PETER PORT
(Guernsey)

Depths in Metres

Conger Rock

Queen Elizabeth II Marina By prior arrangement only

Panel DirOc.WRG.3s5m6M

North Quay

Sill & gates

Locals

South Quay

⊙ Victoria Tr (36)PA

49° 27'·7

49° 27'·5 N

49° 27'·3

WC

St Julian's Pier

WC

Cambridge Pier

RoRo

RoRo

New Jetty

White Rock Pier

Goubeau

Sardrette (6₇)

Boue Gosselin Foul

Foul 4 Area

Royal Channel Island YC

North Esplanade

WC

Victoria Pier

WC

North Pier

Hydrofoil Dock

Oc.G.5s11m14M SS(Port Control)

Arc of vis

Iso.R.2s 22m3M

St Josephs Spire (65) 0.2M

V Victoria Marina (visitors)

Pontoon

Oc.R.5s10m14M

THE POOL

Yacht Track

Small craft fairway

Spire(38)

South Pier

Fish Quay

F.R

Fl.R

Fl.R Fl.R

Cow Bay

Castle breakwater

Tremies

Lighthouse Al.WR.10s14m16M Horn15s.

Albert Marina (Locals)

Albert Pier

Sill

F.R

Viaduct

Guernsey YC

WC

Slip

Castle Cornet

White Patch

Spire(53)

WC

Moorings

Havelet Bay

Oyster Rock

Q.G

Moulinet M Q.R

⊕12 49°27'.53N 02°31'.16W

Belvedere Oc.10s61m14M

Belvedere House 32'

Reffeé Q(6)+LFl.15s

Green White Red

270° 090° G8

Little Russel

G7 085° 265°

G6 298° 118°

G39 312° 132°

350° 170° G5

Ferico

2°31'·5W

Entry formalities

Visiting yachts will be met by the marina dory to issue mooring instructions and deliver a customs and immigration form. This should be completed and deposited in one of the yellow customs boxes ashore or returned to the customs official afloat.

Q Flag It is appreciated if yachts entering from outside the Bailiwick of Guernsey display a Q flag as this assists harbour authorities in identifying new arrivals.

Harbour facilities

St Peter Port is a yachtsman's mecca where all amenities can be found just a short walk or row from Victoria Marina and the outer harbour (The Pool). The marina itself has a shower and launderette block. On Castle Emplacement on the south side of the harbour there are chandleries, marine engineers, electricians and a boatyard. Guernsey Yacht Club at Castle Emplacement and the Royal Channel Islands Yacht Club above the Crown Pub on the waterfront welcome visiting yachtsmen (see *Local information*). There is a wide selection of shops, restaurants, hotels and bars found in the town. The ferry terminals are located on the N side of the harbour near the entrance. Buses and taxis at the waterfront serve the airport.

Fuel (diesel, petrol, (LRP, ULMS))

The fuelling pontoon on Castle Emplacement is operated by Boatworks+. It is accessible about 3–4 hours either side of local HW. There is also a fuelling berth in the QE2 Marina where LPG is available (see *Local information. Supplies and Services*).

Drying out

There are pads in Victoria Marina and QE2 Marina where yachts can dry out alongside. The careening hard N of Victoria Marina is suitable for bilge keelers and yachts with beaching legs.

Marinas

VICTORIA MARINA AND THE POOL
(Plan page 50)

Approach and entry

Visitors have the choice of crossing a half tide sill (dries 4.2m) into Victoria Marina on the W side of the harbour, or mooring to a visitors' pontoon in the outer harbour (The Pool). The decision will depend on the state of the tide, availability of space in the marina and intended length of stay.

Yachts waiting to enter the marina will be directed to the waiting pontoon, or if the marina is full, to The Pool. Getting ashore will involve the tender or there is a water taxi (see *Local Information. Radio Facilities* at the beginning of the chapter). Albert Marina in the SW corner of the harbour is for local residents.

Signals

R/G traffic lights above the marina sill control entry and exit.

Victoria Marina and The Pool

Victoria Marina. Depth over sill in metres

To find depth of water over the sill into Victoria marina:
1. Look up predicted time and height of HW St Peter Port.
2. Enter table below on the line for height of HW.
3. Extract depth (m) of water for time before/after HW.

Ht (m) of HW St Peter Port	Depth of Water in metres over the Sill (dries 4·2 m)						
	HW	±1hr	±2hrs	±2½hrs	±3hrs	±3½hrs	±4hrs
6·20	2·00	1·85	1·55	1·33	1·10	0·88	0·65
·60	2·40	2·18	1·75	1·43	1·10	0·77	0·45
7·00	2·80	2·52	1·95	1·53	1·10	0·67	0·25
·40	3·20	2·85	2·15	1·63	1·10	0·57	0·05
·80	3·60	3·18	2·35	1·73	1·10	0·47	0·00
8·20	4·00	3·52	2·55	1·83	1·10	0·37	0·00
·60	4·40	3·85	2·75	1·93	1·10	0·28	0·00
9·00	4·80	4·18	2·95	2·03	1·10	0·18	0·00
·40	5·20	4·52	3·15	2·13	1·10	0·08	0·00
·80	5·60	4·85	3·35	2·23	1·10	0·00	0·00

Water Available on all marina pontoons and two pontoons in The Pool.
Electricity Available on marina pontoons only.
Depth Victoria Marina is dredged to 2m at CD but depths are less on the westerly pontoons. The bottom is soft mud.
Shelter Excellent in all but easterlies when surge can enter the harbour. In strong to gale force conditions this will penetrate into the marina at HW and life in The Pool can become untenable. Apart from stout fenders and lines, the only option may be to apply for a berth in the QE2 Marina or relocate to the W coast of Herm.

QUEEN ELIZABETH II MARINA (QE2)

(Plan page 50)

This is reserved for local residents although an application can be made for a berth on the E arm for vessels drawing over 2m or requiring an extended stay. The marina has its own entrance 0.4M N of the main harbour entrance and a half tide sill drying 4.5m. Gates ensure total shelter. These are lowered about 3 hours either side of HW depending on whether it is spring or neap tides.

Approach and entry

Approach on 270°, passing close S of Reffée S cardinal light buoy
G8 270° Leading marks in line

Marina leading marks are two rather inconspicuous panels above a white patch on the loose rocks of the breakwater N of the entrance. The front panel is yellow with a RWG directional light and the rear panel is a red square attached to a lamp post. Proceed along the buoyed channel and, when 40m from the breakwater, turn hard to port round the inner port-hand buoy to enter the marina.

At night use a directional light Oc.WRG.3s.

Signals

Signals

Green: Entry permitted. There is at least 2m over the sill
Red: No entry

Electronic depth gauge at entrance indicates the actual depth above the gate in either closed or open position.

BEAUCETTE MARINA

49°30′.14N 02°30′.10W Entrance (Plan page 50)

This unusual marina perched on the NE corner of Guernsey was created by blasting out an 8m wide passage linking an empty granite quarry to the open sea, thereby flooding it. Pond level is retained by a sill. It is privately owned and of the 115 berths, 30 are allocated to visitors. Its isolation will appeal to those seeking the quiet life. Facilities are comprehensive and include a restaurant.

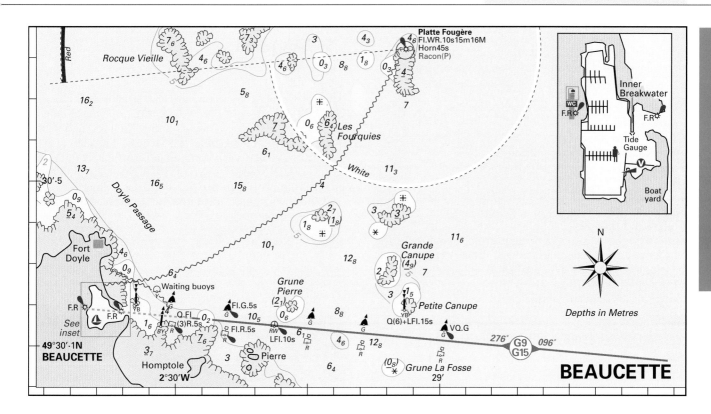

Approaches to Beaucette

All approaches are from Little Russel.

Caution

Entry not advised in strong onshore winds or heavy swell. Channel markers are liable to be changed.

From the north

Approach Little Russel as for St Peter Port (see above). Identify Petite Canupe S cardinal beacon 0.65M S of Platte Fougère LtHo. On passing the beacon turn due W and into the buoyed channel that leads to the marina entrance. There is also a good approach from the NW through the Doyle Passage. This is described under *Approaches to St Peter Port from NW*, page 48.

From the south

Proceed N up Little Russel as for St Peter Port (see above) to pass between Platte beacon tower and Roustel beacon tower. Once past, head towards Petite Canupe S cardinal beacon and proceed as described above.

Access

The sill dries at 2.4m giving access about three hours either side of local HW. Six yellow visitors' buoys are located just to the N of the buoyed approach channel for vessels waiting to enter. These are seasonal (Apr–Oct). Vessels should call the marina for berthing instructions (see *Local information. Radio Facilities*) before entering the Beaucette channel.

Depth

16m at CD.

Entry and berthing

Entry marks are:

G9/G15 276° Front: Situated N of entrance; red arrow on white background Rear: Situated on marina building with windsock: white arrow on red background

The rocks either side of the narrow entrance are painted white. Inside, a concrete wall provides a wave breaker.

There are depth boards situated either side of N head and inside. These indicate depth over the sill.

On entering turn to port and proceed to visitors' berths. Priority is given to vessels departing.

By night

This is possible in settled weather and good visibility using Tautenay light (Q(2)WR.6s7/6M), Petite Canupe beacon (Q(6)+LFl.15s) and the 2F.R lights on the leading marks. The channel buoys are lit (see plan).

Formalities

As a port of entry into the Bailiwick of Guernsey, visitors must complete a customs and immigration form. These can be obtained from the port office.

Supplies and services

16-ton travel-hoist
Customs clearance
Water and electricity on pontoons
Fuel (diesel)
Gas
Launderette
Restaurant ☎ 247066
Toilets and showers
Shop: Dolphin stores is a 5-minute walk away, as is the bus service to St Sampson's and St Peter Port.
Marina office ☎ 245000 *Fax* 247071
Mobile 07781 102302
Email info@beaucettemarina.com

Radio facilities

VHF 80 (0700–2200). Call *Beaucette Marina*.

St Sampson

49°28'.97N 02°30'.66W Pier head

The growth of St Sampson is attributable to the quarrying industry of the 19th century when granite was exported worldwide from its solid wharves and piers. Today this drying harbour 1.5M N of St Peter Port is mainly concerned with commercial traffic carrying bulk cargoes. It is seldom used by yachts but an ambitious engineering project to provide marina berthing for up to 350 shallow-draught local craft was completed in 2005.

St Sampson Marina

Abraham's Bosom

St Sampson Marina looking SE

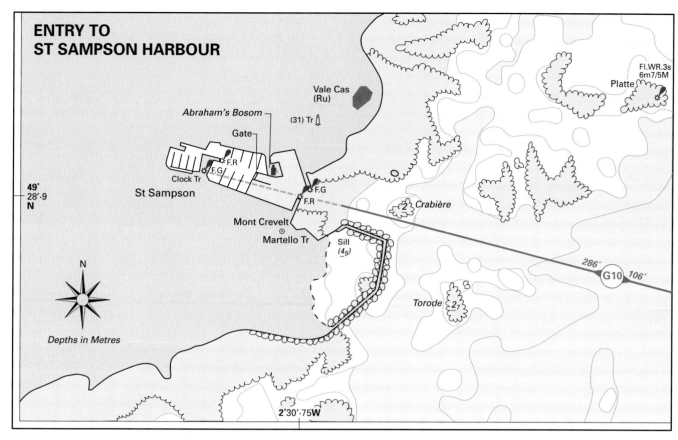

'Space permitting and subject to prior arrangement' there may also be some provision for visitors but at the time of going to press entry for visitors was for commercial services only and there were no special facilities.

Entry

G10 286° *The clock tower in line with white band on southern breakwater head*

Entry signals

R on S pier: large vessels under way and have priority. Keep clear.

By night

The marks are lit, front F.R, rear F.G.

Marina signals

Traffic lights on SW corner of Abraham's Bosom (visible from land).
Green – entry over still permitted
Red – no entry.

Supplies and services

Marine and General Boatyard is the main commercial shipyard in the Channel Islands. It offers a comprehensive range of services to larger vessels including a 75-ton travel-hoist.
Dockmaster (St Peter Port) ☎ 720229
Marine and General Boatyard ☎ 243048
Chandlery: Quayside ☎ 245881.

Fuel

Obtainable at commercial rates by prior arrangement with fuelling companies. The fuelling pontoon is alongside Abraham's Bosom and dries. ☎ 200800.

Radio facilities

VHF 12 (24 hours)

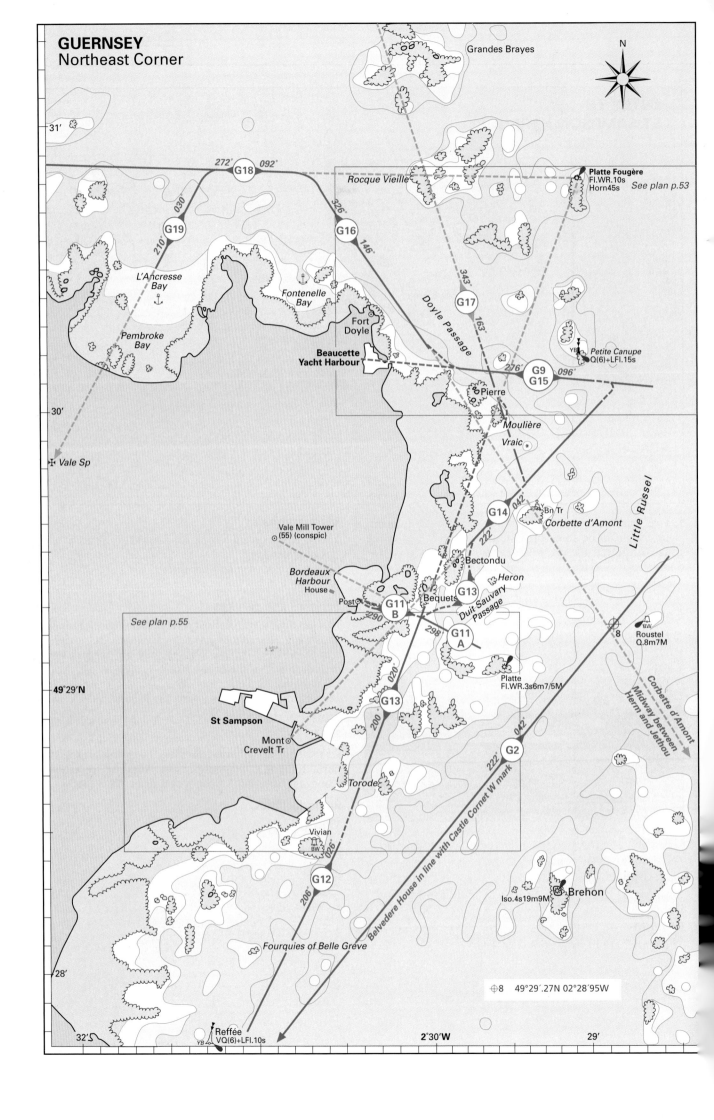

GUERNSEY
Northeast Corner

Grandes Brayes

N

Rocque Vieille

Platte Fougère
Fl.WR.10s
Horn45s   *See plan p.53*

272° **G18** 092°

030°

326°

210° **G19**

G16 146°

L'Ancresse Bay

Fontenelle Bay

343°

163°

Doyle Passage

G17

Fort Doyle

Pembroke Bay

Beaucette Yacht Harbour

YB Petite Canupe
Q(6)+LFl.15s

276° **G9 G15** 096°

Pierre

31'

Vale Sp

Moulière

Vraic ⁎

30'

Vale Mill Tower
(55) (conspic)

042°

Bn Tr

G14 *Corbette d'Amont*

222°

Bordeaux Harbour House

Bectondu

Little Russel

Post

290°

G11 B

Bequets

G13

Heron

Duit Sauvary Passage

Roustel
Q.8m7M

BW

298°

G11 A

8

See plan p.55

020°

Platte
Fl.WR.3s6m7/5M

49°29'N

200°

G13

Corbette d'Amont
Midway between
Herm and Jethou

St Sampson

Mont Crevelt Tr

222°

042°

G2

Torode

026°

Vivian
BW

Belvedere House in line with Castle Cornet W mark

206°

G12

Iso.4s19m9M Brehon

Fourquies of Belle Grève

28'

⊕8 49°29'.27N 02°28'.95W

32'

Reffée
YB VQ(6)+LFl.10s

2°30'W

29'

GUERNSEY

Bordeaux

49°29′.28N 02°30′.30W Pier head

Bordeaux at HW

This shallow drying harbour is 0.5M N of St Sampson and may be of interest to a small yacht able to take the ground. It is exposed to the E.

Approach

G11A 295° Vale Mill in line with the flat-topped Jumelle

Entry

G11B 290° A white post on the end of a short pier, which covers at HW, in line with the gable of a house (partially obscured by trees)

The rock Jumelle has a long flat spur extending some 12m. Hold the transit until 30m from Jumelle then turn to port and round the spur to enter the harbour.

Facilities

None except a bus stop.

Round the island northabout from St Peter Port (by day only)

(See plan pages 44-5)

CHART
BA 807 Guernsey and Herm

Caution

Most of the pilotage in this section should appeal to those looking for a challenge. It passes inside reefs that extend up to 2 miles off the coast and is generally tortuous, particularly in Rocquaine Bay where there are reputed to be 130 rocks. A circumnavigation should only be attempted with local knowledge aboard and in quiet weather with at least 5 miles' visibility. When conditions fall below this minimum the N and W coast between Platte Fougère and Hanois lighthouses should be given substantial clearance.

At the N end of the island are three bays offering secluded pit stops and on the SW corner is Portelet Harbour. With little of interest to the yachtsman in between it follows that a visit to Portelet and its anchorages is more logically achieved south about from St Peter Port, following directions below in reverse (see *Portelet Harbour southabout from St Peter Port*).

All anchorages described (with the exception of those on the S and E coast) are not recommended for use at night as it could be treacherous to leave if the weather changed.

Tidal strategy

As much of the circumnavigation as possible should be made over the LW period and preferably at springs when rocks are visible. With a distance of around 23 miles, target time for a sailing vessel should be about 6 hours, aiming to make the SW corner at LW. Leaving St Peter Port just after half ebb, it is possible to dodge the S-going stream out in Little Russel by keeping close to the shore. At the NE corner, the W-going current will give a good ride down into Rocquaine Bay, but beware of accelerated streams close inshore. From LW up to HW the stream sets conveniently E along the S coast and N up the E coast until HW+0300.

Note Tidal information is based on St Peter Port (St Helier +0005).

St Peter Port north to Fort Doyle 3.5M (3.0m)

(See plan page 56)

Departing St Peter Port take up stern transit G12:

G12 206° White patch on S edge of Castle Cornet open E of Castle Cornet LtHo by its width (shown here open half width)

This transit leads into the Duit Sauvary Passage clearing E of Fourquies of Belle Grève (dries 1.5m) and Vivian BW beacon tower. When NE of this beacon tower and abeam St Sampson's reclamation site take up:

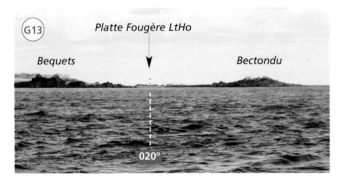

G13 020° Platte Fougère LtHo midway between Bequets and Bectondu (4.4m)

Run up to Bectondu and make a close turn to starboard to pass midway between it and Heron (dries 2.4m). Stop the turn when stern Transit G12 is regained. If this is no longer visible use stern transit:

G14 222° Mont Crevelt Tower (S of St Sampson's Harbour entrance) above the N head of Bectondu. Steer out to pass N of Corbette d'Amont beacon tower

When abeam the tower there is a choice of two entries into Doyle Passage.

Either steer out into Little Russel on stern transit G14 until Petit Canupe S cardinal beacon bears NW then take up Beaucette Marina leading marks:

G9/G15 276° Front: red arrow on white background on the N head. Rear: windsock pole on marina building above white arrow on red background

Note that this leading line crosses a shallow patch (0.2m) 400m short of the entrance.

Continue towards the marina entrance until looking SE identify stern transit:

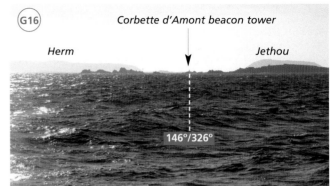

G16 146° Corbette d'Amont beacon tower midway between Herm and Jethou. This leads into Doyle Passage

Or from a position 200m NW of Corbette d'Amont beacon tower look NW to identify sugar-loaf-shaped Rocque Vieille (dries 7.6m) and beyond the whitewashed Grandes Brayes (2m). Take up:

G17 343° Grandes Brayes open to the E of Rocque Vieille. This will clear W of Vraic (dries 0.6m) but a close turn to starboard should be made to clear the E edges of Moulière (dries 4.8m) and Pierre

Return to Transit G16 as described above to enter Doyle Channel.

The turning point onto a W heading is stern transit:

G18 092° Platte Fougère LtHo in line with Rocque Vieille

Fort Doyle west to Grand Havre
3.0M (1.4m)

(See plans page 56 and below)

Transit G18 must be held accurately for almost 2 miles. Now is the time to identify a few marks. Ahead is Rousse de Mer (dries 6.8m) and off the starboard bow is Silleuse (dries 6.4m) and Roque au Nord (ht 0.5m). On the land look for Vale church spire to the SW and Victoria Tower to the SSW, both of which will be needed later.

S of Silleuse the line passes through the narrowest gap in the channel – barely 200m wide.

There is plenty of depth, at least 11m at datum, but it may be necessary to 'borrow' S to clear an isolated rock

(dries 1.2m) to the N. When 0.25M short of Rousse de Mer alter course to WSW and pass 200m S of it and onto Transit G22 as described below.

If early on the tide, branch off the transit G18 and discover several peaceful anchorages on this stretch of coast. All offer good shelter at LW in offshore breezes.

FONTENELLE BAY
49°30'.43N 02°30'.70W

(See plan page 56)

Less sheltered than its neighbouring bays to the W and vulnerable to swell.

There are no formal marks and entry should be made with reference to the chart. Beware of Demie de Fontenelle (dries 4.6m) a half tide rock on the E side.

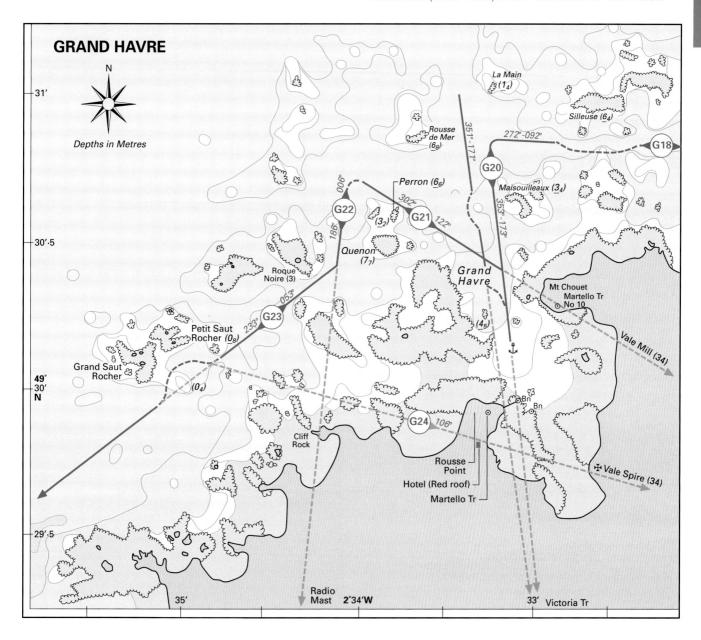

L'ANCRESSE BAY (PEMBROKE BAY)
49°30´.55N 02°31´.45W
(See plan page 56)

L'Ancresse Bay looking south

Entry
When the bay has opened up find:

G19 *210° Martello Tower No. 7 in the S of the bay in line with Vale Church spire (34m)*

Anchorage
There is good holding in sand in the middle of the bay. (see air view page 59). Take care to avoid drying rocks (dries 2.8m) and (dries 0.5m).

Grand Havre
49°30´.18N 02°33´.01W
(See plan page 59)

Entry

G20 *173° From G18 identify:*
Beacon (B) on the end of the quay off Rousse Point is in transit with Victoria Tower. Make sure the correct spire is identified!

Approaching from further N use transit shown on BA chart 807/808 (Victoria Tower in line with Rousse Point 171°) (see plan). This will clear between La Main (dries 1.4m) and Rousse de Mer (dries 6.8m) but crosses a shoal patch of 1.4m 200m W of Maisouilleaux when it will be necessary to borrow a bit to the W. To clear the drying rock (dries 4.5m) further S transfer to G20 on entry to give it a clearance of 175m.

Anchorage
Anchor with reference to the chart. Beware of several drying rocks in the bay. There is a stone slipway on the 130m long quay.

Facilities
Bars, grocery shops and a hotel. Regular buses to town.

Grand Havre looking south

Grand Havre south to Pleinmont Point
9.0M (2.1m)
(See plans pages 59, 62, 63)

Departure from Grand Havre
Proceeding W depart on stern transit:

G21 122° Vale Mill tower closed behind Martello Tower No. 10 on Mt Chouet (shown open for clarity)

Close the transit to give Perron (dries 6.6m) a respectable distance then make a close turn to pass 300m N of the rock and its westerly neighbour (dries 3.2m).

Next look SSW to identify the radio mast in the middle of the island. This is the rear mark for:

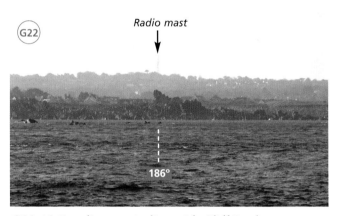

G22 186° radio mast in line with Cliff Rock

This short transit line will clear between Roque Noire (3m) with its drying neighbours and Quenon (dries 7.7m). Looking SW identify Lihou Island and Moulière (2.2m) with its reef. Take up transit:

G23 233° House on Lihou is on the W side of Moulière (2.2m) (here shown too far open)

A minor detour from this transit is required to clear a rocky shoal (0.4m) S of the extensive Grand Saut Rocher (6m) and Petit Saut Rocher (2m) reefs. For the turning point look ESE for the prominent red roof on an hotel on Rousse Point.

G24 106° The N end of the red roof is in line with Vale church spire

Commence a turn to starboard and head for Grand Saut Rocher (6m). When 200m off the rock alter course to port to regain transit G23.

You have cleared the dangers when Hanois lighthouse, if visible, is open to the E of Moulière.

Break off transit G23 to pass N of Moulière.

Continuing SW, a brief alteration onto a WNW heading is now required to find the next transit (G25) as described below. This will clear dangers lurking to the S. If time permits, take a break in Cobo Bay to plan the next stage.

GUERNSEY

COBO BAY

49°28'.66N 02°36'.33W

There are no formal marks for this fair weather anchorage and it is a question of feeling your way in with reference to the chart. When entering or leaving the bay note Boue Vazon (dries 3m) 0.5M SW of Moulière.

Anchorage

SW of local moorings there is good holding in sand.
  Returning to seaward, identify:

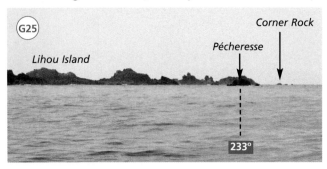

Cobo Bay

G25 233° La Pécheresse (dries 7.9m) to the SW aligned with Corner Rock (0.8m) at the most westerly end of Lihou

Holding this transit accurately is vitally important for clearing between dangers ahead. It will clear between Colombelle (dries 1.5m) and the reef extending W of La Conchée (4m).

Leave Pécheresse close to port to shape a course to pass midway between Corner Rock (0.6m) and Grand Etacré (dries 6.7m). Now is the time to decide whether to continue on to the S coast outside Rocquaine Bay or alter course S into Rocquaine Bay.

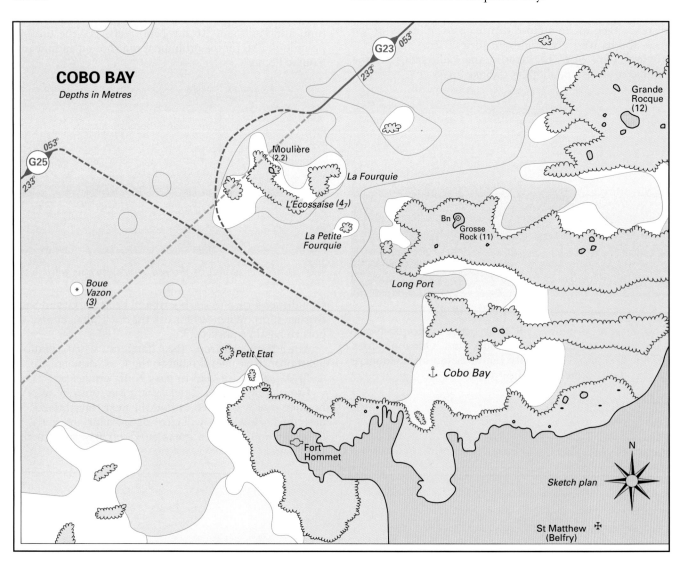

GUERNSEY

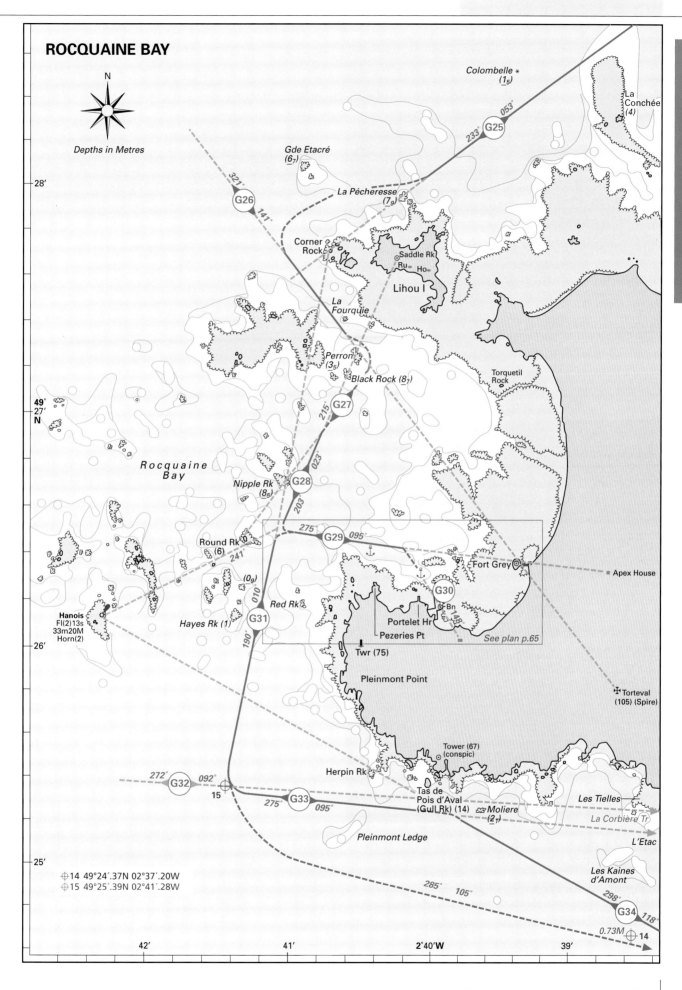

ROCQUAINE BAY

N

Depths in Metres

Colombelle *
(1₅)

La Conchée
(4)

053°

233° G25

Gde Etacré
(6₇)

321°

G26

141°

La Pécheresse
(7₉)

Corner
Rock

Saddle Rk
Ru   Ho

Lihou I

La
Fourquie

Perron
(3₅)

Torquetil
Rock

Black Rock (8₇)

215°

G27

49°
27'
N

*Rocquaine
Bay*

023°

Nipple Rk
(8₅)

G28

203°

275°

G29 095°

Fort Grey

Apex House

Round Rk
(6)

241°

G30

Bn

Portelet Hr

Pezeries Pt

149°

See plan p.65

(0₉)

Red Rk

010°

Hanois
Fl(2)13s
33m20M
Horn(2)

Hayes Rk (1)

G31

190°

Twr (75)

Pleinmont Point

Torteval
(105) (Spire)

Tower (67)
(conspic)

272°   092°

G32

Herpin Rk

Les Tielles

15

275°   G33   095°

Tas de
Pois d'Aval
(Gull Rk) (14)

Moliere
(2₇)

La Corbière Tr

Pleinmont Ledge

L'Etac

Les Kaines
d'Amont

25'

⊕14 49°24'.37N 02°37'.20W
⊕15 49°25'.39N 02°41'.28W

285°   105°

298°   118°
G34

0.73M ⊕14

42'   41'   2°40'W   39'

28'

26'

Looking SE into Roquaine Bay

ROCQUAINE BAY

Entry from N

From a position 400m WNW of Corner Rock (0.6m) identify the white Fort Grey tower, locally known as the 'Cup and Saucer', to the SE and take up:

G26 141° Torteval church aligned with the N side of Fort Grey Tower

Line G26 will leave La Fourquie (dries 6.1m) close to port. When just short of Perron (dries 3.5m) open out the transit and commence a turn to port leaving both Perron and Black Rock (dries 8.2m) to the S of it close to starboard (see view). Turn to starboard onto a heading of 215° with transit:

G27 215° Round Rock (6m) is just open to the S of Nipple Rock (dries 8.5m)

The next transit indicated on BA chart 807 is difficult to identify (2004). Hold G27 until looking astern:

G28 023° Saddle Rock on Lihou Is is aligned with Black Rock

This transit is held until a good 200m E of Round Rock (6m) at which point you can either continue SSE out of the bay using stern transit G31 (described below) or relax at anchor off Portelet Harbour.

PORTELET HARBOUR AND ANCHORAGES

49°26´.15N 02°39´.84W

This minuscule drying harbour has two quays which cover at HW. When there is no swell, bilge keelers can take the ground on firm sand below Trinity Cottages (see aerial views).

Approach

(See plans page 63 and below)

Branch off line G28 when

G29 095° Apex House is aligned with the N side of Fort Grey tower

This clears a rock awash at datum and, further in, La Tour (dries 7.9m). Both will be left to starboard.

Note The rear mark was partially obscured by trees (2004).

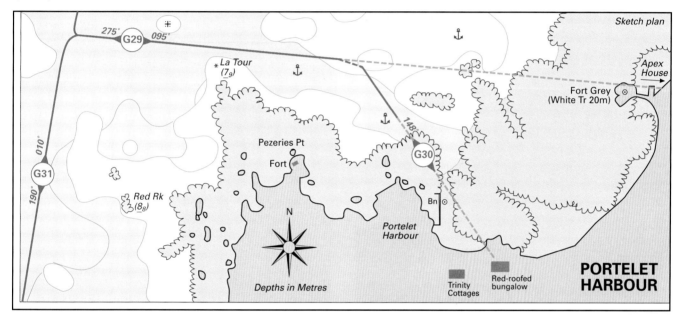

PORTELET HARBOUR

Portelet harbour from the north

A further useful transit for locating a suitable anchoring position N of the harbour is:

G30 *Red-roofed bungalow in line with Portelet Pier beacon 148°*

Note This transit is preferred to that shown on BA 807.

Anchorages

N of Pezeries Point as shown on BA 807 and plan page 65.

Portelet harbour from the WSW. The yacht is anchored NE of Pezeries Point and just S of approach line G29

E of Pezeries Point below the 2m contour NW of small boat moorings.

Facilities

Ashore there is a grocery shop and several restaurants: oysters and mussels are a local speciality.

Departure

Continuing round the island, leave by the arrival transit (see plan page 65):

When a good 200m short of Round Rock, note Hanois lighthouse touching its S edge. At this point take up the final stern transit that leads out onto the S coast:

G31 *010° ⊕15 The westernmost rock off Lihou Is over the eastern edge of Nipple Rock*

Note At 0.5M S of Round Rock the line passes a rock (1.5m) close to port. Depending on the height of tide it may be necessary to open the transit to give a wider berth. As these marks are difficult to identify use Hayes Rock (1m) 0.45M SSW of the break-off point from G29. If you are on the right track you will pass 200m E of this rock. 0.25M on you are clear of all dangers.

Clearing S out of Rocquaine Bay on Transit G31

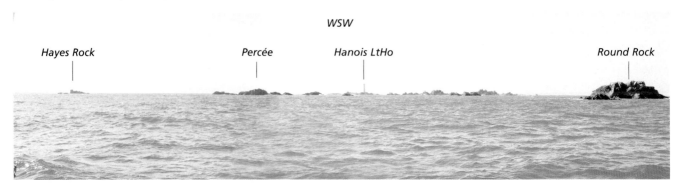

Portelet Harbour southabout from St Peter Port

(See plans pages 44-5, 63, 65, 69)

For a more straightforward passage to Portelet Harbour, go southabout from St Peter Port. Leave at HW St Helier+0230, just before the marina sill closes. There will be a S-going stream to St Martin's Point where it will be slack and on the S coast a W-going stream until LW which is the right time to be in Rocquaine Bay.

All dangers along the S coast will be cleared if you stay just outside the 50m contour – about 1M off.

Pleinmont Point west to St Martin's Point 7.6M (2.0m)

(See plans pages 44-5, 63, 69)

This stretch of Guernsey's coastline is generally steep-to and presents a somewhat confusing succession of similar shaped headlands. There are hazards extending up to 0.5M off, the main ones being Pleinmont Ledge, Les Kaines d'Amont, Les Lieuses, Baleine Rock and the Grunes de Jerbourg.

Locals have their marks for passing inside all but the Grunes. These directions take a moderate route S of most of these dangers, providing short detours into several attractive fair weather anchorages between Pte de la Moye and Jerbourg Point.

The inshore turning point off line G31 and onto the S coast is achieved with:

La Corbière Tower

G32 092° ⊕15 *The conspicuous lookout tower (89m) near La Corbière Point (not to be confused with Pleinmont Tower) bears 092°*

At the same time and subject to good visibility identify the marks for transit:

G33 095° *L'Etac (65m) S of Sark open of Pte de La Moye and midway between the Pte and Grande Lieuse 095° (no view)*

Routeing inside Pleinmont Ledge

This line clears midway between Pleinmont Ledge and Herpin Rock (1.5m). Confirmation can be obtained by taking stern bearings of Hanois LtHo. When on 298° hold transit:

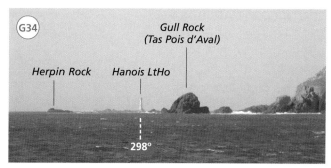

Herpin Rock · Hanois LtHo · Gull Rock (Tas Pois d'Aval) · 298°

G34 298° *Hanois LtHo is seen midway between Gull Rock (14m) and Herpin Rock (1.5m). This clears Les Kaines d'Amont and Les Lieuses*

Les Kaines d'Amont are off the stripey headland Les Tielles

Routeing outside Pleinmont Ledge

An alternative is to pass outside (S) of Pleinmont Ledge then route ESE to the turning point S of Corbière lookout tower. This is:

G35 (⊕14) 000° *Corbière lookout tower bearing N (no view)*

At this point steer towards Jerbourg Pt but note there are dangers extending up to 0.25M off Pointe de la Moye, Icart Point and Jerbourg Point.

To clear S of Grunes de Jerbourg use:

Martello tower · Les Tas de Pois d'Amont · 303°

G36 303° *The Martello tower above Saints Bay is kept well open of the southernmost Tas de Pois d'Amont*

Then turn north onto:

Longue Pierre bn · Brehon Tower · 026°

G38 026° *Brehon Tower is open E of Longue Pierre beacon*

SOUTH COAST ANCHORAGES

The last stretch of the south coast passes some of the island's finest anchorages.

Icart Bay

49°25´.18N 02°34´.70W

Petit Bôt (pronounced 'Bo') **Bay** and its southerly neighbour **Le Portelet** are snug anchorages in offshore winds. Petit Bôt is identified by its Martello Tower (15m). Approach with

G37 353° the tower open of the point

Anchor in 3m E of transit.

Le Gouffre

49°25´.10N 02°35´.30W

This small cove N of Pointe de la Moye offers some shelter in quiet weather. Anchor clear of rocks and moorings.

Pte de la Moye

Le Jaonnet and La Bette

Le Jaonnet and **La Bette** bays in the NE of Icart Bay provide secluded anchorage, but note the drying rocks between them. Approach with reference to the chart.

Moulin Huet Bay

49°25´.41N 02°32´.55W

The main obstruction in this superb bay to the E of Icart Point is the drying rock Mouilière (dries 8.5m) at its centre, which is usually visible. The holding is generally good in fine sand and there are several options depending on wind direction.

Approach and anchor with reference to the chart.

Moulin Huet Bay

Saints Bay

49°35´.23N 02°33´.20W

This small cove offers good holding in sand but beware of a drying rock close in and keep clear of local moorings. A path above the beach leads inland. The beacon marks the entry of old telephone cables. These have now been replaced by a fibre optic cable.

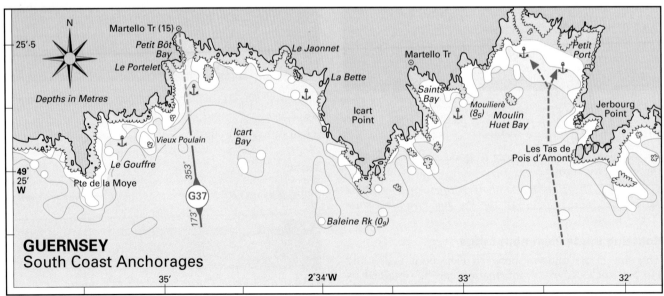

GUERNSEY
South Coast Anchorages

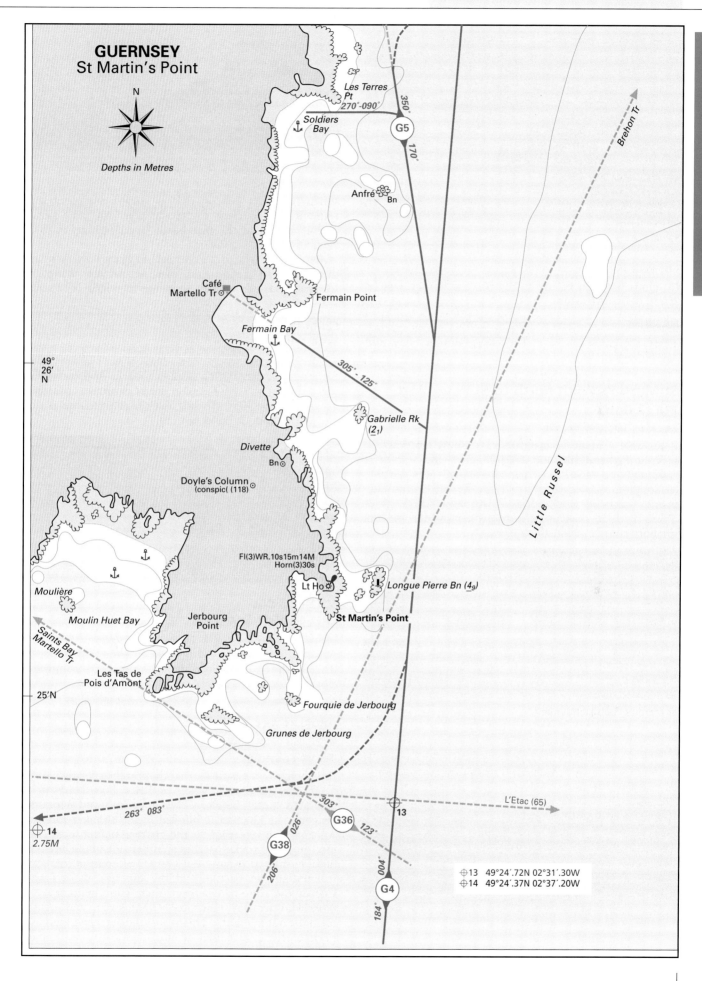

GUERNSEY
St Martin's Point

N

Depths in Metres

Les Terres
Pt
270°-090°

Soldiers
Bay

350°

G5

170°

Anfré
Bn

49°
26'
N

Café
Martello Tr ⊙
Fermain Point

Fermain Bay

305° - 125°

Gabrielle Rk
(2_1)

Divette
Bn ⊙

Doyle's Column ⊙
(conspic((118)

Moulière

Moulin Huet Bay

Saints Bay
Martello Tr

Les Tas de
Pois d'Amont

25'N

Fl(3)WR.10s15m14M
Horn(3)30s

Lt Ho ⊙

Longue Pierre Bn (4_9)

St Martin's Point

Jerbourg
Point

Fourquie de Jerbourg

Grunes de Jerbourg

Little Russel

Brehon Tr

263° 083°

14
2.75M

206°

026°

303°

G36

123°

G38

004°

G4

184°

13

L'Etac (65)

⊕13   49°24'.72N 02°31'.30W
⊕14   49°24'.37N 02°37'.20W

GUERNSEY

Saints Bay

Off Petit Port

In winds between N and E, the best anchorage will be found NE of Moulière.

Facilities

There are cafés ashore at Petit Bôt, Moulin Huet and Saints Bays.

St Martin's Point north to St Peter Port 2M (2.0m)

(See plans pages 45, 50, 69)

If possible arrange to make this last short leg between HW St Helier–0300 and +0100, when the stream is running N up to St Peter Port. Alternatively it is possible to dodge a S-going stream in Little Russel by routeing inside Gabrielle Rock (dries 2.1m) and Anfré (dries 3.3m) with its beacon. Directions below are for the offshore route outside all dangers.

St Martin's Point Lighthouse

G4 004° ⊕13 Vale Mill over the middle shed of a group of three (green) at St Sampsons

G5 350° White Rock light open to the E of Castle Cornet

When Moulinet beacon (M) is abeam, steer out into Little Russel to clear Oyster beacon (0m) and Ferico (0.9m) and open the pier heads (see Approaches to St Peter Port from S above).

Between St Martin's Point and St Peter Port there are three possible anchorages offering perfect shelter in westerlies. They can be untenable in winds between S and E.

FERMAIN BAY
49°26′.12N 02°31′.79W

(See plan page 69)

An attractive bay with a popular beach. Approach with the café open S of Fermain Point with the Martello Tower bearing 305°. Anchor as close to the shore as tide allows. Holding is good in sand.

SOLDIERS BAY
49°27′.06N 02°31′.68W

(See plan page 69)

A small inlet with good holding in sand. Reference to BA 807 shows dangers in the S so approach from the E close to Les Terres Point.

Facilities None, but there are steps to a cliff path.

HAVELET BAY
49°27′.06N 02°31′.68W

(See plan page 50)

A wide bay S of Castle Cornet that can be crowded at the height of the season when St Peter Port Harbour is saturated. Enter between Oyster beacon and Moulinet beacon. The channel is buoyed in the summer months. Anchor with reference to the chart avoiding local craft moorings and rocky patches at either side of the bay. The holding is good in sand but beware of areas of kelp.

Landing can be made at the slip just W of Castle Cornet and close to Guernsey Yacht Club building.

Note Havelet Bay tends to attract swell, making for uncomfortable nights. This is mostly tide-generated and particularly noticeable around HW, especially over spring tides.

Herm

Local Information

STD code: 01481

TRAVEL INFORMATION
Sea only
In the season there is an hourly ferry service between St Peter Port and the island. The Sark ferry calls into Herm several times a week to pick up visitors for Sark
Travel Trident ☎ 721379
Herm Seaway Express ☎ 721379

PORTS OF ENTRY
The official Ports of Entry into the Bailiwick of Guernsey are Braye in Alderney and Beaucette Marina, St Sampson (for commercial vessels only) and St Peter Port in Guernsey. At St Peter Port, all visiting yachts must clear in at the main harbour irrespective of which marina they moor in.

CHARTS
British Admiralty WGS 84
2669 Channel Islands and adjacent coast of France
3654 Guernsey Herm and Sark
807 Guernsey and Herm. Beaucette Marina
808 East Guernsey Herm and Sark. Beaucette Marina
Leisure Folio 5604
9 Guernsey Herm and Sark

Imray C Charts
C33A Channel Islands. Plan: Little Russel
Imray 2500 Channel Islands Chart pack

Stanfords Allweather
16 The Channel Islands
26 Channel Island Harbours (includes Guernsey and the Russel Channels)

French SHOM
6903 Guernsey and Herm
6904 Guernsey Est, Herm et Sark

RADIO FACILITIES
None

NAVIGATIONAL AIDS
None

USEFUL TELEPHONE NUMBERS
Herm Office ☎ 722377 *Fax* 700334

SUPPLIES AND SERVICES
Within the harbour area are: fresh water tap, toilets, showers, gift shops, rubbish collection point.
Basic provisions are obtainable from The Mermaid Tavern shop.
Restaurants The White House Hotel and Ship Restaurant. Reservations ☎ 722159
The Boaters Restaurant (The Mermaid Tavern)

Herm (right) and Jethou (left) from the south

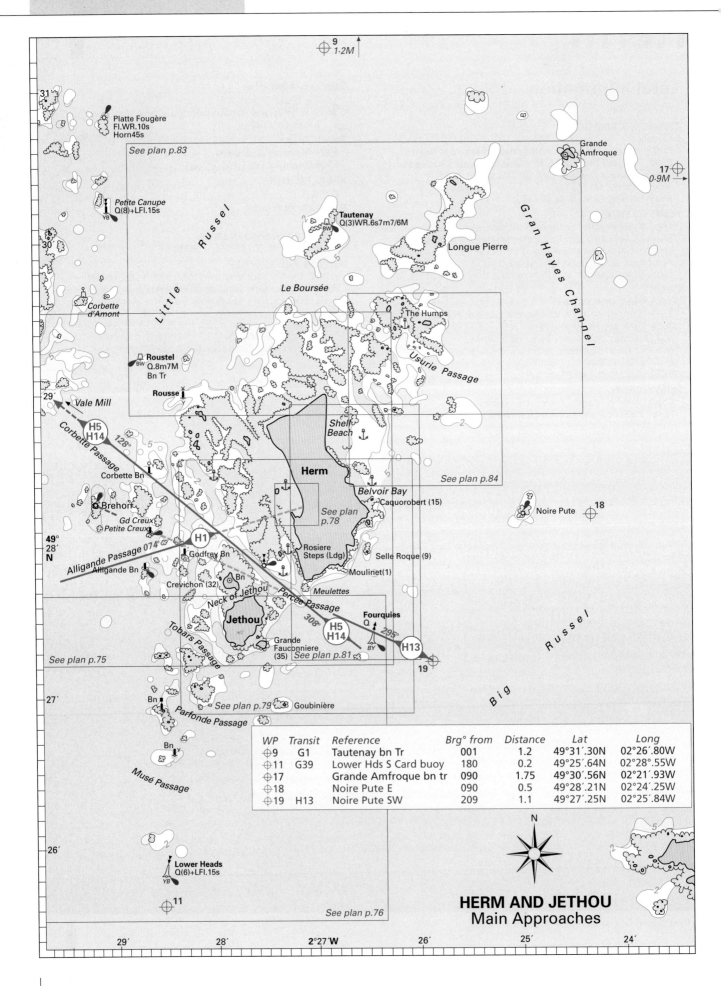

WP	Transit	Reference	Brg° from	Distance	Lat	Long
⊕ 9	G1	Tautenay bn Tr	001	1.2	49°31′.30N	02°26′.80W
⊕ 11	G39	Lower Hds S Card buoy	180	0.2	49°25′.64N	02°28′.55W
⊕ 17		Grande Amfroque bn tr	090	1.75	49°30′.56N	02°21′.93W
⊕ 18		Noire Pute E	090	0.5	49°28′.21N	02°24′.25W
⊕ 19	H13	Noire Pute SW	209	1.1	49°27′.25N	02°25′.84W

HERM AND JETHOU
Main Approaches

Tidal information

Tidal Levels referred to chart datum, as for St Peter Port. A look at the tidal plans in the *Appendix* indicates that the streams around Herm roughly conform to the pattern in the Russels. This is:

N-going from HW−0300 to HW+0300 and S-going from HW+0300 to HW−0300 with slack water around half tide. Close inshore there are subtle variations particularly among the reefs west of Herm and in the Percée Passage S of the island, where currents may exceed 5 knots.

When following the E–W channels the navigator should be particularly vigilant. Here a devious cross set can be experienced and if transits are not held accurately the yacht may quickly be swept towards dangers. *Always allow for tidal set.*

Introduction

A visit to Guernsey would be incomplete without making the three-mile hop across from St Peter Port to enjoy the tranquil charm of Herm. In 1949 the island was purchased in a dilapidated state by Guernsey from the Crown and has since been leased to the Wood family. Thanks to their vision and a strong commitment to conservation, it has been tastefully restored and is well maintained by a permanent community of about 40 people. In the centre of the island is the Manor House with its 12th-century Chapel of St Tugual. Clustered round the harbour are the highly rated White House Hotel and Restaurant, The Mermaid Tavern, self-catering cottages, a campsite and several small boutiques.

Visiting yachtsmen, along with ferry-loads of visitors are welcomed but regulated so the peaceful atmosphere is not threatened. Permission is required to remain on the island overnight and this is available without charge from the administrative office at the harbour.

Jethou and its neighbouring islets Crevichon and Grand Fauconnière are private and landing is prohibited. Herm's minuscule drying harbour and its low-water anchorage to the south offer good shelter with the option of drying out or remaining afloat at all states of tide. There are several idyllic anchorages on the east coast.

Ashore

A walk round the island will take about two hours. Beaches are clean and safe, the best being Belvoir Bay and Shell Beach on the east coast.

The island's sole pub The Mermaid Tavern, sells basic provisions and meals at The Boaters Restaurant.

The White House Hotel (☎ 722159) has two restaurants, The Ship Restaurant which is open to the public and The Conservatory for hotel residents only.

Pilotage

Over a dozen passages cut through the extensive reef that stretches from Grande Amfroque in the NE through Herm and Jethou to the Lower Heads S cardinal buoy. Even given good visibility, sufficient water and large-scale chart BA 808, plying these channels is a challenge to the navigator. With a profusion of marks at close range, pilotage here becomes a precise art calling for a degree of concentration.

Shell beach, Herm   *Visit Guernsey*

In contrast to the deep waters to the south, the north of Herm is an almost impenetrable area of drying sand and reefs. With strong and diverse streams and transits that are difficult to identify without local knowledge, the channels in this area are seldom used by visitors. They should not be attempted until the more straightforward channels in the south have been mastered.

Approaches to Herm

From St Peter Port

When approaching Herm from St Peter Port it is vital to locate key marks well before entering the reefs. Beacons can be difficult to identify against the backdrop of the island. Generally one is in safe water up to the point where Brehon Tower is bearing N. Whether to approach N or S of Jethou will depend on the state of the tide and the navigator's local knowledge.

Northabout (see pages 74–5), the direct Alligande Passage with a succession of beacons and a single transit is the most used channel, but caution is needed below half tide as there are some shallow patches. The LW option is Creux Passage which calls for confident pilotage.

Both these channels converge on a point in the Percée Passage from where you can, with sufficient water, enter the harbour on the leading beacons or proceed down the passage to Rosière Steps deep water landing and anchorage S of the harbour.

Percée Passage, which is a continuation of Corbette Passage (2.2m) provides a deep water NW–SE cut between Herm and Jethou.

Southabout (see pages 76–78), the Sark Ferries regularly ply the Tobars Passage S of Jethou at LW. This has greater depth and easily identified marks but there is little room for error. If uncertain take the easiest, if rather circuitous, option of going S for the Musé Passage or the Lower Heads S cardinal buoy. Approach to Rosière Steps is described under *Rosière Steps Landing* below.

All passages E of Herm are described from W to E.

By night

(See *Herm Harbour. By night.*)

Visitors are not encouraged to approach Herm at night. Locals use Alligande Passage (described below) and enter the harbour on the leading lights.

PASSAGES NORTH OF JETHOU
(See plans pages 75 and 79)

Alligande Passage (0.5m) (W to E)

Used by the Herm ferries, and the only passage that may be taken at night with caution and then only in summer. There are shallow patches so particular caution is required below half tide, when it may be necessary to choose an alternative passage. The key to entry is Alligande beacon (green with an A topmark and lit 49°87′.85N 02°27′.78W) this should be left 200m to starboard. Identify Vermerette beacon (yellow with a V topmark and lit) and take up:

H1 074° Vermerette beacon in line with white patch on end of quay

When 400m short of Vermerette beacon turn to port onto Transit H17 (see *Herm Harbour entrance* below) or to starboard to enter Percée Passage (H5).

Creux Passage (3.0m) (W to E)
(Plan pages 75, 79)

This is the low-water passage from St Peter Port to Herm; there are four doglegs and marks can be difficult to hold with any cross-set.

H2 095° Rosière Cottage (above Rosière Steps on Herm) open to the S of Petit Creux (C) beacon

When 100m from Petit Creux beacon, come to port and make a turn round it, leaving it 60m to starboard, then take up stern transit H3:

H3 257° Victoria Tower in line with Petit Creux beacon will clear N of Etacré (dries 0.9m) and its boue (dries 0.3m) and S of the Boue Lionnais (dries 0.7m)

This transit should be held for 400m then to clear the Boue, alter to 102° using stern transit:

H4 282° Brehon Tower to the N of the highest part of Grand Creux

This course will intercept the Corbette Passage as described under *Approaches to Herm. From the northwest*, below

Percée Passage (Passe Percée) (3.4m) (N to S)
(Plan pages 75, 79)

This NW–SE passage (pronounced 'Per-she') offers a straightforward approach to Herm from either direction.

As a continuation of the Corbette Passage it shares the same transit:

H5/H14 308° Vale Mill open twice its own width SW of Corbette de La Mare beacon

The mill must be kept open by about as much as the elevation of the mill in order to clear Percée Rock W cardinal beacon, also known as Gate Rock, and the sandbank (0.3m) S of Mouette. The above transit will also clear Meulettes (dries 1.7m), a reef off the S end of Herm, and Tinker (dries 2.5m) NE of Jethou.

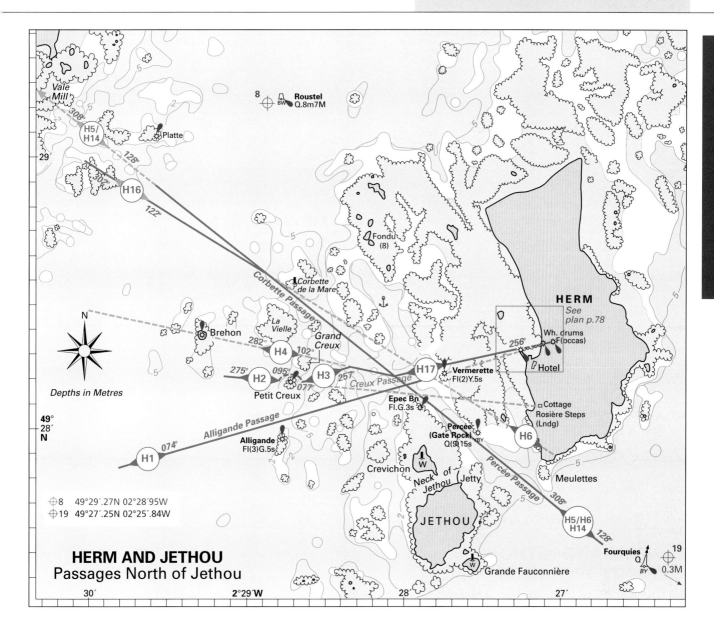

8   49°29´.27N 02°28´95W
19 49°27´.25N 02°25´.84W

HERM AND JETHOU
Passages North of Jethou

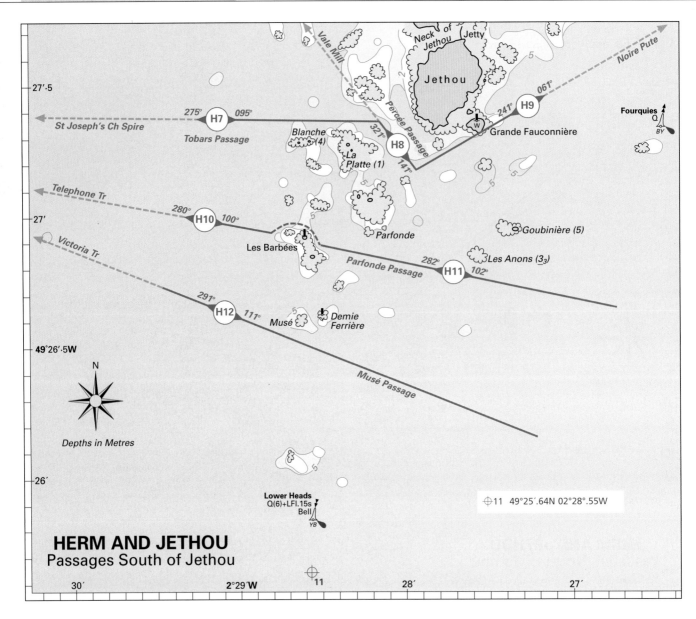

PASSAGES SOUTH OF JETHOU

Tobars Passage (5.0m) (W to E)

This is a more demanding passage and therefore best attempted once local knowledge has been gained. There are three doglegs and three sets of transits.

In very good visibility note that the Bec du Nez of Sark is just obscured behind the slope. When 400m short of Jethou turn to starboard and looking over the port quarter identify:

1. H7 095° Grande Fauconnière white beacon (pepper pot) touching the S slope of Jethou

2. H8 321° Vale Mill by the left (W) side of Brehon Tower

If poor visibility obscures Vale Mill, an alternative is Alligande beacon in the middle of the transit. Hold until:

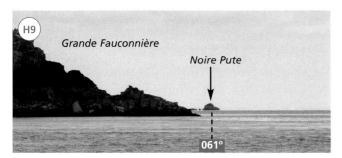

3. H9 *061° Noire Pute open of the southern slope of Grande Fauconnière*

Hold this transit leaving Grande Fauconnière 100m to Port.

Parfonde Passage (2.8m) (W to E)

H10 *280° Telephone Link Tower, with two white dishes (TV mast on chart BA 807/808) just to left (S) of Castle Cornet breakwater LtHo*

After leaving Les Barbées beacon (red can topmark) 100m to starboard (note that a head 100m WNW of the bn dries 1.2m); alter to starboard to avoid Parfonde and ensure the tidal stream does not set you onto Les Anons (dries 3.3m).

Take stern transit:

H11 *282° Victoria Tower just to the N of Les Barbées beacon. Hold for 1M to clear between Les Anons and the Banc des Anons*

Musé Passage (12m) (W to E)
Take stern transit:

H12 *291° Victoria Tower over the N end of Castle Cornet. This leaves Musé Rock 200m to the N and the beacon (M) 300m to the N*

PERCÉE PASSAGE (PASSE PERCÉE) (3.4M) (S TO N)
(See plans pages 75 and 79)

The approach to Herm from the SE and into this passage is the simplest. The key mark is Fourquies N cardinal buoy close N of the rock (dries 2.3m) that it guards. As its position can be unreliable make initial approach into the channel using:

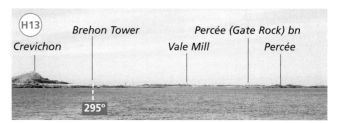

H13 *⊕19 295° Brehon Tower well open to the N of Crevichon*

This line will also clear Meulettes (dries 1.7m) off the S tip of Herm but on closing the 300m wide gap between Herm and Jethou the distant marks to the NW should be identified:

H5/14 *308° Vale Mill open twice its own width SW of Corbette de la Mare beacon*

Since the forward mark may be difficult to see from the S an alternative is to come E a bit to find:

H6 *308° Vale Mill with Percée (Gate Rock) W cardinal lit bn seen to the E and Epec bn (with E topmark and lit) seen to the W*

HERM

See also *Passages North of Jethou. Percée Passage.*

Note Clearing marks for avoiding Meulettes (dries 1.7m) S of Herm and Tinker (dries 2.5m) NW of Jethou are described under *Rosière Steps Landing. Approaches from the S*, below.

From the northwest

(See plan page 75)

Corbette Passage (2.2m) N to S

The direct route from Beaucette Marina or St Sampson to Sark (see plans pages 55 and 59), as it leads into the Percée Passage and out to the S of Herm.

First locate Corbette de la Mare beacon at a distance of no less than 600m. Identify transit:

H16 *122° Sauzebourge Point on Herm in line with Corbette de La Mare Rock*

Pass close W of Corbette de la Mare Rock which is steep-to on its SW side then take up stern transit H5/14 as for Percée Passage, described above.

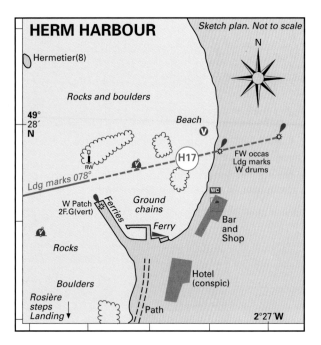

Herm Harbour

49°28'.20N 02°27'.28W Pier head

Space in the inner drying harbour is extremely limited and available only to small bilge keelers and yachts with beaching legs which should moor fore and aft. It is possible to dry out alongside the pier but ferry movements take precedence.

Rosière Steps is the ferry terminal when there is insufficient water in the harbour.

Bilge keelers and multihulls will be in their element on the sandy beach east of the harbour where visitors' moorings and chains have been laid. This area can be very congested at weekends in the summer months and it is not possible to reserve a patch in advance.

Entrance

Depending on draught, there will usually be sufficient water to enter the harbour between HW St Helier–0300 and +0300. Main approaches converge on Vermerette beacon (V) 250m short of Herm pier. When the rock on which it stands is awash there is about 1.0m depth at the pier and its steps.

From a position 80m N of Vermerette beacon locate two white drums above the beach just N of pier end and align with H17 *078°* (see view H1 page 74, plan and air view below).

By night

Lights available are the drums which are lit (F) throughout the summer, Vermerette beacon (Fl(2)Y.5s) and Alligande beacon (Fl(3)G.5s) (see plan page 75).

Local boats return to St Peter Port in the evening on the stern transit as above then round Vermerette beacon and into the Alligande Passage keeping one of the lit drums either side of Vermerette light.

Speed limit

6kn off beaches and in harbour area.

Herm harbour near HW

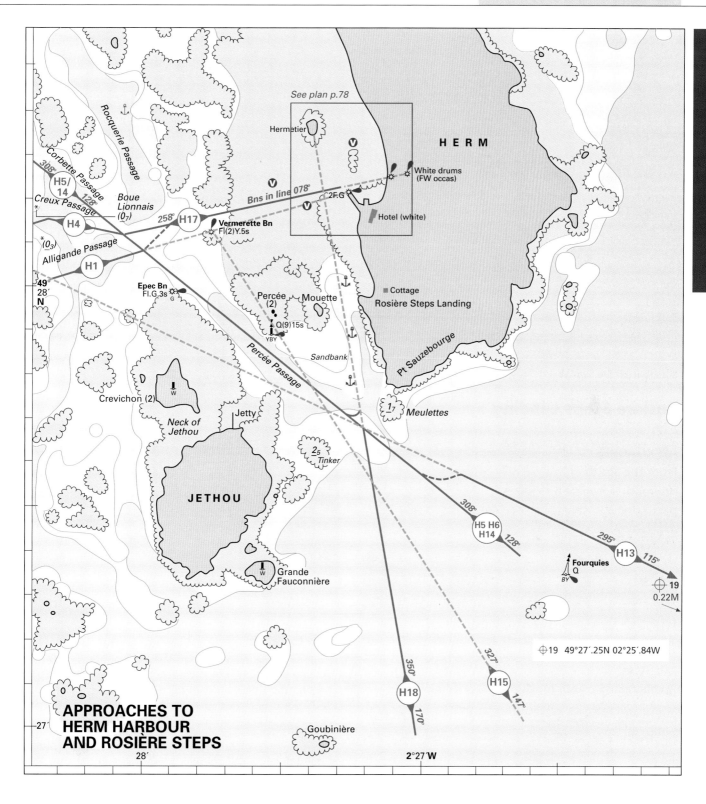

See plan p.78

Hermetier

V

V

HERM

V

Bns in line 078°

2 F.G

White drums
(FW occas)

Hotel (white)

Rocquerie Passage

Corbette Passage

308°

H5/
14

128°

Creux Passage

Boue
Lionnais
(0₇)

258°

H17

Vermerette Bn
Fl(2)Y.5s

H4

*(0₃)

Alligande Passage

H1

**49°
28′
N**

Epec Bn
Fl.G.3s

G

Percée
(2)

Mouette

Q(9)15s
YBY

Cottage

Rosière Steps Landing

Pt Sauzebourge

Sandbank

Crevichon (2)

W

Neck of
Jethou

Jetty

Percée Passage

1₇ Meulettes

2₅
Tinker

JETHOU

W

Grande
Fauconnière

308°

H5 H6
H14

128°

295°

H13

115°

Fourquies
Q
BY

19
0.22M

⊕19   49°27′.25N 02°25′.84W

327°

H15

147°

350°

H18

170°

**APPROACHES TO
HERM HARBOUR
AND ROSIÈRE STEPS**

Goubinière

27′

28′

2°27′W

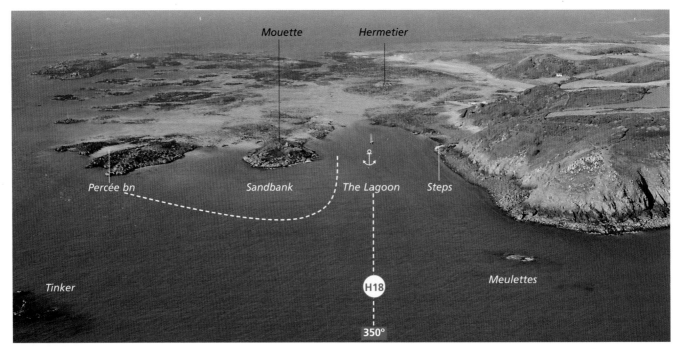

Rosière from the S at LW

Rosière Steps Landing

49°27′.98N 02°27′.20W

APPROACHES

From the south

Approach is from SSE as follows:

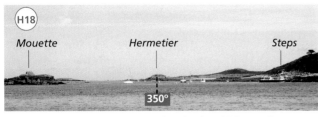

H18 350° Hermetier (Rat Island) should be well open to W of Rosière Steps (midway between the steps and Mouette (5m) to clear between Meulettes (dries 1.7m) and Tinker (dries 2.5m), see air view above.

An alternative transit for clearing E of Tinker is:

H15 327° Vermerette beacon open to the right (E) of Percée (Gate Rock) beacon

Rosière Steps Landing south of the harbour near HW

From the north

If approaching from the N in the Percée Passage avoid taking a short cut into the anchorage ('The Lagoon') by crossing the sandbank (0.3m) S of Mouette. Turn when the N point of Sark is just open of the S point of Herm.

'The Lagoon'

This is a snug anchorage in all but southerlies. Holding is good in sand and shingle if well clear of the rock and weed on the shoreline. Depths at CD are between 0.9m and 3.0m. At springs the whole area to the N dries and there is no flow in the remaining pool of water. At around HW a strong current sweeps S through the anchorage, making the short row to the landing demanding or even dangerous.

Mooring at the landing steps which are used by the ferries is not permitted, but here tenders may be manhandled ashore. A short track leads to the harbour.

Herm east coast (HW springs)

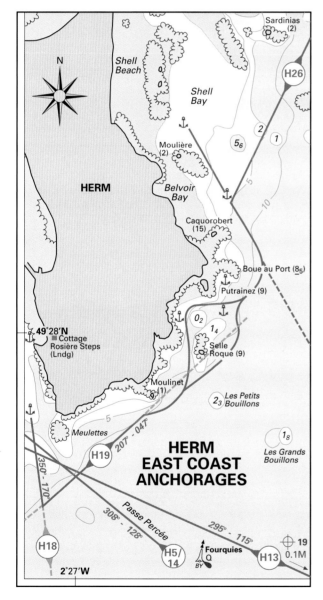

Sardinias (2)

Shell Beach

Shell Bay

H26

Moulière (2)

HERM

Belvoir Bay

Caquorobert (15)

Boue au Port (8₅)

Putrainez (9)

49°28'N

Cottage
Rosière Steps
(Lndg)

Selle Roque (9)

Moulinet (1)

Les Petits Bouillons

Meulettes

207 - 047°

HERM
EAST COAST
ANCHORAGES

Les Grands Bouillons

350° - 170°

H19

308° - 128°

Passe Percée

295° - 115°

H18

H5/ 14

Fourquies
Q
BY

H13

19
0.1M

2°27'W

⊕19 49°27'.25N 02°25'.84W

Herm east coast

APPROACHES

From the east

Approaching from the east is straightforward. The solitary rock Noire Pute (2m) situated one mile ESE of Belvoir Bay is a useful mark, but note it extends 300m N of its small beacon, so it is better to pass S of it. Guard against being set towards reefs to the NE if approaching with a N-going stream.

From the Percée Passage

Hold Transit H5 or H13 carefully and avoid wandering E of the line to risk a conflict with Meulettes. The turning point on to the E coast is reached when the conspicuous *Selle Roque (9m) is bearing 047° and open to the right (E) of Moulinet (1m)*. This is Breastmark H19 (047°):

There is the option of passing inside, with caution, or outside Selle Rocque (9m). 400M N is Putrainez (9m) with Putrainez Bay in between.

ANCHORAGES

Putrainez Bay 49°28'.05N 02°26'.39W

This is a pleasant alternative anchorage to Belvoir further N, particularly at LW.

Belvoir Bay 49°28'.40N 02°26'.34W

This bay lies between Caquorobert (Robert's helmet) (15m) in the S and Moulière (2m) in the N. This is a sheltered anchorage in W to SW winds and the holding is very good in sand. Taking the ground should be avoided as it shelves steeply and is subject to swell. The beach and small café are popular.

Shell Beach 49°28'.60N 02°26'.50W

Made of myriads of rare and exotic shells, this is entered close N of Moulière avoiding drying rocks further to the N. Watch the depth sounder carefully and anchor between Moulière and a group of rocks that dry 6.3m to the NW.

The north of Herm, an area of high rocks, sandbanks and rushing streams

North of Herm

Caution

Like many other Channel Island passages those N of Herm call for local knowledge, good visibility and should be taken between 2 hours either side of LW springs, when the majority of dangers are visible and currents comparatively weak. Much of the pilotage here is of the eyeball variety and should be taken at slow speed (see *Pilotage* page 73).

FROM LITTLE RUSSEL TO BIG RUSSEL BY LE BOURSEE (HAYES PASSAGE) (10m)

Le Boursée (10m) (W to E)

Best taken W to E and in visibility of at least three miles. Proceeding up Little Russel, make for a position 0.4M SW of Tautenay beacon tower (a truncated pyramid with

BW vertical stripes). As a lead into the channel identify Corbette d'Amont yellow conical beacon and align this with Vale Mill (conspic) as a stern transit:

H20 264° *Vale Mill over Corbette d'Amont beacon*

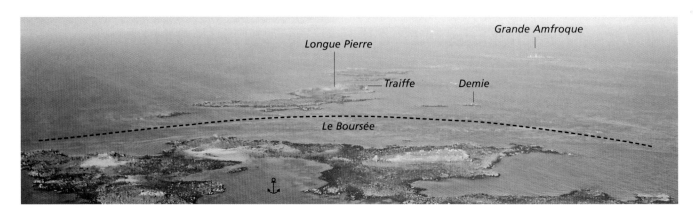

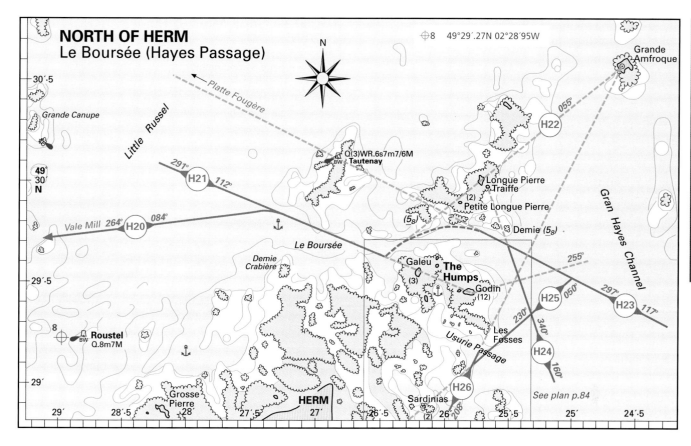

Next identify Godin (12m) and the smaller Galeu (3m) on the Humps. The transit is:

H21 *112° The highest point of Godin just to the N of the highest point of Galeu*

When 600m short of Galeu Island it is time to make the avoiding turn onto a NE heading with the next transit:

H22 *055° Gde Amfroque b/w beacon open to the N of Longue Pierre*

When 300m short of the 5.8m drying rock extending SW of Petite Longue Pierre (2m) commence a shallow turn onto an easterly heading into the middle of the 200m wide channel. Skirt the fringe of rocks to the N, keeping 100m off.

Continue the turn until:

H23 *Platte Fougère light tower (if visible) is just open S of Tautenay Bn Tower*

Steer to hold this transit on 297° into Big Russel until Godin bears 255°.

If proceeding S into The Humps anchorage, the following directions may be used to clear Les Fosses:

From a position 100m S of Demie (dries 5.8m) take up stern transit:

H24 *340° The left (W) edge of Demie in line with the column-like rock Traiffe*
Hold until:

H25 *230° Sardinias (2m) bears 230° and in transit with two isolated trees on the Herm skyline (see plan page 83)*
Hold until:

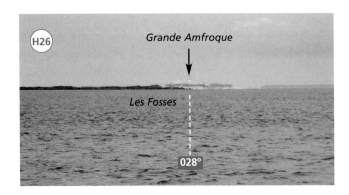

H26 *028° Gde Amfroque BW tower over the exposed end of Les Fosses*

Proceed as for The Humps anchorage as described below.

USURIE PASSAGE AND THE HUMPS ANCHORAGE (S TO N)
49°29′.43N 02°26′.05W
(See plans page 83 and below)

The Humps anchorage

The Humps LW anchorage must rate as one of the most difficult to access in the Channel Islands and calls for local knowledge. Boat owners are requested not to land on The Humps between 1 January and 15 July to protect the important breeding sea bird colonies on these islets. The same applies to Brehon Tower.

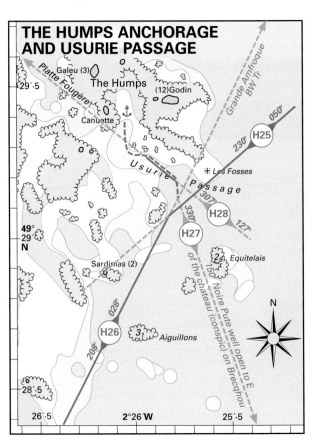

THE HUMPS ANCHORAGE AND USURIE PASSAGE

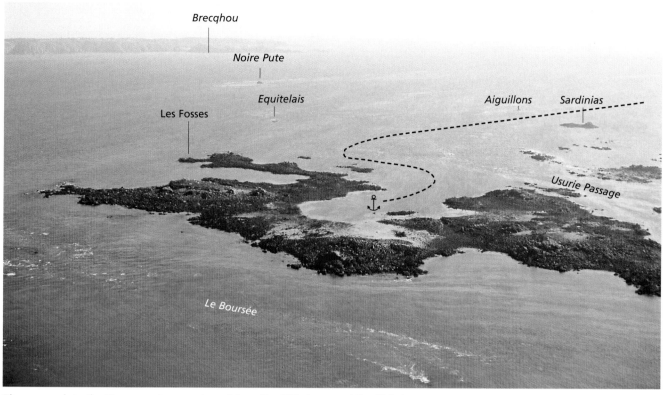

The approach to the Humps anchorage viewed from the NW above and the SE below

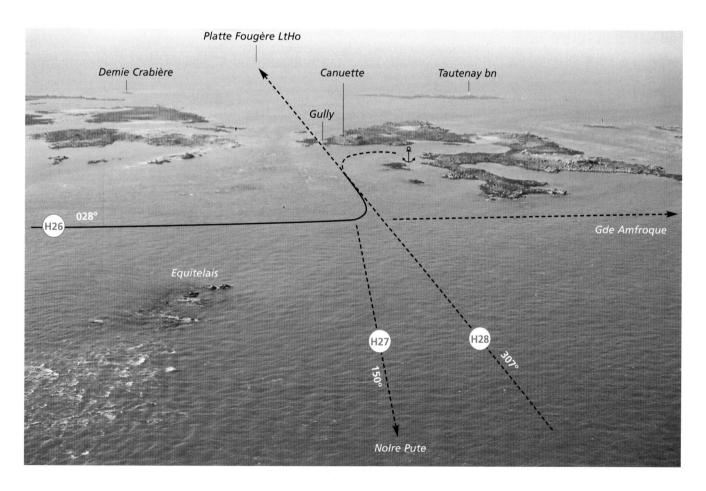

Approach from Belvoir Bay

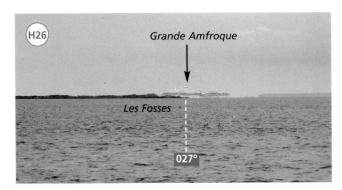

H26 *028° Grande Amfroque BW Tower over the exposed end of Les Fosses*

This is an important transit to be held carefully. It provides safe passage between Sardinias (2m) to the W and Aiguillons (dry 3.1m) and Equitelais (dries 2.9m) to the E. Next be ready for:

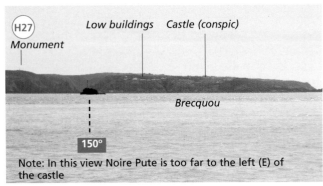

Note: In this view Noire Pute is too far to the left (E) of the castle

H27 *Identify Noire Pute (2m) to the SE on a stern bearing of 150° and well open to the E of the castle (conspic) on Brecqhou,*

alter course to NW and ahead identify Canuette (12m). Keeping a good lookout over the bow make a small westerly diversion onto:

H28 *307° Platte Fougère LtHo in the gully S of Canuette*

Turn N to enter the anchorage. The bottom is sand with some weed and the holding good.

Depth in the anchorage

This is charted as 0.6m at CD. The author found 3.5m at LW when the predicted height at St Helier was 3m.

Looking N into the Humps anchorage at LWS

Sark

Local information

STD code: 01481

TRAVEL INFORMATION

Isle of Sark Shipping Company operates a regular ferry service between St Peter Port and the island. Guernsey office ☎ 724059 *Fax* 713999. The French carrier *Manche Iles Express* (seasonal) links Sark with the other islands and French ports. ☎ 701316 and 01534 880756.

PORTS OF ENTRY

The official Ports of Entry into the Bailiwick of Guernsey are Braye in Alderney and Beaucette Marina, St Sampson (for commercial vessels only) and St Peter Port in Guernsey. At St Peter Port, all visiting yachts must clear in at the main harbour irrespective of which marina they moor in.

CHARTS

British Admiralty WGS 84

808 East Guernsey, Herm and Sark
3654 Guernsey, Herm and Sark

Imray

C33A Channel Islands. Plan: Creux Harbour Approaches
Imray 2500 Channel Islands Chart pack

Stanfords Allweather

16 The Channel Islands
26 Guernsey and the Russel Channels

French SHOM

6904 Guernsey East, Herm and Sark Beaucette Marina
7159P Guernsey, Herm and Sark to Alderney

RADIO FACILITIES

Sark Moorings VHF Ch 10
St Peter Port Radio (west coast) VHF Ch 20
Jersey Radio (east coast) VHF Ch 82

NAVIGATIONAL AIDS

None

USEFUL TELEPHONE NUMBERS

Harbourmaster ☎ 832323 Mobile 07781 101918
Deputy harbourmaster ☎ 07781 106069
(Simon Couldridge) ☎ 07781 132260 *Fax* 832364
☎ 07781 106 065 (Mobile in patrolling dorey)
Email simon@sarkci.com
Sark Tourism ☎ 832345
www.sark.info
Doctor: Sark Medical Centre ☎ 832045

SUPPLIES AND SERVICES

Water from tap (*Creux*) within harbour area.
Showers at the N end of the tunnel.
Petrol and diesel (cans) via harbourmaster.

Bar, restaurant, provisions, bank: walk or tractor up the hill to the village.

Sark from the south

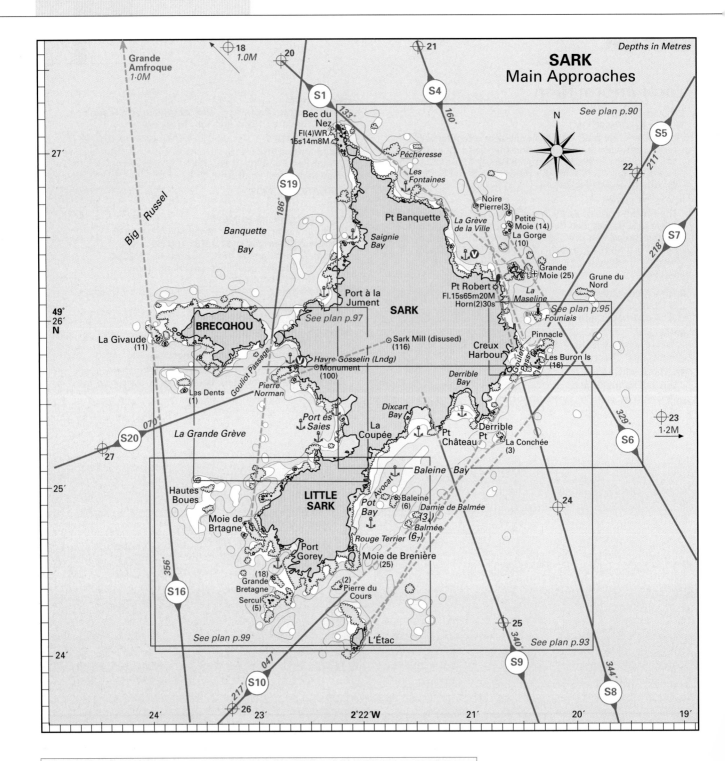

SARK
Main Approaches

Depths in Metres

WP	Transit	Reference	Brg° from	Distance	Lat	Long
⊕18		Noire Pute	090	0.5	49°28'.21N	02°24'.25W
⊕20	S1	Bec du Nez bn NW	322	0.53	49°27'.50N	02°22'.67W
⊕21	S4	Bec du Nez bn NE	042	0.56	49°27'.50N	02°21'.60W
⊕22	S5	Pt Robert Lt Ho	050	1.2	49°26'.95N	02°19'.34W
⊕23		Blanchard E card buoy	090	0.5	49°25'.35N	02°16'.65W
⊕24	S8	Creux Harbour	164	1.0	49°24'.88N	02°20'.20W
⊕25	S9	L'Etac E	085	0.9	49°24'.17N	02°20'.68W
⊕26	S10	L'Etac SW	242	1.0	49°23'.63N	02°23'.39W
⊕27	S20	La Givaude	205	0.7	49°25'.25N	02°24'.40W

Introduction

Sark, the peaceful Channel Island, is a unique place where you can step back in time to an age before cars – there are none. For generations it has managed to retain its independence from the outside world and despite the annual deluge of visitors there is little to disturb the population of some five hundred, other than farm sounds and the call of sea birds.

The island's early history is sketchy. To the Romans it was Sargia. Under the Normans it was held sacred by its monks but was soon abandoned to hermits due to the Black Death and frequent raids by pirates. Sark's modern history starts in 1565 with the arrival of Helier de Carteret, Seigneur of St Ouen in Jersey. He was granted the island by Queen Elizabeth I on condition that it was continually inhabited and capable of defence. This he managed with the aid of 40 families, 35 from Jersey and the remainder from Guernsey. The feudal government they established remains largely intact to this day, the present Seigneur enjoying some of the rights and privileges of his predecessors. Sark is part of the Bailiwick of Guernsey but has its own parliament known as the Chief Pleas.

Rising to 116m (380ft), Sark is hard to miss. A rather sinister aspect from seaward belies the charm of the countryside on top of the plateau. As a place for the crew to stretch their legs it is unsurpassed. Secure the tender at one of the many landing places, scale up a narrow cliff path and walk or cycle the tracks in some of the cleanest air in the realm. For the less energetic, the island may be explored by horse and carriage and there is a tractor-drawn trailer that hauls visitors up the hill from La Maseline Harbour. The village offers basic shopping, two banks, a post office and a good scattering of hotels, restaurants and pubs. The island can be rather creepy after dark and cliff paths are dangerous without a torch.

Little Sark to the S is joined to the main island by a spectacular causeway known as La Coupée.

Brecqhou Island

This island off the W coast is separated by the narrow Gouliot Passage. It is privately owned and landing is strictly prohibited. In recent years a conspicuous fort style residence has been built on the NW corner.

Harbours and anchorages

The bays and coves beneath Sark's cliffs offer sheltered anchorage in offshore winds. Visitors' moorings have been laid in Havre Gosselin (W coast) and Grève de la Ville (E coast). Availability is on a 'first come first served' basis at a charge of £12 per 24 hours. Payment can be made to the official in a patrolling dory or via payment boxes ashore (see Radio facilities and useful telephone numbers above).

The drying harbour of Creux on the E coast was built by the early settlers. It claims to be the smallest in the world and is certainly one of the wonders of Sark. It can only be used by small, shallow-draught boats (and service boats) and with caution.

The adjoining harbour of La Maseline is used by ferries and small cargo vessels. It is unsuitable for yachts.

TIDAL INFORMATION
Tidal levels referred to chart datum
La Maseline Jetty 49°26′.00N 02°20′.60W

MHWS	MLWS	MHWN	MLWN
9.0m	1.0m	3.5m	3.5m

High water at Sark is approximately 10 minutes after St Helier.

Positioned in the middle of the fast-moving stream that ebbs and flows through the Alderney Race just 20 miles to the NE, Sark's currents are vigorous, running approximately SW on the last of the ebb and first of the flood and NE on the last of the flood and first of the ebb. Slack water is around half tide. The shape of the island induces counter currents and reversals round the island which are too complex to show on the Tidal Stream Atlas in the appendix. For example, in the Gouliot, between Sark and Brecqhou, it may touch 7 knots on the top of a big spring tide. Outside Creux and Maseline harbours, the Goulet on the ebb reaches 6 knots.

Inbound to the E coast harbours from Guernsey, the decision whether to go N or S depends on the tide. The fastest streams run approximately NE around high water and SW around low. Thus it follows that from the Bec du Nez to the Grand Moie it is slack at high water and from Sercul to Grande Grève it is slack at low water. Therefore head N coming from the Big Russel at high water but S near low water. When leaving from Sark harbours towards St Peter Port, between half tide up to just before high water, go S. When clear of Sercul, bear away for the Lower Heads buoy. At most other times go N but if it is high water or soon after, circle the Bec du Nez and keep close to the Banquette Bay shore. Keep 200m off the N of Brecqhou, leave Moie Batard 100m to port, then head W across the Big Russel. Naturally, wind direction must be considered in any inshore pilotage around Sark. The high cliffs form a welcome lee but also cause downdrafts and accelerated gusts (see *Appendix. Tidal diagrams*).

Approach and pilotage

There is nothing difficult in arriving within a mile or two of Sark but relevant coastal features should be identified before closing the coast. Initially key rocks tend to be illusive against the backdrop of cliffs with which they merge. Sark waters are not navigable after dark.

Pilotage round the island can be an awesome experience for newcomers. Many channels lie within 0.3M of the shore and rocks are passed close enough to disturb the cormorants. However, inshore waters are generally deep and life will be easier if arrival coincides with half tide, when streams are more or less slack all round the island and many charted dangers are safely covered.

Ashore

The only way to see the island is on foot, with a bike or by horse and cart. Not all bays have footpaths ashore and apart from the harbours, the easiest landings for the village are at Dixcart Bay and Grande Grève.

Sark Information Centre in The Avenue provides an excellent official map of footpaths and landmarks. It is worth visiting La Coupée, the causeway between Sark and Little Sark, and the formal gardens of La Seigneurie. This is the official residence of the Seigneur of Sark.

There are several restaurants ashore specialising in sea food. Dixcart Bay Hotel (☎ 832015) and Aval du Creux Hotel and Restaurant (☎ 852036) and La Sablonnerie Hotel, Little Sark (☎ 832061)are recommended.

If taking an evening meal ashore, be prepared to return to the yacht in total darkness – there is no street lighting!

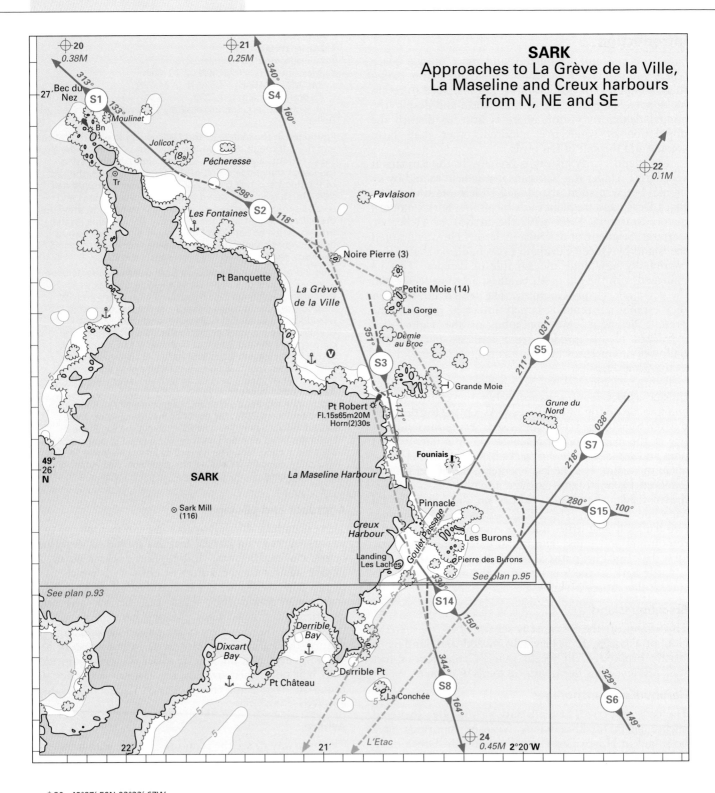

SARK
Approaches to La Grève de la Ville,
La Maseline and Creux harbours
from N, NE and SE

⊕ 20
0.38M

⊕ 21
0.25M

⊕ 22
0.1M

313°

Bec du
Nez

S1

133°

Moulinet

Bn

Jolicot

(8₉)

Pécheresse

Tr

298°

Les Fontaines

S2

118°

340°
160°

S4

Pavlaison

Noire Pierre (3)

Petite Moie (14)

La Gorge

Pt Banquette

*La Grève
de la Ville*

351°

*Démie
au Broc*

V

S3

171°

Grande Moie

031°

211°

S5

*Grune du
Nord*

038°

S7

218°

Pt Robert
Fl.15s65m20M
Horn(2)30s

**49°
26′
N**

SARK

La Maseline Harbour

Founiais

280°

S15

100°

Pinnacle

⊙ Sark Mill
(116)

*Creux
Harbour*

Goulet passage

Les Burons

Pierre des Burons

Landing
Les Laches

See plan p.95

330°

See plan p.93

S14

150°

*Derrible
Bay*

*Dixcart
Bay*

Derrible Pt

344°

329°

Pt Château

La Conchée

S8

S6

149°

22

21′

L'Etac

164°

⊕ 24
0.45M **2°20′W**

⊕ 20   49°27′.50N 02°22′.67W
⊕ 21   49°27′.50N 02°21′.60W
⊕ 22   49°26′.95N 02°19′.34W
⊕ 24   49°24′.88N 02°20′.20W

East coast
(Creux Harbour, La Maseline Harbour, the anchorages)

Approaches

FROM THE NORTH

(See plan page 90)

Inside Pécheresse (dries 8.9m)

The run in from the N on initial transit S1 (⊕20) commences NNW of Bec du Nez. This point is steep-to and overfalls can be expected to the NW of it with wind against tide. The channel N of La Maseline Harbour is narrow (100m wide in one place) and should not be attempted at LW Springs. Coming from Guernsey or the Big Russel the passage is best taken at HW when the stream will be slack between Bec du Nez and the Grande Moie.

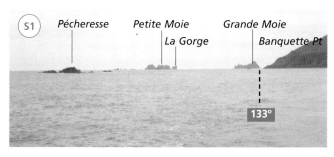

S1 133° (⊕20) 133° W side of Grande Moie in line with Banquette Point clears Pécheresse (dries 8.9m)

With Pécheresse abeam, identify the black above-water rock Noire Pierre (3m) and alter to port for:

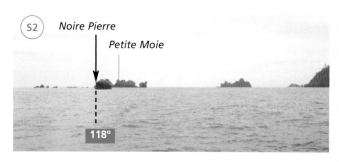

S2 118° N face of Noire Pierre in line with N face of Petite Moie

When 200m off Noire Pierre steer for the gap between Point Robert (with the lighthouse) and Grande Moie.

The dangers in the narrow gap under the LtHo are cleared by S3:

S3 171° Pinnacle Rock of the Goulet just open of the end of La Maseline Jetty

If too open you will be over a patch of Grande Moie drying 1.6m.

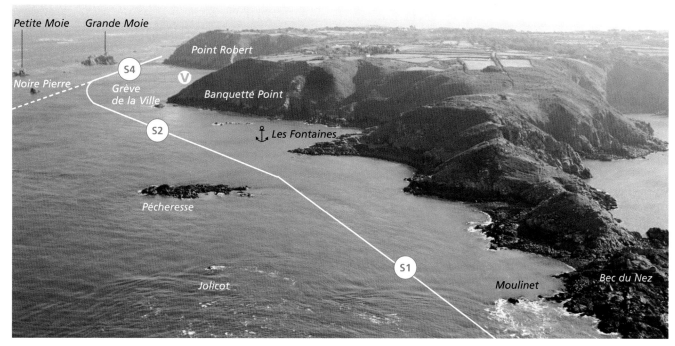

Sark's notheast coast looking south at LWS

Outside Pécheresse (dries 8.9m)

This easier approach, particularly if under sail, avoids overfalls off Bec du Nez and passes E of Pécheresse leaving Bec du Nez 0.5M to starboard. When St Martin's Pt (Guernsey) is open to the right (N) of Bec du Nez find:

S4 160° (⊕21) All Les Burons are open of Point Robert

Hold this transit but leave Noire Pierre to port. Continue as for *Inside Pécheresse* as above.

FROM THE NORTHEAST

S5 211° (⊕22) L'Etac between Les Burons and Sark

This approach from the NE can be used for either La Maseline or Creux Harbour, passing N of Grune du Nord (dries 3.7m).

In the harbour approaches identify Founiais beacon (dries 6.7m) 300m ENE of the pierhead. This can be passed 100m either side (see Transit S15). (For La Maseline entry and information see *La Maseline Harbour. Entry.*)

Goulet Passage (1.2m)

(See plans pages 90 and 95)

If intending to proceed S to Creux Harbour it is necessary to route outside Les Burons. It is prohibited to pass S through the drying Goulet Passage between Creux Harbour and Les Burons so, after passing Point Robert and Grande Moie or on leaving La Maseline take up stern transit:

S6 329° La Gorge with its 'head' looking west open E of la Grande Moie by a distance equal to the distance between the two peaks of la Grande Moie

This transit will clear between Les Burons and the shallows with overfalls to the east. When Les Burons bear due W identify La Conchée (3m) and take up:

S7 218° L'Etac well open to the left (E) of La Conchée

This transit will clear drying rocks off Burons. It can be maintained if proceeding to Creux Harbour or to Baleine Bay anchorages.

FROM THE SOUTHEAST

There are several options if approaching from this direction, typically from Jersey. ⊕24 and ⊕25 are recommended safe-water positions. See plan page 88.

From N to S these are:
1. Transit S6 – described above – skirts S of the troubled waters W of Blanchard cardinal buoy and onto the approach to La Maseline (S 15).
2. Transit S8 ⊕24 Outer approach to Creux Harbour:

S8 344° ⊕24 Pt. Robert LtHo in line with Creux Harbour tunnel

The lighthouse will dip below the headland when less than about 1 mile off. (For Creux Harbour entry and information see under *The Harbours. Creux Harbour,* below.

3. Transit S9 (⊕25) into Baleine Bay aimed at Dixcart Bay.

S9 340° ⊕25 White house above Dixcart Bay over the westward slope of Point Chateau

Note The transit shown on BA chart 808 is unreliable as Sark Mill is no longer conspicuous.

For entry to either of the harbours break off this transit before turning into Dixcart and head NE to join S8, S14 or S15. La Conchée (3m) may be passed either side. See plan page 90.

FROM THE SOUTH

An approach towards the south of the island is best made at low water when marks are visible and from St Helier HW–0500, the stream will run NE for nearly nine hours from Sercul Rock (5m) off Little Sark to Creux Harbour.

BA chart 808 shows the shallows and disturbed water SE of Little Sark and care should be taken not to be swept into Les Vingt Clos (dries 1.9m) or Balmée (dries 6.7m), when the stream is running.

Outside (E of) L'Etac

(See plan page 88)

The easiest option is to approach well outside all dangers. Pass 0.5M S of L'Etac then steer 060° to reach Transit S9 *340°* for Dixcart Bay, or S8 *344°* Outer approach to Creux Harbour or S6 *329°* for La Maseline.

Inside (W of) L'Etac

(See plans pages 88, 90 and below)

There are two passages, both of which require positive identification of key marks and precise pilotage.

1. **Outside Pierre du Cours S10** (⊕26)
   Starting from a position 0.75M off the S point of Little Sark bearing 030° make a positive identification of Pierre du Cours (2m) and La Conchée (3m) 2M beyond and SE of Derrible Point. Then take up S10 as shown overleaf.

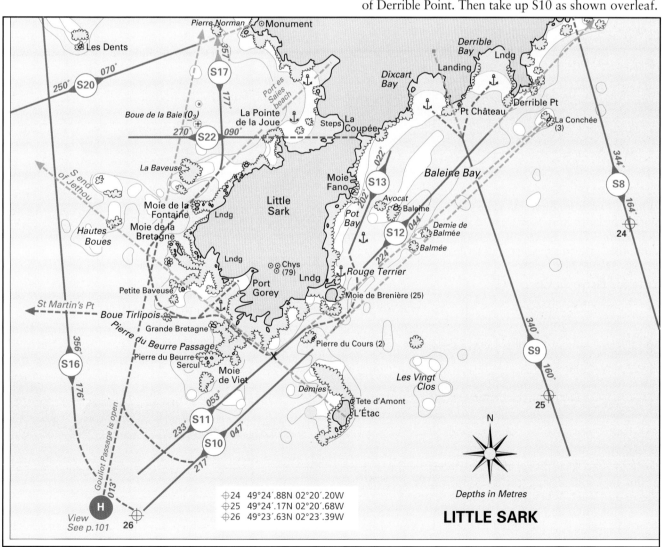

⊕24 49°24′.88N 02°20′.20W
⊕25 49°24′.17N 02°20′.68W
⊕26 49°23′.63N 02°23′.39W

Depths in Metres

LITTLE SARK

Looking NE over L'Etac at the south end of Sark

S10 047° ⊕26 *La Conchée well open to the E of Pierre du Cours and Balmée (dries 6.7m) (if above water)*

When 200m from Pierre du Cours leave it close (50m) to port in order to keep well clear of the Demies that extend NW from l'Etac. Steer out to leave Balmée to port or take the inshore passages described under *Passages across Baleine Bay* below.

2. Inside Pierre du Cours S11

S11 053° *La Conchée and Balmée (if above water) on the edge of Moie de Brenière (25m)*

Steer to pass W of Pierre du Cours (2m) by more than 150m to avoid drying rocks extending W to NW of Pierre du Cours. When the rock bears S, steer E to avoid rocks S of Moie de Brenière. When Balmée is seen open E of La Conchée, come round to the N, leaving Moie de Brenière 200m to port.

PASSAGES ACROSS BALEINE BAY

Passage N to Dixcart Bay may be made inside Balmée (dries 6.7m) and Demie de Balmée (dries 3.4m) with transit:

S12 044° *Les Burons chimney in the 'V' of Derrible Pt (see air view below)*

Note that a shelf extends W of Balmée and there are drying heads 100m to the S of Baleine.

Passage N inside Baleine (6m) and Avocat (dries 3.7m) may be made using stern transit:

S13 202° *Daylight just showing through the hole in Moie de Brenière*

Beware of Avocat which may be covered and rocks drying 5m extending 100m E from Moie Fano.

The harbours

Creux Harbour

Location 49°25´.80N 02°20´.60W Pierhead

The harbour dries out completely and is prone to surge. It is therefore suitable for small shallow draught boats and only in fair weather. Access is HW St Helier ± approximately 2 hours. Anchoring outside the harbour, Les Laches, is prohibited.

Entry

On closing the harbour on Transit S8 as described above under *East coast. From the SE* transfer to entry transit S14.

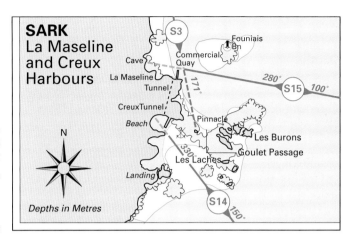

S14 330° The beach at the back of the harbour fills the entrance

La Maseline and Creux Harbour at LWS

Note This will only just clear drying rocks S of Les Burons so it may be necessary to borrow a bit to port.

Depths

At half tide there is 4m at the pierheads and 3m at the embarkation steps just inside the entrance on the N side. Entry can be made about 2 hours either side of HW.

Mooring

Dry bow to E wall and stern to anchor keeping well clear of embarkation steps at S end of the pier at all times. Drying out alongside may be possible subject to available space.

The bottom is generally firm sand with a pebble beach on the W side opposite the entrance.

La Maseline Harbour

49°25′.97N 02°20′.57W Jetty head

This deep-water commercial harbour is connected to Creux Harbour by a tunnel cut through the cliff.

Entry

Preferred entry is from NE, which provides a clear view of any activity in the harbour. If entering from E beware of cross-set. Either way give Founiais (dries 6.7m) with its with its beacon a clearance of 100m. A useful transit for an easterly entry or departure is shown below.

S15 *280° Cave just open of the pierhead*

Depth

Least depth is 4m.

Mooring

The quay is reserved for commercial vessels but coming alongside briefly is possible when it is clear. The harbourmaster may grant permission to lie alongside overnight but the vessel should not be left unattended and should be ready to move at any time.

Anchoring NW of the jetty is possible with harbourmaster's approval, but keep well clear of ferry movements. It can be uncomfortable in all but light winds from between NW and SE. Northwesterlies produce a swell.

Notes: East coast anchorages (N–S)

(See plan page 88)

Caution

With a wind shift or a turn in the tide a tranquil anchorage can become exposed and anchors may drag. It is inadvisable to leave an anchored yacht unattended or out of effective control anywhere off Sark.

LES FONTAINES

49°26′.78N 02°21′.62W

Sand and shingle with fair holding. Anchor well clear of reefs with La Gorge of La Petite Moie on the edge of Banquette Point.

GREVE DE LA VILLE

49°26′.57N 02°21′.05W

Good shelter in southwesterlies. Anchor close in to stone steps in 4–7m. Visitors' moorings available. Good access to village by cliff path.

DERRIBLE BAY

49°25′.41N 02°21′.07W

Good holding in firm sand anywhere in the bay but swell can penetrate, making it uncomfortable. Used by ferries. Good access to shore by zig-zag path.

DIXCART BAY

49°25′.33N 02°21′.48W

(For approach and entry see *East coast approaches. From the SE.*)

Good holding in firm sand. Popular with French and Jersey yachts due to good access to hotels, restaurants and shops. Swell can penetrate in southwesterlies.

POT BAY AND ROUGE TERRIER (LITTLE SARK)

49°24′.78N 02°21′.87W

Protected fair weather anchorages under high cliffs with a landing and cliff path to the top where there is an excellent hotel/restaurant. Holding is good in sand.

West coast anchorages

Approaches from the west

N of Brecqhou (Banquette Bay)

An approach to Sark between Bec du Nez and Gouliot Passage presents no major navigational obstacles. There are two small bays, Saignie Bay in the N and Port à la Jument in the S. See *W Coast Anchorages (N–S)*.

South of Brecqhou (La Grande Grève)

Sark's most frequented anchorages within easy reach of St Peter Port are located in La Grande Grève. These are described in (N–S) order below and under *Notes: W Coast Anchorages (N–S)*.

Pilcher Monument (conspic)
Gouliot passage
Visitors' moorings
Landing
Pierre Norman

GOULIOT PASSAGE (3.6m)

Between Banquette Bay and La Grande Grève is the Gouliot.

Shooting through this narrow passage between Sark and Brecqhou has long provided Channel Island yachtsmen with a bit of excitement. On spring tides the stream courses through the gap at 5–7 knots, but it should be taken at half tide when the stream is slack. Stemming it head on can prove slow, if not impossible. Consult the *Appendix. Tidal diagrams.*

The passage is clean on both sides with a least depth of 3.6m. It is important to observe the transits as described below in order to keep clear of isolated drying rocks and shoal areas lurking at either end of the passage.

Passage north

(See plan page 88)

S18
Moie de St Pierre
Bec du Nez
022°

S18 022° Bec du Nez just seen through the Gouliot Passage

This will clear dangers all the way to Bec du Nez. If proceeding to Herm do not turn W until well past Boue de Grune Gouliot (0.8m) NE of Brecqhou.

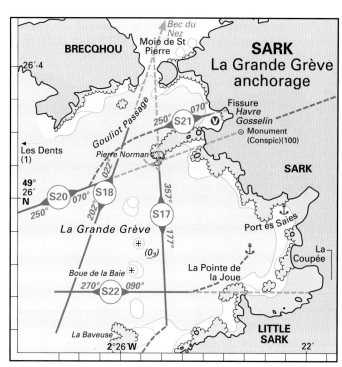
SARK La Grande Grève anchorage

Passage south

(See plan page 88)

S19
Moie de St Pierre
Moie de la Bretagne
Brecqhou
Castle
186°

S19 186° Moie de la Bretagne open of Moie de St Pierre

TO HAVRE GOSSELIN S20 ⊕27 S21

49°25'.77N 02°22'.68W

Approach from the SW using recommended ⊕27. In the absence of any boats in the cove, it is easily located by reference to the consipicuous Pilcher Monument (100m) on the skyline to the S. To clear Les Dents (1m) S of Brecqou the distant approach is made on transit S20:

S20
070°

S20 070° ⊕27 Pilcher Monument in line with Sark Mill
Note Sark Mill is no longer conspicuous.

SARK

Closer in a further danger to be avoided is Pierre Norman (drying 8.8m) on the outer SW corner of Havre Gosselin. The transit available to clear this is:

S21 070° Gosselin Fissure over to the left of Pierre Norman

With Gouliot Passage opened up as above (S18) come to port to round Pierre Norman by 200m. This transit above will also clear the drying rock (2.6m) S of Brecqhou on the W side of Gouliot Passage.

TO PORT ES SAIES

(View I page 101)
49°25´.35N 02°22´.43W

Approach is straightforward with the bay opened up but adequate clearance should be given to isolated dangers in the bay as described above (see also *Approaches from the S. Inside La Baveuse*, below).

TO LA GRANDE GREVE S22 090°

(E of La Coupée)

49°25´.38N 02°22´.59W

This approach passes between La Baveuse (drying 7.6m) and Boue de la Baie awash at LW, to the N of the line. The marks for this transit are shown at top of right-hand column:

Pierre du Beurre Passage

S22 090° S edge of of La Coupée in line with Pointe de la Joue

When 400m from Pointe de la Joue turn to port and come to anchor NE of the point.

Approaches from the south

(See plan page 88)

W of Les Hautes Boues

This is the easiest route passing outside all dangers. From a position 1.2M SW of L'Etac identify La Givaude (12m) to NNW off the westernmost tip of Brecqhou then take up the transit shown below.

S16 356° Grande Amfroque (17m) open W of La Givaude clears all dangers to W of Sark

Break off this line for La Grande Grève or Havre Gosselin anchorages as required (see *West coast anchorages. Approaches from W*).

Inside La Baveuse

(See plans pages 93, 97 and below)

The passage S of Sercul (5m) and then inside La Baveuse (dries 7.6m) is difficult. Start from a position 0.8M SW of Sercul ⊕26 at LW when the stream is slack and marks are visible. Identify Transit S10 (page 94) and make a slow turn to NW. When the peak of Moie de St Pierre (at the Gouliot) bears 013° and is open its width to W of Moie de la Bretagne, steer on this transit with care, leaving Boue Tirlipois (drying 1.1m) 200m to starboard (see View H under *Pierre du Beurre Passage* below).

When Petite Baveuse (6m), which extends westward at LW, is 250m abeam, steer to leave Moie de la Bretagne (17m) at least 100m to starboard. Then come round to starboard, steering to leave Moie de la Fontaine (17m) at least 100m to starboard.

At this point proceed NE towards Port Es Saies to pass between La Baveuse and the shoreline. Entry to La Grand Grève anchorage is described above under *Approaches from the West*. If proceeding N across the bay to Havre Gosselin anchorage (see under *Sark Anchorages* below) beware of an isolated danger in the bay, Boue de la Baie (awash at CD), and its neighbour (dries 0.3m). Use the transit line S17 as follows to clear E of this (and see plans pages 93 and 97).

S17 357° *Pierre Norman (dries 8.8m) in line with the middle of Gouliot Passage*

PIERRE DU BEURRE (BURRE) PASSAGE (APPROX. 3.6m) (E–W)

(See plan below and air view page 98)

Caution

Little Sark is no place to be at HW due to powerful currents, swell and a lack of reference points. This inshore passage that elbows its way through the rocks around the bottom of Little Sark is best attempted at LW Springs in quiet weather, good visibility and with sound knowledge of the area or a local expert aboard. There is 3.6m in the passage at CD and at one point the passage is only 20m wide. Pilotage is by rock recognition rather than transits. Marks must be positively identified.

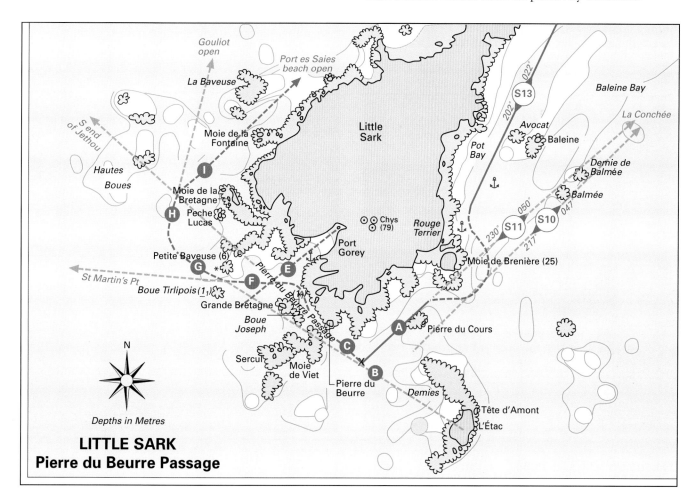

LITTLE SARK
Pierre du Beurre Passage

When the author made this passage from east to west, timed over LW with a predicted height of 2.5m at St Helier a minimum depth of 3.6m was found.

Starting from Dixcart Bay, a position 200m E of Moie de Brenière was reached by the inshore route across Baleine Bay (S13). This is described under *Approaches to the East Coast. From the South*. Alter heading towards Pierre du Cours and hold until the beach SW of Moie de Brenière comes into view, then take up:

S11 *053° La Conchee and Balmée on the East edge of Moie de Brenière*

In view A above and on the plan, Balmée is almost closed behind the E edge of Moie de Brenière and La Conchée is not visible. This is favoured by Sark pilot instructor Dick Adams as it gives more clearance of the drying extension on the W edge of Pierre du Cours.

Hold until 180m SW of Pierre du Cours which is the turning point into the passage (marked with a red X on the plan). Identify key marks as shown in View B.

Enter with View C on a NW heading:

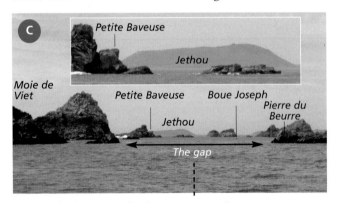

S end of Jethou is in the 'bottom step' of Petite Baveuse

This transit will lead through a narrow gap between Pierre du Beurre (dries approximately half tide) on the Sark shoreline and Moie de Viet (10m) to the S.

With Pierre du Beurre abeam identify the small isolated Boue Joseph (dries approximately 1.2m) lying midway between Grande Bretagne (18m) and the Sark shoreline.

Pierre du Beurre

Before Grande Bretagne comes abeam make a small alteration to starboard to within 20m of the shore in order to leave Boue Joseph 20m to port (View D). Then return to a northwesterly heading with C until:

The beach at Port Gorey is open

Now alter course to port towards the southern point of Guernsey:

The southern point of Guernsey

Hold this heading until, looking astern, Mark G is identified:

The chimney of Moie de Viet (10m) is on the peak of L'Etac

Turn to starboard onto a NW heading to hold these marks for clearing between Boue Tirlipois (dries 1.1m) to the S and Petite Baveuse (6m) to the north (see air view on following page).

Next look N for View H:

The Gouliot Passage is open

Turn onto a NNE heading to leave Les Hautes Boues to port and Moie de la Bretagne (17m) with Piquillon and Peche Lucas SW of it 100m to starboard.

When Moie de la Bretagne is on the quarter identify and head towards Port es Saies beach to the NE (View I):

The beach at Port es Saies is open

Moie de la Fontaine should be left 100m to starboard. Pass midway between La Baveuse (dries 7.6m and 0.2m) and the shoreline.

With Pointe de la Joue abeam either take up the leading marks S22 090° for entry to Grande Grève anchorage (see *Approaches from the S. Inside La Baveuse*) or proceed N using Transit S17 357° to clear E of dangers in the bay (see *Approaches from the W. To La Grande Grève*).

Sark Mill

Notes: West Coast anchorages (N–S)

(See plan page 88)

SAIGNIE BAY
49°26′.53N 02°22′.10W

Sand and shingle with fair holding. Anchor in 3–5m. Exposed to NW.

PORT A LA JUMENT
49°26′.17N 02°22′.42W

Sand and shingle with fair holding in 3m. Exposed to NW. Path up to hotel at top.

HAVRE GOSSELIN
49°25′.77N 02°22′.68W

Popular small deep-water cove exposed to W and SW. Can be swelly particularly at springs when it is not recommended for overnight stay. Easy landing in SE corner with 299 steps and steep zigzag path the top. The reward is an outstanding view. Most of the anchorage is now taken up by visitors' moorings. For entry see *West Coast anchorages* above.

LA GRANDE GREVE
49°25′.38N 02°22′.59W

A snug anchorage in easterly winds under La Coupée. The bottom is fine sand and shingle and there are steep railed steps from the beach up to La Coupée. An alternative is Port es Saies in the N corner of the bay with good holding in sand. For entry see *West coast anchorages. Approaches from the west* above.

PORT GOREY
49°24′.54N 02°22′.80W

A narrow cove prone to HW swell and strictly a fine weather LW anchorage. Holding is good in sand at the entrance but there are boulders further in. The crumbling remains of a 19th-century silver mine are conspicuous on the skyline above the small beach. Landing is possible on S side with path to the top and a hotel.

Approach

Starting from position 0.5M WSW of Sercul, approach with the beach open on a bearing of 050° and with the

Chimneys   Grande Bretagne   L'Etac

Moie de Viet

Port Gorey

Sercul

Petite Baveuse

Boue Tirlipois

050°

Port Gorey

conspicuous mine chimney on the starboard bow. This will leave Grande Bretagne (18m) 100m to starboard (see *Pierre Du Beurre Passage, View E*).

Departure

Make good a course of 230°. If proceeding into the Big Russel, hold to pass between Grande Bretagne (18m) to the SE and Boue Tirlipois (dries 1.1m) to the NW. You are clear of all dangers when L'Etac bears E and Grande Amfroque is open W of La Givaude on 356° (see S16 on page 97 and air view on page 101). If proceeding N, follow directions under *West Coast anchorages. Approaches from the S* above.

Jersey

Local information

STD code: 01534

TRAVEL INFORMATION

There are regular flights to most UK and continental airports and ferry links with Portsmouth, Poole and Weymouth in the UK and Carteret, Granville and St-Malo on the French coast.

Air
British Airways ☎ 711711
Flybe (British European) ☎ 498284
Aurigny Air Services ☎ 744735
Blue Islands

Sea
Condor Ferries ☎ 0845 1242004
Manche Iles Express ☎ 766566

PORTS OF ENTRY

Official Ports of Entry into the Bailiwick of Jersey are St Helier and Gorey

CHARTS

British Admiralty WGS 84
2669 Channel Islands and adjacent coast of France
3655 Jersey and adjacent coast of France
1136 Jersey – North Coast
1137 Approaches to St Helier
1138 Jersey – East Coast
3278 St Helier Harbour
3656 Plateau des Minquiers and adjacent coast of France
Leisure Folio (5604)
4 Guernsey to Jersey
6 SW Approaches to Jersey

Imray C Charts
C33A Channel Islands Plan: Gorey
C33B Channel Islands (South) Plans St Helier Approaches, St Helier Yacht Harbours
Imray 2500 Chart pack

Stanfords Allweather Charts
16 The Channel Islands
26 Channel Island Harbours with Plan Jersey south coast and approaches

French SHOM
6938 Abords de St Helier
6939 Jersey – Côte Est
7160 Jersey à Guernsey – Plateau des Minquiers
7161 des Iles Chausey à Jersey. Plateau des Minquiers

RADIO FACILITIES

Jersey
Jersey Radio VHF Ch 82
☎ 741121 *Fax* 499089

MMSI 00232 0060
Hrs of watch: 24
VHF Ch 16, 82, 25, 67 (small craft distress and safety working)
DSC Ch 70
Weather Bulletins at 0545, 0645, 0745, 1245, 1845, 2245 UTC
Strong wind and gale warnings: On receipt and at 0307, 0907, 1507, 2107 UTC
(See *Introduction. Sources of weather information*)
Navigation warnings On receipt and at 0433, 0833, 1633, 2033
Link calls: Ch 25 only
VHF Direction Finding Vessel transmits and receives bearing from Station on Ch 16 or 82
Note The aerial position for D/F purposes is 49°10´.85N 02°14´.30W Lookout tower Point La Corbière
St Helier Pierhead Control Ch 14 Hours of watch: 24. Range: approx 5 miles
St Helier Pierheads Information Service Transmits wind speed and direction at St Helier Pierhead Control every 2 minutes Ch 18

NAVIGATIONAL AIDS

Racons (Radar beacons):
Demie de Pas light tower 49°09´.00N 02°06´.15W (T) 10M

USEFUL TELEPHONE NUMBERS

Rescue Centre ☎ 885504
Jersey Radio ☎ 741121
St Helier Marina Office ☎ 885508
St Helier Harbour office ☎ 885588
Fax 885599
Email: jerseyharbours@jersey-harbours.com
www.jersey-harbours.com (Harbour office)
Elizabeth Marina Office ☎ 885530
La Collette Yacht Basin ☎ 885529
Jersey Tourism ☎ 500700
Royal Channel Islands YC ☎ 741023
St Helier YC ☎ 732229

SUPPLIES AND SERVICES

For general supplies see under separate marinas
Chandlery, fuel, bottled gas, charts, sail repairs
South Pier Marine ☎ 711000
Marine Engineers
DK Collins Marine ☎ 732415
Fox Marine Services ☎ 721312
Marine Electronics
South Pier Marine ☎ 711000
Marine & Vehicle Electrics ☎ 853717

St Helier

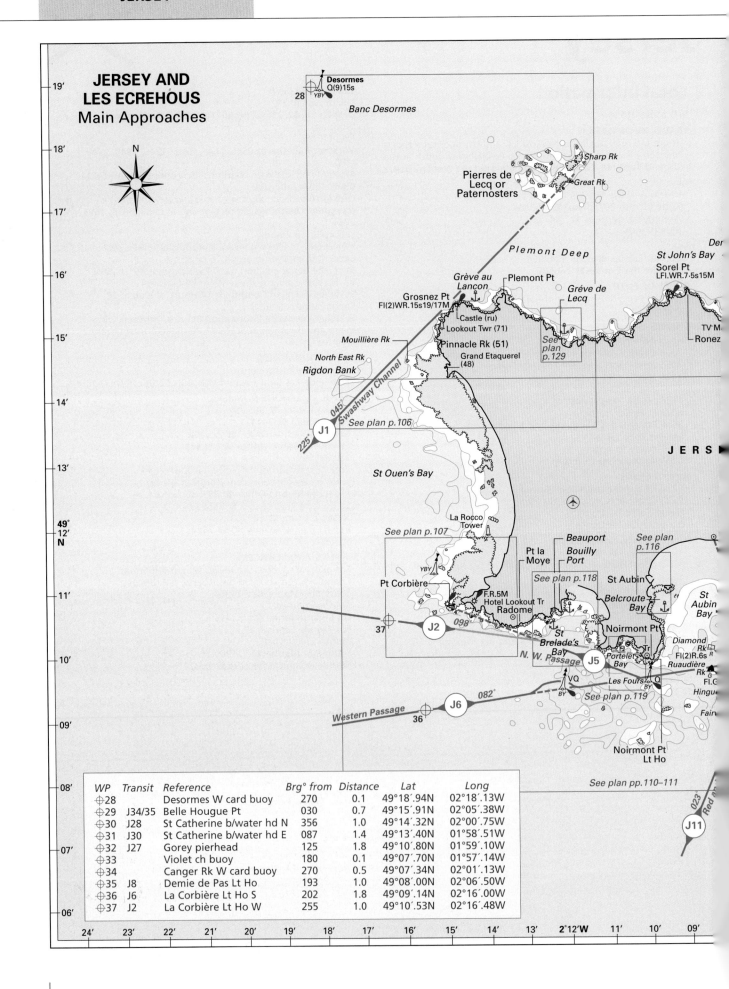

JERSEY AND LES ECREHOUS
Main Approaches

N

Desormes
Q(9)15s
28 YBY

Banc Desormes

Pierres de Lecq or Paternosters

Sharp Rk

Great Rk

Plemont Deep

Der
St John's Bay
Sorel Pt
LFl.WR.7·5s15M

Grève au Lancon

Plemont Pt

Grève de Lecq

TV M
Ronez

Grosnez Pt
Fl(2)WR.15s19/17M

Castle (ru)
Lookout Twr (71)
Pinnacle Rk (51)

See plan p.129

Mouillière Rk

Grand Etaquerel (48)

North East Rk
Rigdon Bank

Swashway Channel

045

See plan p.106

225°

J1

JERS

St Ouen's Bay

La Rocco Tower

See plan p.107

Beauport
Bouilly Port

See plan p.116

Pt la Moye

See plan p.118

St Aubin

Pt Corbière

YBY

Belcroute Bay

St Aubin Bay

F.R.5M
Hotel Lookout Tr
Radome

St Brelade's Bay

Noirmont Pt

Diamond Rk
Fl(2)R.6s

37

J2

098°

N. W. Passage

J5

Portelet Bay

Ruaudière Rk R

Fl.G

Les Fours

VQ
BY

See plan p.119

Hingue

Western Passage

082°

J6

36

Fair

Noirmont Pt
Lt Ho

See plan pp.110–111

023°
Red an

J11

WP	Transit	Reference	Brg° from	Distance	Lat	Long
⊕28		Desormes W card buoy	270	0.1	49°18′.94N	02°18′.13W
⊕29	J34/35	Belle Hougue Pt	030	0.7	49°15′.91N	02°05′.38W
⊕30	J28	St Catherine b/water hd N	356	1.0	49°14′.32N	02°00′.75W
⊕31	J30	St Catherine b/water hd E	087	1.4	49°13′.40N	01°58′.51W
⊕32	J27	Gorey pierhead	125	1.8	49°10′.80N	01°59′.10W
⊕33		Violet ch buoy	180	0.1	49°07′.70N	01°57′.14W
⊕34		Canger Rk W card buoy	270	0.5	49°07′.34N	02°01′.13W
⊕35	J8	Demie de Pas Lt Ho	193	1.0	49°08′.00N	02°06′.50W
⊕36	J6	La Corbière Lt Ho S	202	1.8	49°09′.14N	02°16′.00W
⊕37	J2	La Corbière Lt Ho W	255	1.0	49°10′.53N	02°16′.48W

JERSEY

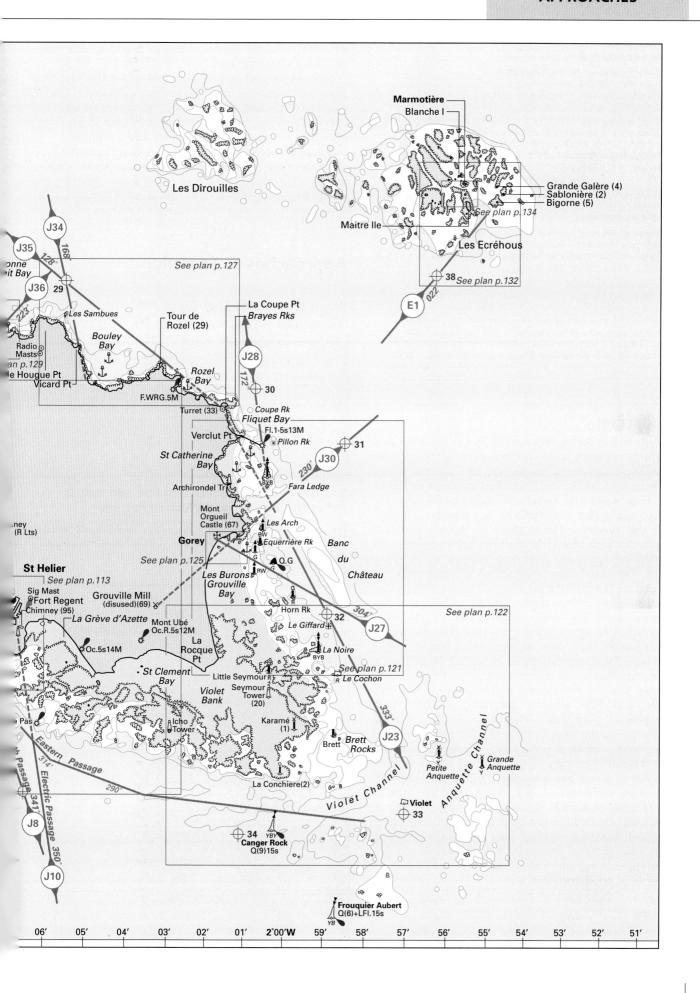

Marmotière
Blanche I

Grande Galère (4)
Sablonière (2)
Bigorne (5)

Les Dirouilles

Maitre Ile

See plan p.134

Les Ecréhous

J34

J35

128°

168°

J36 29

223°

38 *See plan p.132*

E1 022°

onne
it Bay

Les Sambues

Bouley
Bay

Radio
Masts

See plan p.127

Tour de
Rozel (29)

La Coupe Pt
Brayes Rks

e Hougue Pt
Vicard Pt

F.WRG.5M

*Rozel
Bay*

J28

172°

30

Turret (33)

Coupe Rk
Fliquet Bay

Verclut Pt

Fl.1·5s13M
✳ *Pillon Rk*

J30 31

230°

*St Catherine
Bay*

BYB

Fara Ledge

Archirondel Tr

Mont
Orgueil
Castle (67)

Les Arch
BW

Gorey

See plan p.125

Q.G
Equerrière Rk

G
RW G

Les Burons
*Grouville
Bay*

*Banc
du
Château*

304°

See plan p.122

St Helier

See plan p.113

Sig Mast
Fort Regent
Chimney (95)

Grouville Mill
(disused)(69)

La Grève d'Azette

Mont Ubé
Oc.R.5s12M

Horn Rk

32

J27

333°

ney
(R Lts)

Oc.5s14M

La
Rocque
Pt

Le Giffard

La Noire
BYB

See plan p.121

· *St Clement
Bay*

Little Seymour

Le Cochon

*Violet
Bank*

Seymour
Tower
(20)

Pas

cho
Tower

Karamé
(1)

Brett *Brett
Rocks*

J23

*Petite
Anquette*

Grande
Anquette

314°

Eastern Passage

290°

La Conchiere(2)

Violet Channel

Anquette Channel

J8

341°

Electric Passage 350°

Violet
33

J10

34 YBY
Canger Rock
Q(9)15s

Frouquier Aubert
Q(6)+LFl.15s
YB

| 06′ | 05′ | 04′ | 03′ | 02′ | 01′ | **2°00′W** | 59′ | 58′ | 57′ | 56′ | 55′ | 54′ | 53′ | 52′ | 51′ |

TIDAL INFORMATION

Tidal levels referred to chart datum

St Helier 49°11′N 2°07′W

MHWS	MHWN	MLWN	MLWS	MTL
11.0	8.1	4.1	1.4	6.1

St Helier is a Standard Port for the Channel Islands and it is more accurate if all tidal calculations are based on St Helier rather than Dover when cruising in this area. HW St Helier is approximately HW Dover −0500. With spring tide means of 11.0m and 1.4m Jersey can claim the greatest tidal range of the islands. Equinoctial spring tides can be awesome, when height predictions modified by strong winds or extremes of barometric pressure may cause flooding and the exposure of vast areas of seabed.

Areas noted for rough seas and overfalls in strong wind against tide conditions are Grosnez point (with the Rigdon Bank) off the NW corner and Point La Corbière and Noirmont Point off the SW corner.

The *Tidal Atlas* shows the flood setting eastward and the ebb westward along the south coast. On the N coast the flood is generally SE and the ebb NW. The E coast presents something of an anomaly which is indicated on the large-scale tidal diagrams in the *Appendix* but not in the *Tidal Atlas*. The flood sets generally S offshore while inshore it is northerly for half the period. There is a similar contra-flow towards the latter part of the ebb. Inshore eddies also occur on the SW corner.

Introduction

The Bailiwick of Jersey, which includes Les Ecréhous and Les Minquiers reefs, is the southernmost territory of the British Isles, and being the closest to France it is not surprising that the Normans left their strongest influence here. Their laws and system of government form the backbone of Jersey law and the Norman French they spoke still survives. The exploits of Jersey's seafarers between the 16th and 19th centuries are legendary and well documented in the Maritime Museum at St Helier Marina. The island's principal port of St Helier embraces several interesting historical sites. Elizabeth Castle that shelters the entrance was the official residence of the Governor until the 18th century, one of its most distinguished residents being Sir Walter Raleigh, whose term began in 1600. Part of the castle's breakwater is Hermitage Rock, reputed to be the home of St Helier, hermit, missionary and patron saint.

Today Jersey is the most commercial of the Channel Islands and has all the amenities to satisfy a cosmopolitan population. Despite a large influx of visitors during the season, there remain many areas of natural beauty and tranquillity in and around the island where it is possible to get away from it all. In recent years the States of Jersey has done much to improve facilities for visiting yachtsmen. Land reclamation has created three marinas, making St Helier a practical port of call or a longer-term base. Bilge keelers and multihulls can enjoy the option of small drying harbours such as Gorey and St Aubin which have a character all their own. In suitable conditions of wind and tide, the island's coastline offers a number of good anchorages.

Ashore

First time visitors will find all the information they need at Jersey Tourism Centre in Liberation Square off St Helier Marina. It is a short walk north across Royal Square to find the shopping precincts and a wide range of cafés and restaurants.

Sites of interest around the harbour are the Maritime Museum adjoining the Marina and Elizabeth Castle, which is reached at low tide by a causeway. The developing Waterfront Centre has an Aqua Centre with multiplex cinema, fast food outlets and a nightspot.

There is a comprehensive bus service, the terminus is off Liberation Square and several car rental depots nearby. It is worth taking the half hour coastal route along to Gorey for a visit to Mont Orgueil Castle. Alternatively, go west via St Aubin to St Ouen's Bay with its 5-mile beach – a popular venue with surfers.

Approaches to St Helier

From the north and west

(See also plans on pages 104–5 and 110–111)

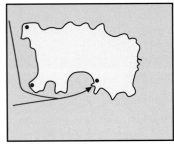

Grosnez Point to Point La Corbière and into St Helier NW Passage and Western Passage

Grosnez Point at Jersey's NW corner and Point Corbière at its SW are vital reference points when making a landfall from the north or west.

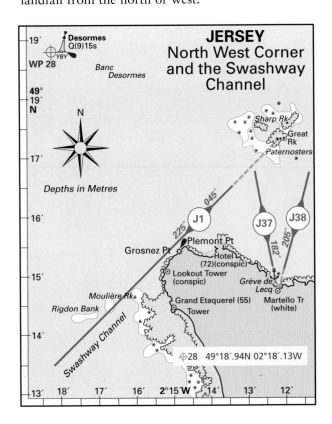

The approach channels in from the west run within a mile of the south coast and marks should be positively identified from a safe water position.

The sea off Grosnez Point can be rough in wind against tide conditions when the Rigdon Bank should be given a good clearance. In quiet weather the Swashway Channel may be used by day only.
The stern transit is:

Pt Corbière LtHo looking E towards St Helier

J1 *045° Great Rock of the Paternosters open of Grosnez Point*

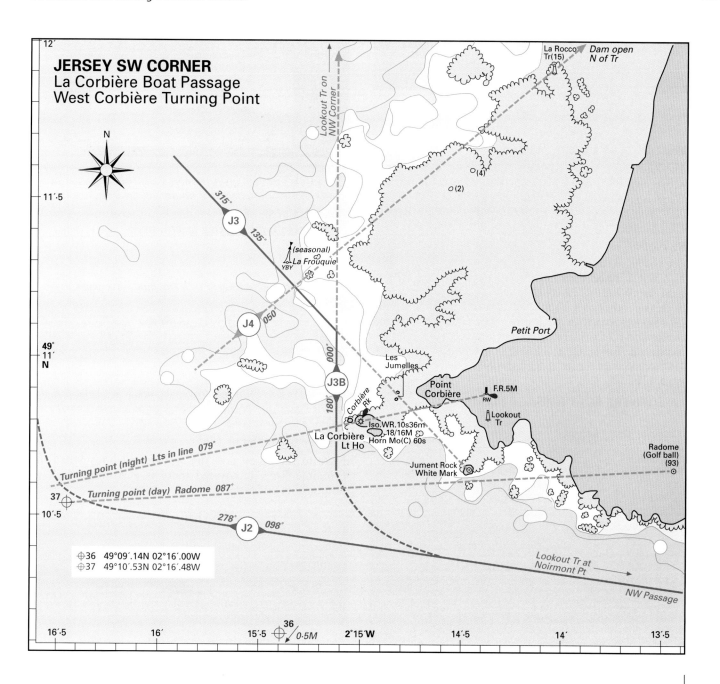

This will pass between Rigdon Bank (minimum depth 3.1m) and Moulière (or Mouillière) Rock (dries 0.6m) leaving it 200m to port. It should be held until La Corbière lighthouse bears SSE when course may be altered towards Pt Corbière.

Round the point at a distance of 1 mile off the light to clear outlying dangers. This is achieved by keeping the top of the lighthouse level with the skyline.

With the lighthouse abeam run S until you identify Noirmont Pt light tower. When this comes onto an easterly bearing commence a turn onto:

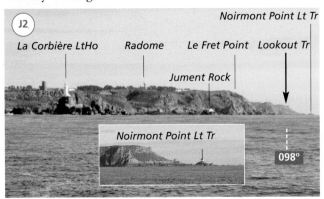

J2 098° ⊕37 The lookout tower on Noirmont Point open S of Le Fret Point

West Corbière turning point

The Radome (93m) (known as The Golf Ball) on Point la Moye, makes a useful mark for a turning point by day. When it is open SE of the white-painted Jument Rock on 087° you are clear to commence a turn (see plan page 107).

By night

Approach in the white sector of Grosnez Point light Fl(2)WR.15s and then into the W sector of La Corbière light (Iso.WR.10s). Leave the LtHo at least 1M to port – in clear conditions a back bearing on Point Robert light (Fl.15s) on Sark can be useful. When the F.R (on the shore) and La Corbière light come in line (079°) identify Noirmont Tower light (Fl(4)12s) and when this bears 100° commence a turn to join the NW passage (see plan page 110).

LA CORBIÈRE BOAT PASSAGE (1.2M)

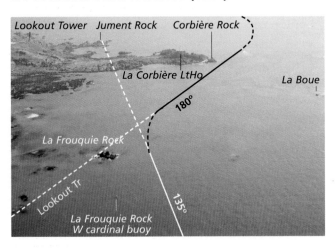

By day only

This short cut inside reefs to the W of Point Corbière provides a spectacular view of its lighthouse. The passage now prohibited to commercial traffic, has claimed several casualties over the years, not least the French ferry *St Malo* in 1995, which struck La Frouquie Rock (dries 9.8m). The rock is now guarded by a W cardinal buoy (April–October). The passage carries a least depth of 1.2m at chart datum and should not be attempted in anything other than quiet weather with no W swell. If in doubt stay out.

Approach from the north

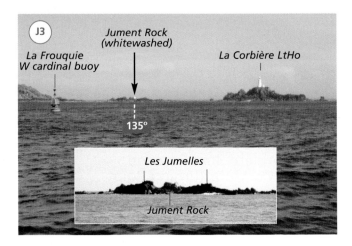

J3 135° White patch on Jument Rock between the two heads of Les Jumelles (dry about 9m and 8m)

When 200m SE of La Frouquie buoy, steer just to the W of the LtHo until, looking astern, find:

J3B 000°. The Lookout tower on the NW tip of the island bears due N, with La Frouquie if visible well open of the headland

Take up a heading of 180°.

Note In the absence of the W cardinal buoy when the Frouquie Rock is covered there is a striking mark to pinpoint its position:

J4 050° La Rocco Tower bearing 050° with the dam open its width to the N

When 400m off La Corbière Rock, which is steep-to, steer round it at a distance of 100m off. When the lighthouse bears 030° steer out on 130° to pick up mark J2 as described above and enter the NW passage.

NORTHWEST PASSAGE (8.5M)
(See plan page 110)

Continue E on line J2 *098°* keeping the lookout tower well open of Noirmont Point in order to clear Les Kaines (dry 8.5m). When St Brelade's Bay opens up take up

stern transit for this passage:

J5 290° La Corbière LtHo open S of La Jument white painted rock will clear Les Kaines (dry 8.5m)

This should be held until abeam Noirmont Point when course should be altered into the Western Passage (see below and plan page 110).

By night

Hold Noirmont light Fl(4)12s on a steady bearing of no more than 095° to enter the red sector of La Corbière light. Identify Passage Rock N cardinal buoy (VQ), Les Fours N cardinal buoy (Q) and Ruaudière buoy (Fl.G.3s) beyond. As La Corbière light turns from red to white, steer to pass midway between Noirmont Point light and Les Fours (leaving Passage Rock buoy 0.5M to starboard) until the leading lights for the Western Passage come in line as described below.

WESTERN PASSAGE (4.0M)

J6 082° ⊕36 Grève d'Azette lighthouse in line with Dog's Nest beacon

This passes over Passage Rock, but if you borrow to the N to leave the Passage Rock N cardinal buoy to starboard the whole channel then carries 6m.

By night

The same transit is used, but since the Dog's Nest beacon is not lit, the mark becomes Mont Ubé light (Oc.R.5s46m12M) in line with Grève d'Azette LtHo (Oc.5s23m14M).

From the south
(See also plan pages 110–111)

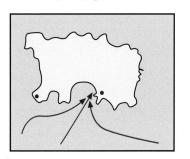

Caution

Reefs extend W from Demie de Pas light tower to Passage Rock N cardinal buoy off St Brelade's Bay.

Picking your way between them using some of the passages described below may be demanding as marks must be positively identified from safe water which can be up to 4 miles off. Transits may also be difficult to hold accurately with the stream setting E or W.

It may be safer to make for a poisition W of Passage Rock N cardinal buoy to approach by Western Passage, or a position S of Demie de Pas light tower to approach by South Passage.

DANGER ROCK PASSAGE (5.8m)

J7 044° Fort Regent signal mast just open S of breakwater end

The signal mast is hard to identify at a distance but the conspicuous white-painted pierhead control tower makes a good alternative.

This passage leaves Danger Rock (1.2m) 400m to starboard and two rocks (depth 0.3m and 0.9m) with Grunes aux Dardes (dry 1.8m) 200m to port so the line must be held exactly.

By night

The passage is unlit. Use the Red and Green Passage (see *Entry to St Helier Harbour* below) if there is sufficient water over the Fairway Rock (1.2m).

SOUTH PASSAGE (8m)

Once identified with binoculars the marks are conspicuous. With Demie de Pas light tower abeam to starboard, Les Têtards Rocks (one awash at LW and another depth 1.8m) lie 300m to port. Identify Hinguette buoy (R) which will be left 100m to port in this passage.

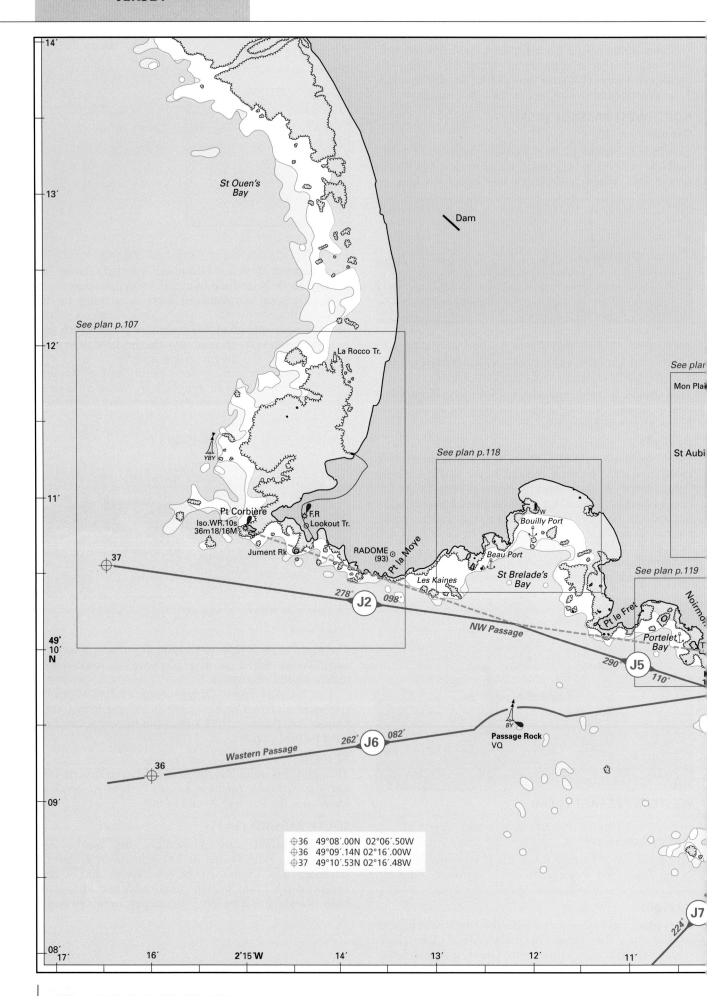

JERSEY

St Ouen's Bay

Dam

See plan p.107

La Rocco Tr.

YBY

See plan p.118

Mon Plai

St Aubi

Pt Corbiere
Iso.WR.10s
36m18/16M

F.R
Lookout Tr.

Bouilly Port

See plan p.119

37

Jument Rk

RADOME
(93)

Pt la Moye

Les Kaines

Beau Port

St Brelade's
Bay

Pt le Fret

Noirmo

278° J2 098°

NW Passage

290° J5 110°

Portelet
Bay

T

Western Passage 262° J6 082°

Passage Rock
VQ
BY

49°
10'
N

49°
10'
N

36

⊕36 49°08'.00N 02°06'.50W
⊕36 49°09'.14N 02°16'.00W
⊕37 49°10'.53N 02°16'.48W

J7
224°

APPROACHES TO ST HELIER

JERSEY

Depths in Metres

N

BW Mark

See plan p.113

ST HELIER

8m1M
ubin's

La Vrachière
Boat Passage

Oc.R.5s12M

⊕35 49°08'.00N 02°06'.50W

rosse
Rk

St Aubin's Bay

J12

Sig Mast
Fort
Regent

Rocquemin

Elizabeth
Castle
YBY

F.G

Gros du Château

Oc.G.5s11M

F.G

Mont Ubé
Oc.R.5s46m12M

G

Chimney
(95)

W

Les Grunes
du Port

Diamond Rk
Fl(2)R.6s

Grève d'Azette
Oc.5s23m14M

R

W

R

Q.G

Dog's
Nest

G G

et

Fl.G.3s
Bell

Ruaudière
Rk

G

Danger Rock Passage

Red & Green Passage

Fl.(4)R.15s

Grunes
aux Dardes

Middle Passage

Fairway
Rock

Hinguette

South Passage

Mo(D)WR.12s
11m12/9M
Horn(3)60s

1.8

Danger
Rock

Demie
de Pas

Icho
Twr

Les Têtards

341°

338°

314° - 134°

Eastern Passage

J8

J9

350°

J10

161°

158°

170°

La Corbière LtHo

290°

J20
J21

023°

339°

J11

J13

203°

159°

Electric Passage

⊕
35

110°

09'   08'   07'   06'   2°05'W   04'   03'

J8 341° ⊕35 The black and white vertical stripes on the sea wall between the twin heads of Gros du Château

By night

Unlit. Use the Eastern Passage below.

Inshore alternative to South Passage (2.5m)

Used by small craft. By day only.

J9 338° Elizabeth Castle breakwater end on (BW stripes) in line with Platte Rock beacon (R)

This unofficial passage runs parallel to South Passage but 400m closer inshore. It is useful when South Passage marks are difficult to identify.

Shape a course to pass not more than 0.5 M W of Demie de Pas light tower then align the marks. This transit must be left 200m short of E Rock buoy (G) when course should be altered W to join Red and Green Passage J11.

'ELECTRIC PASSAGE'

J10 350° Demie de Pas light tower in line with power station chimney

This unofficial passage may be used when approaching from the SE but must be left, steering 314°, to join the South Passage when 500m from Demie de Pas light tower, Hinguette buoy (R) will be left to port.

By night

This transit may be used by night if the chimney is floodlit.

From the east

EASTERN PASSAGE (7m)

There are no leading marks for this wide passage which joins the Red and Green Passage 0.5M S of Platte beacon.

By night

Keeping in the white sector of Demie de Pas light (Mo(D)WR.12s), steer to leave it 300m to starboard and the Hinguette port buoy (Fl(4)R.15s) 400m to port until the Red and Green Passage lights (front Oc.G, rear Oc.R.5s) are in transit on 023°.

Entry to St Helier Harbour

RED AND GREEN PASSAGE (SHOAL PATCH 1.2m)

This passage covers the final entry to St Helier Harbour and its marinas via Small Road.

It is unsuitable as an entry passage S of East Rock buoy as it passes over Fairway Rock (1.2m). The marks can also be difficult to identify at a range of more than 1 mile.

J11 023°. Two thin metal dayglo red columns, the rear on land and the front on a white painted caisson E side of the RoRo berth

By night

Front mark (Oc.G.5s11M) and rear mark (Oc.R.5s12M) in transit. Despite their intensity the marks can be difficult to identify against the mass of background lighting.

LA VRACHIERE LOCAL BOAT PASSAGE (DRIES 5.3m) (W–E)

To reduce the volume of traffic in the Small Roads at peak periods, Jersey Harbours encourage local boat owners, rather than first-time visitors, to make use of

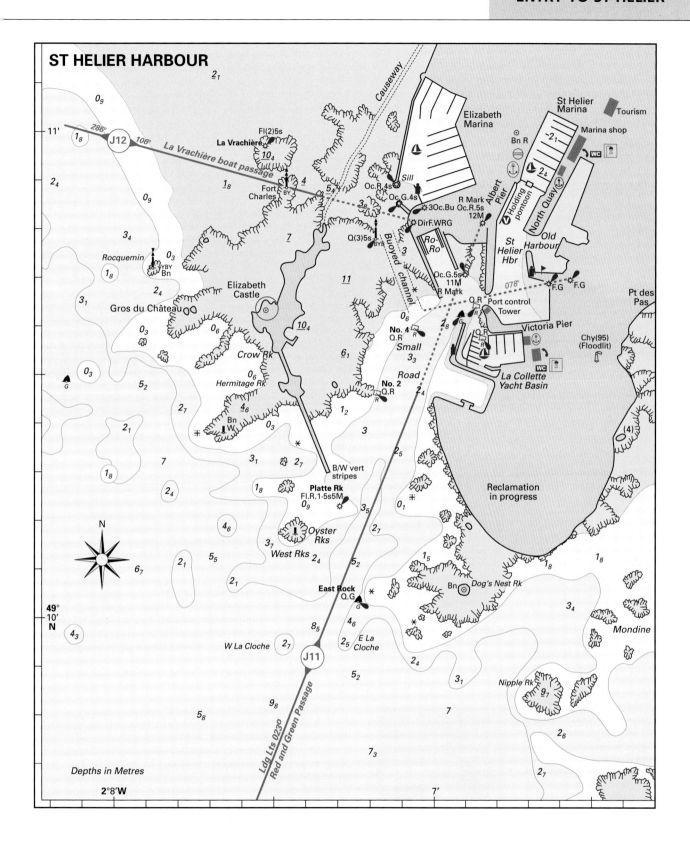

ST HELIER HARBOUR

Causeway

2₁

0₉

11' 286° 106° La Vrachière boat passage

Fl(2)5s
La Vrachière
10₄

1₈ J12

2₄

0₉

Fort Charles 4 5₄

BY

1₈

3₄

Rocquemin 0₃

YBY Bn

1₈

2₄

Gros du Château

3₁

7

3₈

Q(3)5s BYB

Buoyed channel

Elizabeth Castle

10₄

0₃

0₆

0₆

Crow Rk

Hermitage Rk

5₂

0₃

Sill

Oc.R.4s

Oc.G.4s

☀3Oc.Bu Oc.R.5s
R Mark 12M

DirF.WRG

Ro-Ro

Oc.G.5s
11M
R Mark

0₆

Elizabeth Marina

St Helier Marina Tourism

Bn R 2₁ Marina shop

2₄ WC

Albert Pier

Holding pontoon

St Helier Hbr Old Harbour

North Quay

078° F.G F.G

Pt des Pas

11

Q.R

0₆

No. 4
Q.R

1₈

Small 3₃

Road

No. 2
Q.R

2₄

Q.R
R

Port control Tower

Victoria Pier

Chy(95)
(Floodlit)

WC

La Collette Yacht Basin

(4)

0₃

G 0₃

5₂

2₇

4₆

Bn

2₁

7

1₈

2₄

3₁

2₇

B/W vert stripes

1₈ 0₃

Platte Rk
Fl.R.1·5s5M
0₉

3₅

3₇ West Rks 2₄

Oyster Rks

4₆

5₅

2₁

6₇

N

49°
10'
N

4₃

W La Cloche 2₇

1₂

3

2₅

0₁

1₅

Reclamation in progress

1₈

Dog's Nest Rk

Bn

3₄

Mondine

2₆

1₈

East Rock
Q.G
G

*

4₆

2₅ E La Cloche

8₅

2₄

3₁

Nipple Rk 9₁

J11

5₂

9₈

Ldg Lts 0230
Red and Green Passage

5₈

7₃

7

2₇

Depths in Metres

2°8'W

7'

JERSEY

this passage when there is sufficient water over the crossing point of Elizabeth Castle causeway (dries 5.3m). The table below shows depths over the causeway relative to the digital depth display at Elizabeth Marina entrance. At opening and closing time, approximately half tide, there is about 0.5m over the causeway crossing point.

Indicated depth over sill (m)	Depth over causeway crossing point
2.1m	0.5m
2.6m	1.0m
3.1m	1.5m
3.6m	2.0m
4.1m	2.5m
4.6m	3.0m

J12 106° The dayglo red marks positioned S of Elizabeth Marina entrance should be held in transit until 100m N of Fort Charles E cardinal Q(3)5s, when course may be altered for the marina entrance or St Helier Harbour pierheads

The passage passes 100m S of La Vrachière beacon (Fl(2)5s), shown here at HW.

By night

Keep in the W sector of Dir.WRG.4m1M positioned on the nearer day mark. When 2 lights (3Oc.Bu.8s4m1M) in the Elizabeth Marina entrance are in transit on 076° you may, subject to traffic signals, enter the marina or break off S to follow the lit buoyed channel into the Small Road.

St Helier Harbour

49°10′.57N 02°06′.87W Pier head control tower

TRAFFIC CONTROL SIGNALS

Traffic signals are exhibited from the top of the pier head control tower when there are commercial traffic movements

F.R	Stop, vessels shall not proceed
Fl.R	Serious emergency. Stop and await instructions
F.G	Vessels may proceed. One-way traffic
F.G, F.G, FW	Vessels may proceed. Two-way traffic.
Oc.Y	Vessels less than 25m may enter or leave contrary to main signals

VHF

Port Control work on VHF Ch 14 and approaching vessels are advised to keep a listening watch for shipping movements. Range is about 5 miles. If berthing information is required, port control is in contact with marina staff. There is no marina channel.

Speed limit

A speed limit of 5 knots applies in the Small Road.

Entry formalities

If arriving from outside the Bailiwick of Jersey a customs and immigration declaration form must be completed on arrival. These may be obtained and delivered at marina offices.

Marinas

ST HELIER MARINA

Located in the upper harbour in the town centre, this is the most sheltered of the three marinas.

Entry Approximately 3 hours either side of HW over a sill (dries 3.5m), with hinged gate which operates when tide level is 2.2m.

Entry signals Lights are displayed above the entrance and have the same meaning as Pierhead Control signals (see *Traffic Control Signals* above). A depth display and board indicates depth over the sill.

Retained depth 2.3m minimum. Deep draught yachts are advised not to manoeuvre within the marina when the gate is closed as there are shoal depths in places.

Waiting areas La Collette Yacht Basin or No 5 pontoon SW of the entrance.

Shore facilities In addition to a comprehensive facilities block there is a marina shop that keeps long hours during the season and a DIY laundry.

Fuel The fuel berth is located at South Pier in the main harbour and operated by South Pier Marine. The berth dries at 3.2m. There is a depth board below the pumps.

Hours of opening (tide permitting) Mon–Fri 0830–1700; Sat 0900–1700; Sundays and holidays 0900–1700 (see harbour plan).

Drying out A scrubbing pad is situated in the NE corner with water and electricity on hand. It is totally dry for approximately 5 hours. Pre-booking with the marina office is necessary.

☎ 01534 885508 Fax 01534 879549

LA COLLETTE YACHT BASIN

Well placed for chandlers, marine engineers and sailmaker, but some distance from the town. St Helier Yacht Club on nearby South Pier welcomes visiting yachtsmen. Bar with food facility.

St Helier Marina

La Collette yacht basin. It is an exceptionally low spring tide and the channel is almost dry

Elizabeth Marina

Entry All states of tide, although the narrow buoyed channel has a least depth of 1.8m at MLWS when a close eye should be kept on the sounder – the bottom is soft mud.

Entry signals None.

Facilities Pontoons C and D are reserved for visitors. As popular holding points while waiting for the tide they are often congested. Water and electricity are available on C but water only on D.

Drying blocks situated in SE corner are dry for approximately 6 hours from half ebb. Fishermen have priority so check with marina staff.

Fuel See *St Helier Marina* above.

Haul-out 16-ton slipway hoist and 65-ton docking hoist. Maximum stay ashore is 3 months.

Shore facility block including showers. The marina office is manned 3 hours either side of HW and longer periods during the season. Snack shop (seasonal only).

☎ Marina office 01534 885529.

ELIZABETH MARINA

Situated W of Albert Pier with 590 berths. A limited number of berths are available to visitors staying for a minimum of 1 month. Pre-booking is necessary.

Entry Over a sill (dries 3.5m) with hinged gate which operates approximately 3 hours either side of HW. A depth display and board indicate depth over the sill after tide level has reached 2.2m and the gate has been lowered. The entrance is narrow and the current can attain 4 knots at spring tides. The rate is displayed on a digital gauge.

Traffic signals One-way traffic is controlled by traffic lights at the entrance and have the same meaning as Pierhead Control Signals (see *Traffic Control Signals* above). A relay light positioned on W breakwater is visible when approaching from the Small Road. A warning alarm sounds (0730–2300) when the gate is rising and the traffic lights go to red. They change every 10 minutes.

Waiting buoys 5 yellow buoys positioned either side of the approach channel are available to yachts waiting to enter. Most of the area dries at MLWS.

Retained depth 5.6m.

Shore facilities The facilities block consists of a large foyer, toilets, showers, wash-up, washing machines and driers. It is adjoined by the marina office and chandlery.

Fuel Diesel and petrol are available at the fuelling berth near the entrance. This is operated during marina shop hours by Freeport Marine staff with whom arrangements should be made.

Pump-out facilities (free) Available adjacent to the fuelling berth. Enquire at the marina shop.

Drying out There is a scrubbing pad close to the entrance. Arrangements should be made with the marina office.

☎ Marina office 01534 885530 *Fax* 01534 885593
☎ Freeport Marine 01534 888100
Fax 01534 888088

St Aubin Harbour and south coast anchorages

49°11′.21N 02°10′.04W N Pierhead

Historical note

From earliest times and until the development of St Helier as a deep-water harbour in the 19th century, St Aubin served as the island's port. This western corner of the bay enjoys almost total natural shelter from winds and swell, and extensive firm sands meant ships could take the ground and discharge their cargoes into carts. The addition of piers and fortifications in the 17th and 18th centuries gave further protection and created the town. The Old Court House Inn overlooking the S arm dates from this era. Its restaurant and bars are a popular venue.

Approach

(See plan on pages 110–111 and caution page 109)

From the south

MIDDLE PASSAGE (6.0m)

S of western passage intersection

First identify on BA chart 1137 several features on the W side of St Aubin Bay:

Pignonet S cardinal pole beacon
Les Grunes du Port port-hand buoy
St Aubin Fort with Platte Rock pole beacon and Grosse Rock pole beacon (G) close SE of the fort
Mon Plaisir House. Martello tower No.2

With good visibility and positive identification of marks (J13) Middle Passage may be used for entering the W side of St Aubin Bay.

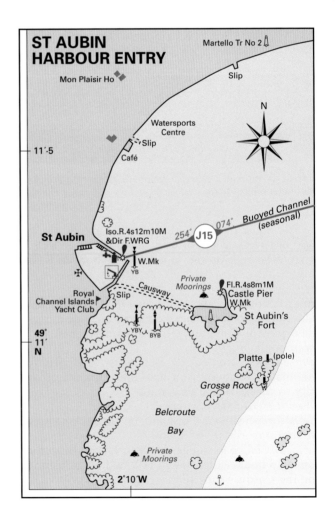

J13 *339° Mon Plaisir House in line with St Aubin Fort*

The line clears E of both Danger Rock (1.2m) and Frouquie of the Grunes aux Dardes (dry 0.9m) by 500m and W of Ruaudière Rock (dries 1.2m) by 400m. If extended N of its junction with Western Passage it will clear close E of Les Grunes du Port port-hand buoy. When abeam alter course N into the bay. Hold until N of the Fort and the harbour entrance has opened up.

SILLETTE PASSAGE (6.1m S OF WESTERN PASSAGE INTERSECTION)

This passage provides a transit that may be adapted to clear close W of Les Grunes du Port (dries 2.1m) when approaching from the S. Once past, borrow E to avoid Les Junées (0.9m)

J14 *000° Martello Tr no. 2 on the E side of Grosse Rock*

From the southeast

Use the South Passage. When East Rock buoy (G) is abeam alter course for St Aubin Fort to pass N of it and into the entry channel.

Caution

A strong cross-set may be experienced using N–S channels S of St Aubin Bay.

From St Helier Harbour

Subject to sufficient rise of tide use La Vrachière local boat passage (see *Entry to St Helier Harbour*) or depart via Red and Green Passage and proceed as from southeast.

Entry to St Aubin Harbour

J15 *254° N pierhead light on a white mast*

Enter by the channel which is buoyed during the season. There is a depth board at the entrance.

By night

St Aubin N pierhead light Iso.R.4s12m10M and DirF.WRG. Enter in the W sector of the directional light. St Aubin Fort Pier light Fl.R.4s8m1M. White Mast.

Shelter

Total from prevailing W to SW winds with some fetch entering the harbour in strong northeasterlies.

Access

The harbour and approaches dry out and entry is only possible approximately 2 hours either side of HW. At neaps the tide barely fills the harbour and there is only 1.5m at the entrance at the top of a 7.6m tide.

Mooring

There are no visitors' moorings but there is limited space alongside the N arm up to the hand crane.

Nearby anchorages

In settled weather and with light offshore winds, bilge keelers can dry out between the harbour entrance and the mole at St Aubin Fort. Deep keel yachts have the option of remaining afloat at all states of tide in Belcroute Bay (see plan) or, with caution and in calm conditions, to dry out alongside the N end of the W side of St Aubin Fort mole. Here the yacht should not be left unattended.

Harbour facilities

Fuel Diesel only by arrangement with local boatyards 6 days a week. Petrol is available from a nearby garage.
Water From tap on N arm.
Crane A 4½-ton crane jointly operated by boatyards in the area is situated on the S arm.
Drying out There is a pad and two drying out grids. Book in advance through the St Helier harbour office or in case of emergency check availability with local boatyards.
Boatyards and chandlers Jackson's Yacht Services and Gallichan Marine, both in The Bulwarks.
Yacht club The Royal Channel Islands Yacht Club overlooking the S arm welcomes visiting yachtsmen to their clubhouse. Showers, bar and restaurant available.
St Aubin village Telephone box on W side of parish hall, post office, supermarket and a variety of shops close by. Bus and taxi services into St Helier. Some of the best restaurants on the island.
Telephone numbers
St Helier harbour office ☎ 885588
Fax 746592 Emergency out of hours ☎ 733908
Jackson's Yacht Services ☎ 743819
Gallichan Marine ☎ 746387
Royal Channel Islands Yacht Club ☎ 741023

South coast anchorages

(See plan pages 110–111)

ST BRELADE'S BAY

49°10′.64N 02°11′.84W

A wide bay sheltered between W through N to E but exposed to southwesterly swell. Most of the middle and E part is inaccessible, being strewn with rocks. There are two attractive anchorages on the W side and there is one entry transit into the bay. Do not close the bay until it has fully opened up and the marks have been identified:

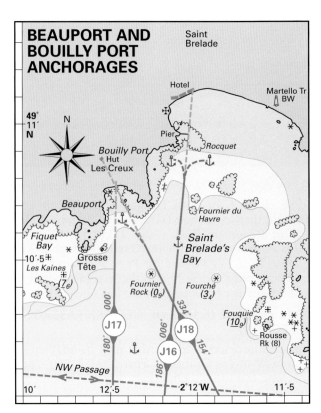

J16 006° The E end of St Brelade's Bay Hotel (marked Hotel on BA chart 1137) above white patch on end of jetty

Pigonet

Beauport and Bouilly Port

BEAUPORT

49°10′.62N 02°12′.40W

On entering St Brelade's Bay a small cove distinguished by its sandy beach and conspicuous pinnacle rock will open up. Beauport anchorage is considered by many to be the most beautiful anchorage on the island. There are two approaches passing either side of Fournier Rock (dries 0.9m):

W of Fournier Rock (3m)

J17 000° The middle of Beauport beach bearing N will give 200m clearance

E of Fournier Rock (3m)

J18 334° Pinnacle Rock below red-roofed hut on skyline will give 125m clearance

Bouilly Port

It is possible to venture further on transit J16 to anchor 400m from the jetty just S of Rocquet beacon. Sound in carefully, avoiding fishermen's moorings and pot markers.

PORTELET BAY

49°10′.13N 02°10′.61W

Historical note

The Janvrins were a leading maritime family in 17th and 18th-century Jersey, owning the largest fleet of merchant ships in the island. Many were built in St Helier for trading and privateering in Canada and Newfoundland. On return to his native isle in 1721, Philippe Janvrin fell victim to the plague and died in quarantine aboard his brigantine *Esther* anchored off Noirmont. He was buried on the islet Ile ès Guerdains, in this bay.

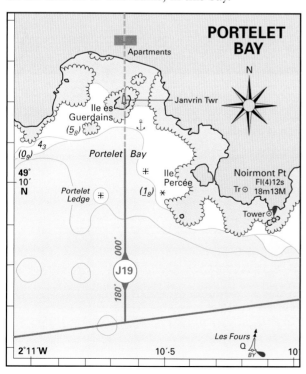

J19 000° Janvrin Tower in line with white tank on roof of the flats behind

Avoid the drying ledges on the W side of Noirmont Point by approaching with Janvrin Tower bearing due N. When just off the islet alter course to starboard to anchor SE of it. Space is tight and it would be as well to remain on board and maintain an anchor watch. This is a good spot for safe swimming out of the tide and there is an excellent, very popular beach, a short row away.

BELCROUTE BAY

49°10′.43N 02°09′.60W

Provides excellent shelter from W and SW winds, but dries at 3.5m and is cluttered with small craft moorings. Anchoring off is recommended and the holding in sand is good. The approach from the S using BA chart 1137 is straightforward noting dangers to the N of the bay, and an isolated drying rock (3.3m) in the S. See *St Aubin Harbour. Approach from the south* above.

Gorey Harbour

49°11′.80N 02°01′.34W Pier head

Gorey Harbour from the SW near HW

Historical note

'The Village the Oysters Built'. Gorey, known as the drying harbour nestling beneath Mont Orgueil Castle (meaning Mount Pride), first appears in 13th-century records as 'Portus Gorryk', a landing place for boats coming from France. Over the years its rough piers came and went but a boom in the oyster fishery business in the early 19th century saw its development into the port of today. Large fleets of oystermen, mostly from the east coast of England, crammed the harbour, and rows of cottages on the pier and in the nearby village were erected for the newcomers. Over-dredging killed the industry but its place was taken by shipbuilding. At its height in the 1860s, large schooners up to 250 tons were being built on the waterfront for trading as far afield as Newfoundland.

Access

The harbour dries completely and is accessible 3 hours either side of HW St Helier.

Shelter

Exposed between S and SE and can be very uncomfortable when gales from this sector combine with large spring tides.

CHARTS WGS 84
BA 3655 Jersey and adjacent coast of France
BA 1136 Jersey – north coast
BA 1138 Jersey – east coast
Imray C Charts
C33A Channel Islands (North) Plan: Gorey
Imray Chart Pack 2500
TIDAL INFORMATION
Tidal levels referred to chart datum
St Catherine's Bay 49°13′N 2°01′W

MHWS	MHWN	MLWN	MLWS
11.1m	8.0m	4.1m	1.4m

TRAVEL INFORMATION
Gorey Pier office ☎ 853616 (hours determined by ferry movements and tides)
VHF Ch 74 during hours
Public telephone boxes on the pier and near bus station at its root.

La Conchière

There is a frequent bus service to St Helier. During the season there are occasional ferry services between Gorey and the French ports of Carteret, Portbail and Granville.

APPROACHES TO GOREY

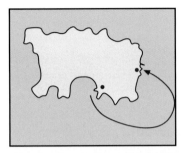

From the West (St Helier)

(See plans pages 104–5, 111, 121, 122)

Approach along the S coast to round the SE corner by the Violet Channel ⊕33, the Anquette Channel or the Brett Boat Passage short cut. Aim to be off St Helier no later than half flood and at the SE corner at St Helier HW−0200 when the N-going eddy is building up inshore along the E coast. This will ensure a fair stream all the way, sufficient water and arrival off Gorey just before HW.

If setting out from St Helier, leave by the Red and Green Passage (J11) then the Eastern Passage. Round Demie de Pas light Tower at a distance of 0.2M and when due SSE of the tower, take up a heading of 110°. A transit that will ensure a safe distance off this rocky coastline is shown below (see plan page 111).

J20 290° La Corbière LtHo open of La Moye Pt

In poor visibility an alternative that may be used with caution is as follows:

J21 292° Noirmont Point Lt Tr well open to the S of Demie de Pas Lt Tr

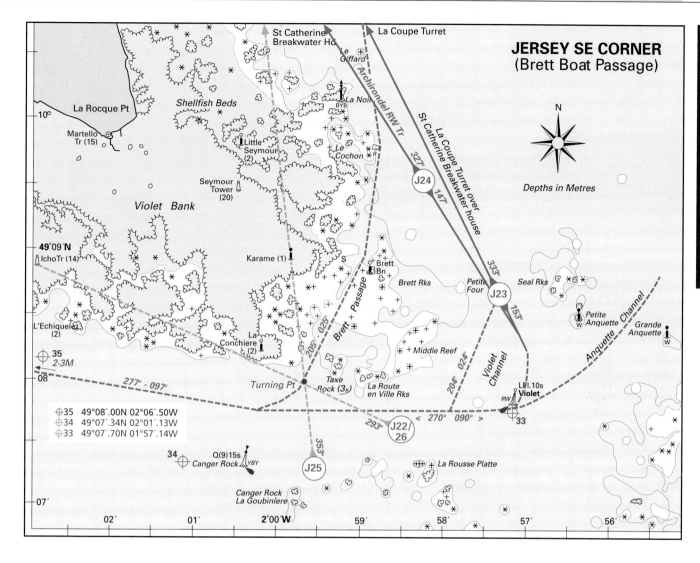

When S of Icho Tower (14m) alter course to make good 097° to pass midway between La Conchière (2m) with its bent beacon and Canger Rock W cardinal buoy.

Violet Channel (9.0m)

Identify the Violet Channel RW safe-water buoy ⊕33 a further 2M to the E and proceed towards it with due regard for a strong northerly set which will be experienced here from HW St Helier −0200 to +0300. To assess any set towards Taxe Rock (drying 1.4m) and La Route en Ville Rocks (drying up to 2.0m) Transit J22 is useful as a clearing line:

J22 *293° Icho Tower open SW of La Conchière Rock (2m) with its beacon clears SW of Taxe Rock and La Route en Ville Rocks*

Pass the Violet Channel buoy either side and take up a northerly heading until the next set of marks are identified. This transit will be held all the way to Gorey Outer Road

Violet Channel buoy

J23 *333° La Coupe turret over St Catherine Breakwater Ho – a prominent white building at the root of the breakwater (Verclut Point). (See plan page 121)*

La Coupe turret

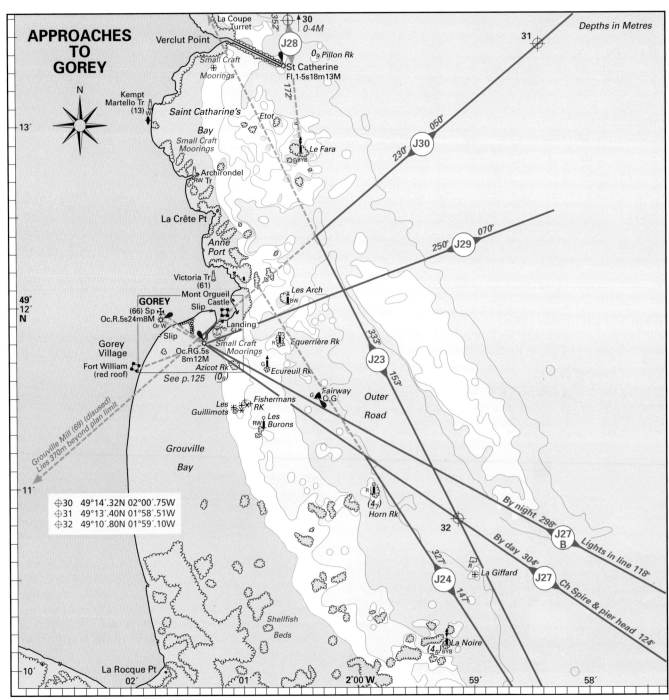

APPROACHES TO GOREY

⊕30 49°14´.32N 02°00´.75W
⊕31 49°13´.40N 01°58´.51W
⊕32 49°10´.80N 01°59´.10W

The turret is often difficult to find, even with binoculars, in which case a useful alternative is as follows.

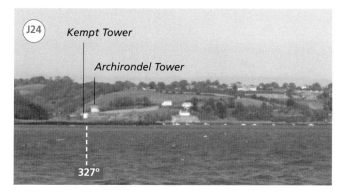

J24 327° Archirondel RW Martello Tower in line with Kempt Tower behind it or open to the left

Anquette Channel (8.0m)

NE of the Violet Channel buoy is a clean channel 0.75M wide between Grande Anquette and Petite Anquette beacons – a useful alternative to the Violet Channel if proceeding to Carteret on the Normandy coast.

BRETT BOAT PASSAGE (1.0m) (S–N)

Chart BA 1138 Jersey – east coast
(See plan page 122)

With sufficient water and good visibility this passage with rocks drying 2m or more on either side provides a useful short cut. Before entering the passage obtain the Brett Passage Turning Point, just under 0.5M SE of La Conchière beacon. This may be fixed by a cross-cut of 2 transits, as follows.

1. J25 353° Karamé beacon in line with St Catherine breakwater end, if visible

2. J26 293° Icho Tower (14m) open SW of La Conchière Rock (2m) with its beacon, at which point turn smartly onto 025°. (For view see J22 above)

Leave Brett beacon 300m to starboard then make good 010° to Le Cochon R and Le Giffard R can buoys, both of which should be left to port. Finally, identify the leading day marks for entry to Gorey J27 304° ⊕32 as described under *Entry to Gorey*.

By night

J27B 298°
The only possible approach from the W is by the Violet Channel buoy (LFl.10s) ⊕33 and then onto the leading lights (see *Entry to Gorey* below).

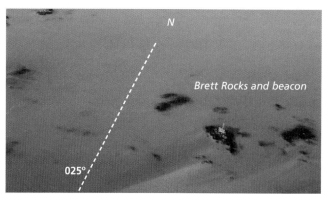

Brett Rocks looking N at an exceptionally low spring tide. The passage is almost dry

Grande Anquette

Brett beacon. It may be submerged at HW springs

FROM THE SOUTH AND SOUTHEAST

Inbound from Granville, Iles Chausey or St Malo a yacht will be navigating on a falling tide, having departed around HW. The prevailing stream will be NW to W-going, although during the early hours of the ebb there is a more northerly element off the SE corner. Care should be taken to avoid being set towards the reefs that extend some 8M SE from the island to the Normandy coast, forming an almost impenetrable barrier. Two buoys that should be identified en route but given a respectable offing are Frouquier Aubert S cardinal and Canger Rock W cardinal ⊕34. From the latter, take Brett Boat Passage, Violet Channel or Anquette Channel onto the E coast.

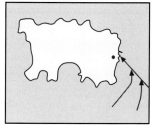

By night

Route via Frouquier Aubert S cardinal buoy, Canger Rock W cardinal buoy ⊕34, Violet Channel buoy (LFl.10s) ⊕33 and the leading lights as described under *Entry to Gorey* below.

FROM THE NORTH

(See plans pages 105, 121, 127)

The approach from the N will normally be with the S-going flood tide, having cleared the Alderney Race around LW St Helier. Route S to pass midway between the Paternosters and Les Dirouilles reefs. Follow the

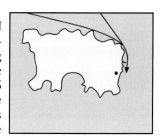

coast to the NE corner, (⊕30) keeping at least 0.5M off. When St Catherine Breakwater head bears S, take up Transit J28 to clear dangers off the corner. If bound from Guernsey, Herm or Sark, it might be preferable to route via Desormes W cardinal buoy (⊕28) and pass S of the Paternosters. Follow the coast as described above (see *Between Sark and Jersey. Dixcart Bay to Gorey* page 19).

J28 172° ⊕30 Le Fara E cardinal beacon open of the end of St Catherine breakwater clears Coupe Rock (2.7m) and Brayes Rocks (dries 1.8m) off La Coupe Point and Pillon Rock (0.9m)

Leave the breakwater end 100m to starboard and clear Fara E cardinal beacon by at least 0.2M. Note this reef extends some way E of the beacon. Steer due S until Gorey pierhead (whitewashed) bears 250° and with sufficient water enter with:

J29 250° Fort William red-roofed house on the distant beach just open to S of Gorey pierhead

Alternatively, route further S leaving Les Arch BW beacon and Equerrière beacon 400m to starboard and pick up the leading marks in Outer Road (J27 or J27B).

By night

Approach the N coast by the same route. Stay in the W sector of Sorel Pt (LFl.WR.7.5s) and keep at least 1M off the coast.

FROM THE NORTHEAST

Inbound from Carteret or Les Ecréhous the unmistakable landmark of Mont Orgueil Castle should be kept on a bearing of not less than 230°.

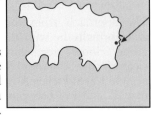

Closer in and given good visibility it should be possible to locate Grouville Mill (69m) and transit:

J30 230° ⊕31 Grouville Mill open to S of Mont Orgueil Castle

This transit avoids trouble with the reef surrounding Le Fara off St Catherine Bay and enables the navigator to keep any set in check. From half flood to half ebb there is a strong N-going stream inshore.

When 1M mile off, edge S to enter on J29 as above or the leading marks J27 as below.

By night

Until established on the leading lights, keep at least 1M off all coastal dangers. Lights for reference are in N–S order:

St Catherine Fl.1.5s
Gorey Road buoy Q.G
Violet Channel buoy LFl.10s
⊕32 is positioned on the day entry marks (J27).

Entry to Gorey

J27 304° ⊕32 Gouray (not Gorey) church spire over the white patch on the end of the pier

By night

J27B Leading lights in line
Front Oc.RG.5s8m12M
Rear Oc.R.5s24m8M
Identify Gorey Inner Road Starboard buoy Q.G 0.7M SE of the pierhead. This will be left 80m to starboard. Note that Gorey Castle is floodlit between 2100 and 0000 LT throughout the year.

Caution

Note that the leading line by day passes over Azicot Rock (dries 0.9m) 400m short of the pierhead.

Entry formalities

Gorey is an official port of entry for vessels arriving from outside the Bailiwick of Jersey. A customs and immigration declaration form must be completed on arrival. These may be obtained and delivered at Gorey Pier office.

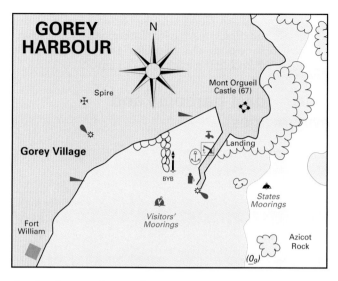

Gorey harbour at half tide

Anchoring and mooring

Outside the harbour

Anchor E of pierhead clear of private moorings. The holding is good in sand. There are 2 deep-water moorings situated about 200m E of pier head. These are orange, flat-topped and marked 'States of Jersey'.

St Catherine Bay to the N offers a further possibility (see below).

Within the harbour

150m W of the pierhead are 12 yellow visitors' buoys. They dry out around LW. Further into the harbour are 5 wall berths alongside where visitors may dry out, and several fore and aft moorings set up on the beach.

Facilities

Fuel Premier Service Marine Engineers ☎ 01534 759688 supply petrol and diesel (duty free) from pumps at pierhead steps. Open 3 hours either side of HW up to 1800 LT, unless the wind is above Force 5. Out of hours by arrangement.

Water At fuelling berth and crane.
Electricity Operated by card obtainable from harbour attendant. There are points at fuelling berth, crane and on each lamppost on the pier.
Crane Max 7 tons.
Shower and toilets Available near fuelling berth.
Scrubbing Either alongside or on the grid near half tide steps. Arrangements should be made with the harbour attendant.
Chandlers None.
Marine and *electrical engineers* On call.
Ashore There is a good selection of bars and restaurants on the pier and in nearby Gorey Village, which has a good shopping centre. Visit the medieval fortress Mont Orgueil for an insight into Jersey history. Discovery Pier in the pierhead building provides a novel experience of the island's maritime environment.

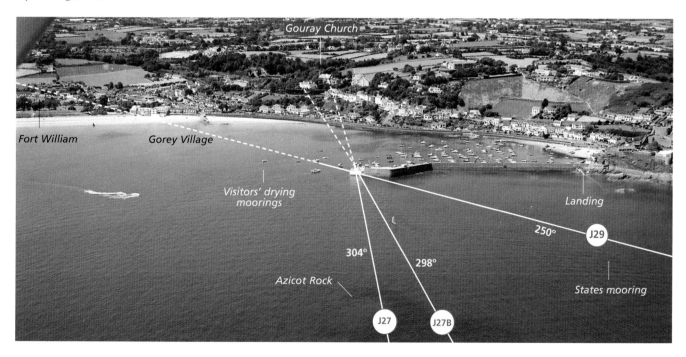

Gorey to Grosnez Point (E–W)

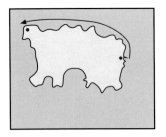

St Catherine Bay

49°13′.33N 02°00′.65W Breakwater head

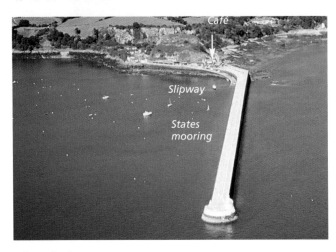

Historical note

N of Gorey is St Catherine Bay with its breakwater that stretches almost 0.5M out to sea and known as 'The harbour that failed'. This grandiose construction dates from the mid-19th century and was intended to form part of a large fortified harbour in response to the fortification of nearby French harbours of Cherbourg, Granville and St Malo. The stub of the southern breakwater with its red and white tower still remains at Archirondel. The project was doomed from the start, as a harbour peppered with rocks and shallowing waters due to silting is of little use. When the threat from France diminished it was abandoned to remain something of a folly.

Entry

Entry and departure is by the N end of the bay using BA chart 1138 Jersey – East Coast. Note Pillon Rock (0.9m) 0.2M ENE of pierhead, Coupe Rock (2.7m) and Brayes Rocks (dries 1.8m) off La Coupe Point. For marks to clear, see *Gorey. From the north*, transit J28.

Shelter and anchorage

The bay is sheltered in all but easterlies. Anchor just S of the middle of the breakwater in 3m or more, but do not close it as rocks and debris extend out to 100m along its length. The holding is good in sand and mud but beware of areas of kelp. Anchoring further into the bay is possible about 0.5M SW of the breakwater clear of private moorings.

A states mooring is situated 200m SE of the slipway. Landing can be made on the slipway at the root of the breakwater. At the top is a café, telephone box and a stop for the bus to Gorey and St Helier. Nearby is the clubhouse and dinghy park of St Catherine's Sailing Club.

Further S next to the Martello Tower (13m) is St Catherine's RNLI lifeboat station and slip.

North coast harbours and anchorages

JERSEY NORTH COAST

(See plans pages 104–5 and 127)

The contour of Jersey resembles a S-inclined wedge shape. The N coast, in contrast to the S, is generally high, with spectacular stretches of steep cliffs towards its W end, sloping to a more hospitable verdant landscape of wooded valleys and farmland in the E. To be appreciated fully it needs good weather with an absence of onshore winds which can produce swelly conditions, particularly at springs. There are 3 small fishing harbours and a handful of anchorages. There are no dangers more than 0.5M offshore.

Proceeding E–W, pass St Catherine breakwater head with stern Transit J28 to clear rocks immediately N of it (for view see page 124). Before turning NW to follow the coast find transit:

J31 *290° Belle Hougue Point is open of conspicuous*

Tour de Rozel (29m) with its white mark

ROZEL

49°14′.23N 02°02′.65W Pier head

A small drying fishing harbour with a cluster of gift shops, a pub (Rozel Bay Hotel), several restaurants and an hotel. The pier was built in the early 19th century to provide shelter for the overflow of oyster boats from Gorey. Today it is the domain of small fishing craft and holidaymakers but is only occasionally visited by small yachts able to take the ground.

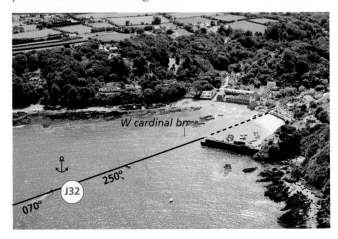

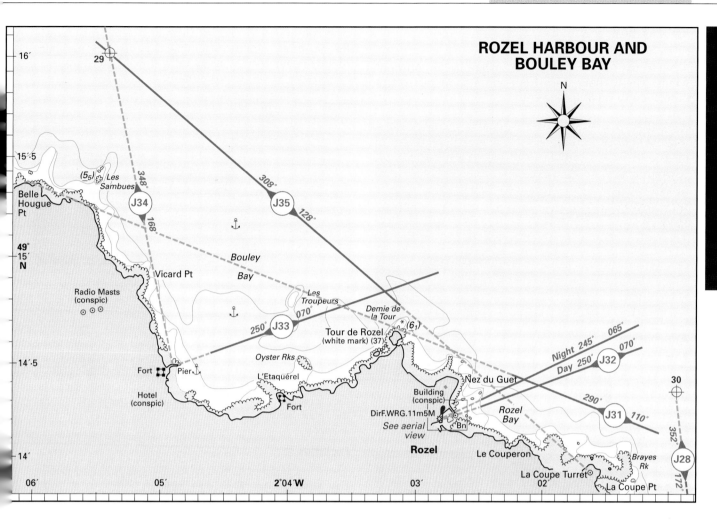

ROZEL HARBOUR AND
BOULEY BAY

Approach

From Transit J31 identify the white patch on the end of Rozel pier and take the following transit:

J32 250° A conspicuous buff-coloured gable open of white patch on pierhead

Note the official rear mark is a slender white light beacon on the slipway on an approach bearing of 245°, but this is seldom visible from seaward hence the above alternative. There is a buoyed entry channel (seasonal).

By night

Approach in the white sector of DirF.WRG light.

Anchoring and mooring

Due to the maze of moorings and lines in the harbour, the recommended anchorage lies outside, S of the approach line and clear of moorings. The bottom is mainly sand. Just inside the pierhead are landing steps which may be used briefly by tenders and small craft for off-loading. In suitable conditions and space permitting, a bilge keeler or multihull could safely ground on a sand and shingle beach to the N of the slipway opposite the entrance. Care should be taken not to get 'neaped'.

Shelter

Very good in westerlies and more sheltered than Gorey or St Catherine's Bay in a southerly. Exposed in easterlies when the anchorage and harbour can be untenable with heavy swell.

Supplies and services

Water Standpipe on pier.
Fuel Nil.
Crane Hand operated.
Stores No shops, but there are several snack bars and restaurants in the harbour area.
Transport There is a bus service to St Helier.

Departure

Continuing W leave Rozel on Transit J32 and when Tour de Rozel bears W steer 290° to leave Demie de La Tour (dries 6.1m) off the Tour de Rozel 500m to port.

BOULEY BAY

49°14′.50N 02°04′.70W

A wide bay offering sheltered anchorage in offshore winds. The harbour dries 1.6m and a short pier offers protection to small fishing craft.

Approaches

From east

Steer into the bay between Tour de Rozel and Les Troupeurs (1.8m) with:

J33 250° *the right (W) side of Fort Lester over the white patch on the pierhead*

From west

A line to clear Les Sambues:

J34 168° ⊕29 *The root of Bouley Pier just open of Vicard Point clears Les Sambues (dry 3.4m and 5.5m), the rocky patches extending 0.5M off Belle Hougue Point*

If continuing W and not intending to put into Bouley Bay a more comfortable distance off Les Sambues (0.4M) is obtained by using the following stern transit.

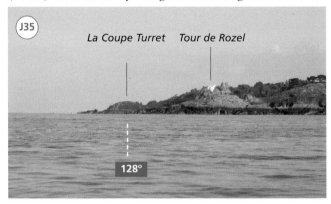

J35 128° ⊕29 *La Coupe Turret well open of N edge of Tour de Rozel*

Anchoring

There is a buoyed channel (seasonal) to the mooring area. Anchor 200m SE of the pierhead clear of moorings. The holding is good in sand. Landing crew alongside is possible in calm conditions and with sufficient water. Use the steps, which have a depth board, or the ladder nearer the pier head. There are few fixing points for lines ashore.

Facilities

There is a hotel (The Black Dog Bar), a pub, and Bouley Bay Dive Centre ☎ 01534 866990. The bus to town takes 30 minutes.

BONNE NUIT HARBOUR

49°15′.09N 02°07′.17W Pier

A small fishing harbour beneath a backdrop of hills over 400ft high. The harbour dries to sand and shingle with rocky patches nearby. It is well traversed with mooring chains and prone to surge in northerlies, so taking the ground is not recommended. As with Rozel, anchoring off and entering by dinghy is the best way to see this quaint harbour with its hotel, cafés and pub. Anchor

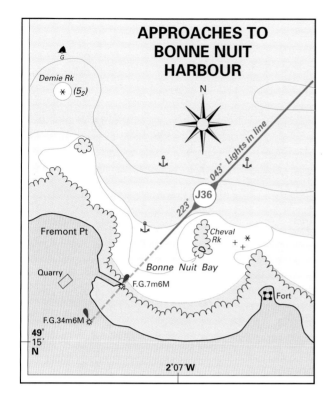

J36 223° The leading marks in line. Rear: red mark on hill. Front: pier head

By night

Entry possible with caution with both fixed green leading lights (F.G.6M).

Departure

If proceeding W identify the starboard buoy guarding Demie Rock (dries 5.2m) and leave it to port and keep 0.5M off the coast.

GRÈVE DE LECQ

49°14′.98N 02°12′.12W

Grève de Lecq has a popular bathing beach with several bars and cafés but the stone pier is destroyed.

The Demies (dry 5.2m) lie 600m north of the E arm of the bay and are the main obstacles in the approach. There is only 0.5m at LWS between the Demies and the beach to the S but from 2m–4m may be found between them and the ruined pier. Approach and anchorage is therefore best made W of the Demies.

clear of fishermen's buoys in 2m midway between the pierhead and Cheval Rock.

Historical note

Bonne Nuit takes its name from the priory established here in the 12th century. Not long after the monks returned to France it became a notorious rendezvous for smugglers, which may explain why the atmosphere in certain weathers can be eerie. Since it was a possible landing place for an enemy, La Crete Fort with its barracks was built in the 18th century.

Approach

Identify the above-water Cheval Rock (0.3m) ENE of the pierhead and marked with a pole and radar reflector. Enter with:

The pierhead at Bonne Nuit

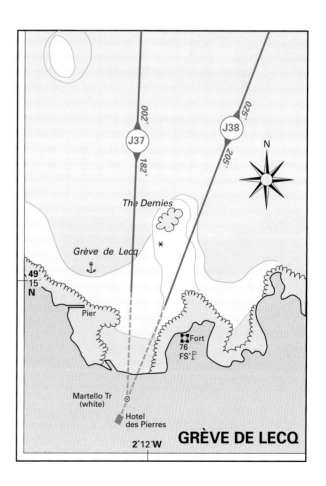

Approach from the north

When 0.5M off the shore, note the conspicuous Martello Tr (white) which is the key to clearing the Demies.

Approach W of the Demies

J37 182° The east wing of Hotel des Pierres is open to the right (W) of the tower

Approach E of the Demies

J38 205° The tower almost obscures Hotel des Pierres
Both lines will clear The Demies by approximately 160m.

Anchorage

BA chart 1136 shows cables running out from the slipway. An anchorage should be found 180m N of the ruined pier and well clear of these.

GREVE AU LANCON (PLEMONT)
49°15′.60N 02°14′.14W

Although shown as an anchorage on BA charts the bay is seldom visited due to the prevalence of swell. Holding is good in sand but beware of discontinued submarine cables.

Les Ecréhous and Plateau des Minquiers

Local information

TRAVEL INFORMATION
Not applicable

PORTS OF ENTRY
Official Ports of Entry into Bailiwick of Jersey are St Helier and Gorey

CHARTS WGS 84
BA 3655 Jersey and Adjacent coast of France
BA 2669 Channel Islands and Adjacent coast of France
BA 3656 Plateau des Minquiers and Adjacent coast of France
SHOM Chart 7161 Des Iles Chausey à Jersey. Plateau des Minquiers
Imray Chart Pack 2500

RADIO FACILITIES
See *Jersey Radio*

NAVIGATIONAL AIDS
None

USEFUL TELEPHONE NUMBERS
None

SUPPLIES AND SERVICES
Les Ecrehous None
Plateau des Minquiers Except for the toilet (the southernmost in the British Isles!), there are no facilities on the island and visitors must bring their own water and supplies with them.

Les Ecréhous looking south

Les Ecréhous

Note: Les Ecréhous has various spellings, including Les Ecrehous and Les Ecrehou.

Historical note

This rocky archipelago between Jersey and Normandy is part of the Parish of St Martin in Jersey and has an interesting history.

Its name, which has varied much over the centuries, is thought to derive from the Scandinavian words *skerholm* meaning 'rocky islets'. In 1203 they were given to a Norman monastery on condition that the monks maintained a light and said masses for the King. The priory ruins still exist on Maître Ile.

The reef has seen its fair share of wreckings. The first reported was in 1309 when a boat returning from a seaweed-gathering trip was holed at low tide. The captain, thinking the rocks would never be covered, discharged all women passengers on a small rock while the crew swam to safety on La Marmotière. Night fell, the tide rose and at dawn the rock (since known as Pierre des Femmes) was bare. There is a tradition that on stormy nights the shrieks of the drowning can still be heard.

As with Jersey's other offshore possession, Les Minquiers, disputes with the French over sovereignty were not resolved until 1953 when the matter was settled in favour of Jersey. Even so it has since been necessary to defend the flag on occasions. In 1993 invading French fishermen succeeded in hauling down the Union Jack from the flagpole on La Marmotière and replacing it, briefly, with the tricolour and the banner of Normandy.

Three of the rocks have been elevated to the status of island, Maître Ile, La Marmotière and Blanche Ile. All have small buildings known as huts, which just manage to stay above water on the top of spring tides. Their Jersey owners use them as occasional retreats but there have been several notable long-term residents, the most recent being a 14-year stint by the self-styled King of the Ecréhous – Alphonse le Gastelois. He managed quite nicely on a staple diet of wild rabbit, fish and seaweed, supplemented by a bit of help from Jersey friends.

Ashore

There are no restrictions to landing and exploring Marmotière and Maître Ile but visitors should respect the privacy of residents and their properties.

Les Ecréhous is more family friendly than Plateau des Minquiers. Low water springs uncovers large areas of sand leaving natural pools for bathing. This should be undertaken with caution keeping a close eye on the tide.

Wildlife

The reef, which is a protected site, supports a diverse range of wildlife. In addition to breeding colonies of cormorants, shags, oystercatchers and terns, it is a stopover for migrants in the spring and summer. Marine mammals such as bottle-nosed dolphins are common and more recently grey seals have been spotted in the summer months.

TIDAL INFORMATION
Tidal levels referred to chart datum
49°17'.10N 1°55'.50W

MHWS	MHWN	MLWN	MLWS	MTL
10.9m	8.4m	3.8m	1.3m	6.1m

HW +0400 NNW 1.0–2.0 HW+0500 NNW 0.5–1.0

TIDAL STREAMS (referred to St Helier)
In the channel running NNW to Marmotière and round its E side.
HW–0100 the stream is slack
HW NNW 1.0–2.0 increasing to 2.5-5.0 or more then decreasing to: HW+0400 NNW 1.0–2.0, HW+0500 NNW 0.5–1.0 (slack), HW+0600 SSE 1.0–2.0 increasing to 2.0-5.0 and even 6.0 E of Marmotière, then decreasing (see plan).

Timing a visit

The area should be regarded as open sea at HW springs and can be very rough when accompanied by southerlies. A first visit should be made at neap tides in settled weather, light northwesterlies are best, with good visibility and no risk of fog.

The approach from the SW is best timed on a rising tide to arrive about HW–0200 when the stream is fairly slack. Locals aim to arrive at half ebb having taken a fair stream from the E coast. At that time the sandy ridge joining the two islands is uncovering and rowing ashore becomes easier towards LW. Caution: Dinghy work and bathing can be dangerous and particular attention should be paid to streams.

Depths

The anchorage and moorings S of Marmotière can be approached at all states of tide with a least depth at the moorings of 1.5m LWS. The Pool (plan p134) has recently been silting, the sand is ridged, and deep draught vessels that cannot take the ground should enter with

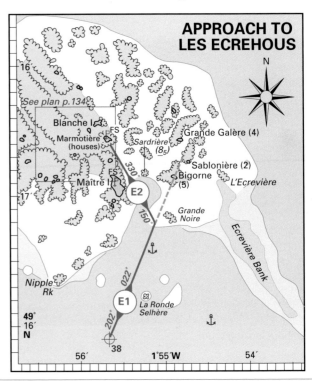

WP	Transit	Reference	Brg° from	Distance	Lat	Long
⊕38	E1	La Bigorne Rk	202	1.3	49°15'.94N	01°55'.65W

Entry viewed from the south (HW)

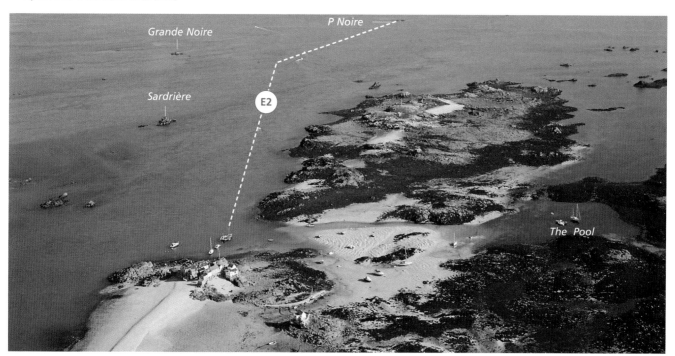

Entry viewed from the north (LW)

caution, if at all. 1m may be found in places to the W at LWS but there is more water at neaps. A reef of *Sargassum muticum* (Japanese seaweed) was reported in the pool in 1995.

Approach (by day only)

Approach from the SW (⊕38) with La Bigorne Rock (5m) on a steady bearing of 022°. This key rock to the E of Maître Ile is identified by its tusk shape – its name derives from a Jersey French word meaning pickaxe. It should be positively identified as early as possible and when on the above bearing take up:

E1 022° ⊕38 La Bigorne Rock midway between Grande Galère (4m) N and Sablonière (2m) S will clear rocks either side of the approach

When just under 400m short of La Bigorne Rock, look NW to identify the second set of marks:

E2 330° A black board in line with Marmotière flagpole above vertical white stripe

This transit should be held accurately to clear the drying rock La Sardrière in the centre of Le Sond E of Maître Ile. Approaching the N tip of Maître Ile, a slight deviation to the E may be necessary to avoid drying rocks.

Anchorages

S of La Marmotière

Close S of La Marmotière are several mooring buoys which are private and should not be used without the owner's permission. Alternatively there is good holding, if limited swinging room, for anchoring S of this mooring area. Here the yacht will be just clear of the strong tidal stream in Le Sond.

The anchorage off La Marmotière can be congested at weekends

Drying anchorages and moorings

The aerial view shows several areas in the SW quadrant of La Marmotière where it is possible to dry out on a sandy bottom. There is a States of Jersey maintained mooring buoy (dries) located W of La Marmotière.

The Pool

This offers the possibility of remaining afloat at LW, if only just at spring tides. Access is about 2hrs either side of HW. Proceed to the States mooring W of La Marmotière, avoiding the S extremity of the islet, then

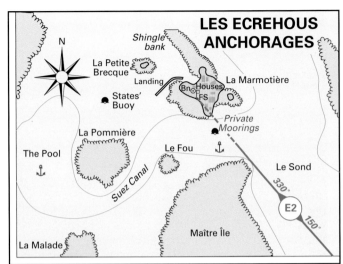

The anchorage off La Marmotière

head SW for the private mooring buoys in The Pool. This route will leave La Pommière (dries 3.2m) close to the S. Once familiar with the area entry may also be made via the narrow 'Suez Canal' (also known as 'The Gully') given sufficient water and before Le Fou, Malade and Pommière Rocks are covered. There are no formal marks and a LW reconnaissance is best made beforehand with the dinghy.

The Pool at LWS viewed from the southwest. The yacht is aground, supported by beaching legs

Plateau des Minquiers

48°58′.16N 2°03′.60W (States mooring)

Historical note

This reef, known locally as The Minkies, is Britain's most southerly outpost and at LW springs uncovers a larger area than that of Jersey. Together with Les Ecrehous and the Paternosters, it is a protected RAMSAR site on account of its unique wildlife. For centuries the rare ormer shellfish, considered a local delicacy, has been gathered here at very low 'ormering' tides. Despite the reef's notoriety for treacherous rocks and strong tidal streams, the approach from the N in settled weather with good visibility is straightforward, as is departure to the SE as long as the line is held accurately. The charted S channel must be used for entry or departure with caution.

Maîtresse Ile is large enough to hold a dozen or so small houses, most of which were built by the quarrymen who toiled on the reef in the 18th century. Fort Regent overlooking St Helier is reputed to have been built of granite transported by barge from the Minkies. By the early 19th century local fishermen, fearing there would soon be little left of their valuable fishing grounds, threw the quarrymen's tools into the sea, but they had already had enough and in 1807 emigrated to work for the French on Chausey. Their names can still be seen carved on the rocks.

For centuries French and Jersey fishermen shared the harvest of the Minkies, their harsh lives being immortalised in Victor Hugo's famous novel *The Toilers of the Sea*. In 1953 sovereignty of the reef was confirmed in favour of Britain and the French removed all their buoys. Since then the States of Jersey, with the help of Trinity House, have maintained an excellent system of buoyage and marks around the reef.

Timing a visit and selecting an anchorage

A visit over HW neaps is the best time to make a first acquaintance. Settled weather is essential with at least 3M visibility for identifying marks. Aim to be at the N entrance around half flood so entry is made on a rising tide with decreasing current. Piloting in at an average speed of 4 knots allow about half an hour to reach the Pool (see plan on page 137). At least 3 hours remain to take in some extraordinary scenery before returning on the ebb. From the highest point at the N end of Maîtresse Ile it is possible, on a clear day, to pick out the spire of St Malo Cathedral.

The reef is at its best at LW springs when it becomes the haunt of low water fishermen. The best option is to

Rocher Blanc

TIDAL INFORMATION
Tidal levels referred to chart datum
48°58′N 2°08′W

MHWS	MHWN	MLWN	MLWS	MTL
11.6m	8.9m	4.0m	1.4m	6.5m

Tidal streams referred to HW St Helier

1.0M N of Demie de Vascelin starboard buoy, marking the entrance to the N approach channel to Maîtresse Ile;
HW−0600, W 1.7–0.7 then slack and turning anti-clockwise to:
HW−0500, SE 0.4–0.2 increasing to:
HW−0300, ESE 5.0–2.0 then decreasing to:
HW E 0.4-0.2 slackening and turning anticlockwise to:
HW+0200 WNW 2.3–1.1 with a maximum:
HW+0400 WNW 4.0–1.5

The stream runs SSE and NNW down the channel passing W of Maîtresse Ile with a maximum of 3.5 knots SSE at HW−0400 and 3 knots NNW at HW+0200 (see *Appendix*).

NE of Maîtresse Ile it can attain 7 knots through the Gauliot Passage, occasionally used by locals in small craft.

S of the S Minquiers and SE Minquiers buoys the stream runs E or SE from HW−0500 to HW St Helier with a maximum of 5 knots at springs and W or NW from HW+0100 to HW−0600 with a maximum of 4.7 knots at springs.

Caprice in the Pool off Maîtresse Ile. The fishing boat is on the States mooring

take the ground, if practicable, in the Pool (dries 1.2m) with its clean sandy bottom and total protection afforded by borders of drying rocks.

Ashore

There are no restrictions to landing and exploring Maîtresse Ile but visitors should respect the privacy of residents and their properties. In the Spring tread carefully to avoid nests and fledglings.

There is a Jersey Impots (Customs) hut on the Island which is fitted out with bunks and basic rations for emergency use. The landing pad at the North end of Maîtresse Ile may occasionally be used by Search and Rescue helicopters.

Les Demies (Demics) Sandbank

Access to the Pool is limited by the depth over the Sandbank S of Les Demies, locally known as the Demics.

This was reported as drying 4.3m in 1995 but in 2005 there is evidence that it has reduced to 3.0m. The cautious limit for crossing at half-tide may be extended to HW springs St Helier −0300 to +0400 and more at neaps. The author has found as much as 2.5m depth at LW neaps.

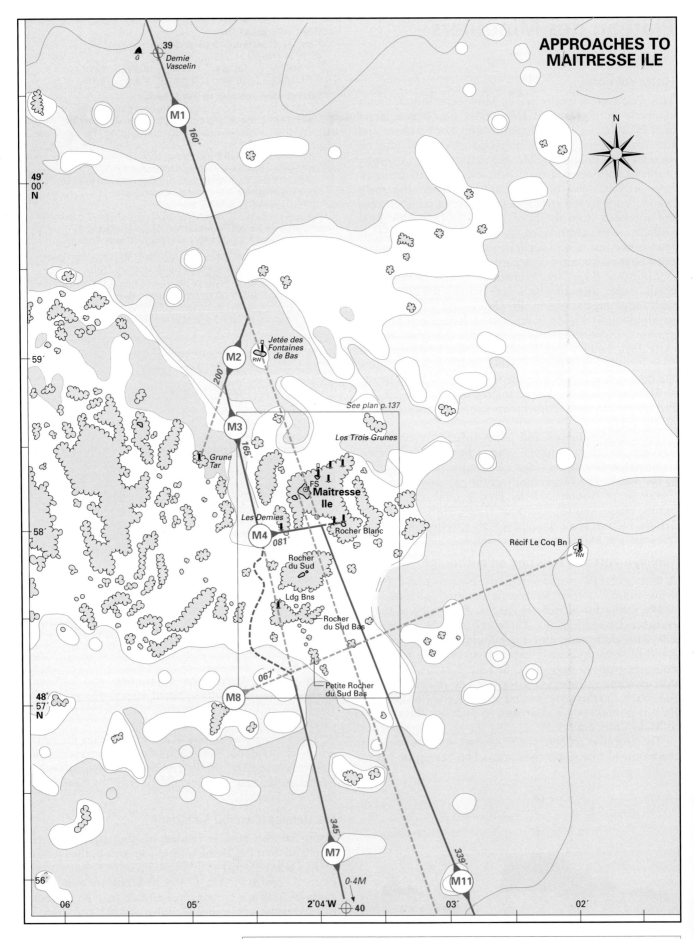

APPROACHES TO
MAÎTRESSE ÎLE

N

39
G
Demie
Vascelin

M1
160°

49°
00′
N

59′

Jetée des
Fontaines
de Bas
RW

M2
200°

See plan p.137

M3
165°

Les Trois Grunes

Grune
Tar

58′

FS
Maîtresse
Île

Les Demies

Rocher Blanc

M4
081°

Récif Le Coq Bn
RW

Rocher
du Sud

Ldg Bns

Rocher
du Sud Bas

067°

48°
57′
N

M8

Petite Rocher
du Sud Bas

345°

M7

56′

0·4M
40

339°

M11

06′   05′   2°04′W   03′   02′

WP	Transit	Reference	Brg° from	Distance	Lat	Long
⊕39	M1	Demie de Vascelin buoy	090	0.1	48°00′.80N	02°05′.00W
⊕40	M7	Maîtresse Île FS	175	2.85	48°55′.40N	02°03′.60W

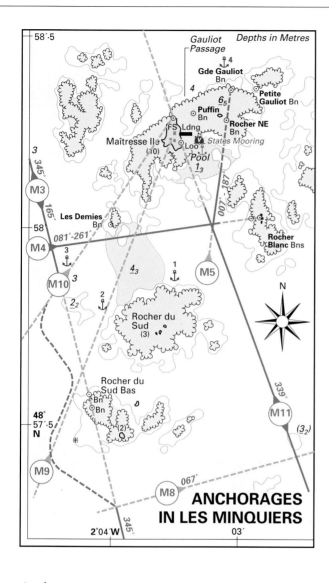

Looking NE over the sandbank south of Les Demies towards Maître Ile and The Pool. It is LW springs

Looking NE over Maîtresse Ile towards the anchorage north of Grande Gauliot. Les Trois Grunes (drying 9.4m) are visible at the top of this view

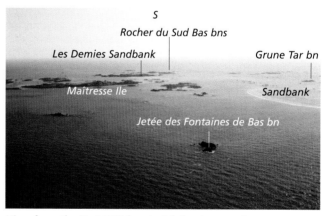

View from the N at LWS (see text following page)

Anchorages

There are a number of alternatives if you wish to remain afloat. The most straightforward of these are as follows (see photos):

1. E of sand bar by Les Demies. This is approximately 400m SE of the beacon
2. S of Les Demies, west of the sand bar. The stream may run hard in a SSE direction after LW
3. SW of Les Demies in the main channel on the Rocher du Sud en Bas marks (M3)
4. NW of Gde Gauliot. To reach this anchorage from the N, round the Jetée des Fontaines de Bas beacon, leaving it to port and steer 151°, with due attention to the tidal stream, on a line between Puffin beacon and Jetée des Fontaines de Bas beacon (astern on the reciprocal 331°). This course leaves the Jetée des Fontaines rocks, drying 7.4m close to port and a rock drying 1.8m close to starboard.

Caution

In view of the dangers in the approach to the anchorage NW of Grande Gauliot it should not be attempted without local knowledge on board.

Approaches to Maîtresse Ile (The Pool) (by day only)

Northern approach (drying 1.6m)

The following sequence of photographs were taken on a visit under sail. Predicted height of HW St Helier was 8.1m (neaps).

HW–0300 Departure from St Helier marina by S Passage (see *St Helier. From the south* on page 111). Start point is 0.5M W of Demie de Pas LtHo.

HW–0100 At the Demie de Vascelin green unlit buoy with radar echo-enhancer (⊕39). This is the key mark for entry and is left close to starboard. Maîtresse Ile is the largest feature to the left (E). The first transit is:

M1 160° ⊕39 Jetée des Fontaines de Bas RW beacon in line with Maîtresse Ile flagstaff

At weekends a resident may fly the Union flag making the flagstaff easier to identify. When 200m from the beacon alter to starboard towards a single mark.

M2 200° Grune Tar beacon, a white column with 'T' topmark. Hold on a steady bearing and look for the next distant transit to the S:

M3 165° Rocher du Sud Bas beacons in line

The forward northernmost mark is a pole with two red balls as topmark and the rear S mark is a white concrete column.

Caution

In September 2005 the sandbank NE of Grune Tar (dries 4m) had drifted E and S into the channel, reducing its width at CD to less than 100m and it now obstructs the channel. Keel boats may be unable to pass at LWS.

With the sandbank running down the W side of the channel and drying rocks to the E, there is little room to deviate from transit M3. This should be held accurately until Les Demies beacon pole with D topmark is abeam. Look E for the next transit (M4) and make ready to turn to port.

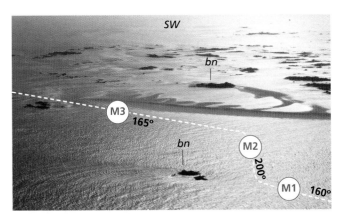

The sandbank northeast of Grune Tar beacon at LWS

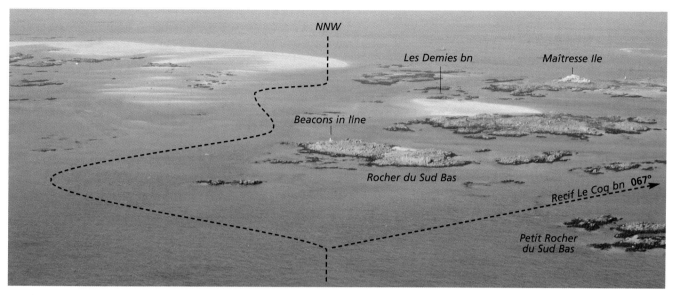

Southern approach on an exceptionally low tide. The sandbank obstructs the channel

M4 081° The Rocher Blanc beacons in transit

The forward mark is a red beacon and the rear E mark is a white painted rock topped with a white pole and **+** topmark. When just short of Rocher Blanc turn to port onto the final transit.

M5 007° The Rocher NE RW beacon is in line with La Grande Gauliot beacon pole with open diamond topmark

Hold this transit until M6 marks are in transit:

M6 The most southerly chimney on Maîtresse Ile is in line with the toilet, then head towards the States of Jersey orange mooring buoy in The Pool

Southern approach (0.3m)

This entry is not easy and should only be attempted after using it for departure, and identifying the dangers at low water.

Entering from the S, leave the SE Minquiers E cardinal buoy 1M to starboard and steer for Maîtresse Ile on 342°. From a distance of not less than 2M, identify the leading beacons on Rocher du Sud Bas.

Rocher du Sud Bas beacons

M7 345° ⊕40 With the beacons in line make good 345° and identify Récif Le Coq beacon, a RW pole with heavy wire guys, 2M to starboard

Hold transit of **M7** ⊕*40* until:

Breast mark **M8** *067° Récif Le Coq beacon is just open to the N of the Petit Rocher du Sud Bas rocks (dries 7.3m)*

This transit is the turning point for clearing W of rocks SW of Rocher du Sud Bas (see air view on page 139).

Alter to port to make good a WNW course. Hold until:

M9 NNE The huts on Maîtresse Ile are open to the W of the northernmost Rocher du Sud Bas beacon (pole with two red balls)

Steer a NNE course, with allowance for stream, leaving the beacons 100–200m to starboard. When abeam, alter course to make good NW until:

M10 NE the flagstaff on Maîtresse Ile is just open to the W of Les Demies (Demics) beacon

Regain the transit line **M3** to realign both Rocher du Sud Bas beacons astern on 165°. If proceeding to The Pool turn to starboard with Rocher Blanc beacons in line on 081° (M4).

Departure southeast

If there is 4m or more at the States buoy in The Pool, and it is not below half tide, it is possible to leave by this passage on a single transit. The marks are hard to identify from a distance and entry should only be attempted when thoroughly familiar with the area.

There is a toilet on Maîtresse Ile, which is painted on the S side with black/white bands (see view M6 above).

The lower half of the flagstaff is also painted with black/white bands.

The stern transit is the alignment of both these marks.

Britain's southernmost toilet

M11 339° The flagstaff in line with the toilet

Hold accurately for at least 2M with due allowance for the tidal stream.

Maîtresse Ile at the top of a large spring tide. There is little to see

Iles Chausey

ILES CHAUSEY

Local information

STD 00 332 33
Location 48°51′.44N 01°48′.57W
1.2M SE of Crabière de L'Est light beacon

TRAVEL INFORMATION
  Granville–Chausey ferry (April to September)
  Compagnie Corsaire ☎ 08 25 13 80 50/02 33 50 16 36
  Fax 02 33 50 87 80
  www.compagniecorsaire.com

PORTS OF ENTRY
  French mainland port

CHARTS WGS 84
  British Admiralty 3656 Plateau des Minquiers and adjacent
  coast of France
  SHOM 7134 Iles Chausey is essential
  7161 Des Iles Chausey à Jersey. Plateau des Minquiers
  (It is not yet established in WGS84 (2005))
  Imray Chart Pack 2500

RADIO FACILITIES
  Jersey Radio
  Granville Signal Station Chs 16, 80

NAVIGATIONAL AIDS
  None

USEFUL TELEPHONE NUMBERS
  Police ☎ 02 33 52 72 02
  CROSS ☎ 02 33 52 72 13

SUPPLIES AND SERVICES
  La Boutique general store and bakery (☎ 02 33 50 24 01)
  for basic provisions including Camping Gaz.
  Restaurants and bars Le Bellevue ☎ 02 33 50 80 30.
  Hotel du Fort ☎ 02 33 50 25 02.
  Water There is a standpipe on the main slipway.
  Fuel None.

Introduction

This intriguing archipelago of rocks, islets and sandbanks lies 6M NW of Granville on the Normandy coast and 20M SE of St Helier.

Unlike the chaotic sprawl of its neighbouring reef, the Plateau des Minquiers, it is compact with a well defined perimeter and measures a quarter of the size: 6M from E to W and 2.5M from N to S. Dominating the reef is Grande Ile with its conspicuous lighthouse, a fort, two hotels, a small church, a store and a scattering of cottages and gites. It supports Chausey's permanent population of about 100 who live mostly by fishing and catering for the stream of day-trippers from Granville. Among its distinguished residents are the Renault family who converted one of the island's forts into a private holiday château.

The famous maritime painter and ocean traveller M Marin-Marie had his studio here.

The archipelago is penetrated by several narrow well marked channels, most of which converge on Chausey Sound, the main anchorage and landing on the E side of Grande Ile.

Historical note

The earliest residents were monks from nearby Mont St Michel but Chausey's history has been far from peaceful. The forts, begun in the 16th century, are evidence of years of rivalry between France and Britain for control of the Baie du Mont St Michel. Their fate was not secured until 1802 when they came under the administration of the Commune of Granville and the British dropped their claim to the archipelago as one of their Anglo-Norman possessions.

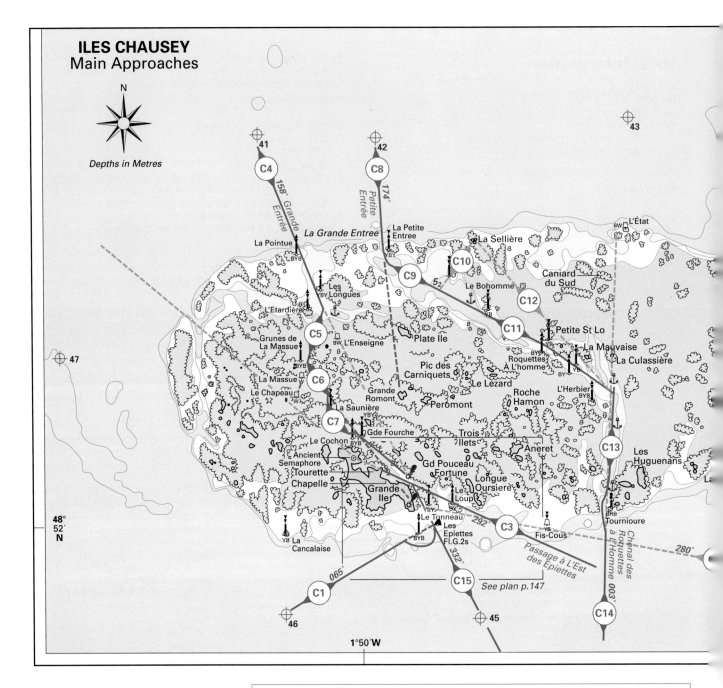

ILES CHAUSEY
Main Approaches

N

Depths in Metres

WP	Transit	Reference	Brg° from	Distance	Lat	Long
41	C4	L'Enseigne Col NW	339	2.0	48°55'.53N	01°51'.46W
42	C8	L'Enseigne Col N	012	1.9	48°55'.53N	01°49'.80W
43		L'Etat	000	1.0	48°55'.67N	01°46'.20W
44		Anvers W card buoy	270	0.3	48°53'.87N	01°41'.54W
45	C15	Grande Ile LtHo	147	1.2	48°51'.17N	01°48'.38W
46	C1	Cancalais W card bn	180	0.7	48°51'.24N	01°51'.16W
47		L'Enseigne Col W	270	2.6	48°53'.67N	01°54'.32W

A 'threat' of a different kind came from the exploitation of Chausey's much sought-after blue-tinged granite. For nearly 900 years until the early 20th century, armies of quarriers worked on every part of the reef, shipping out vast quantities of stone for the building of quays and ramparts in ports as far afield as London and Bordeaux.

Ashore

A large part of Grande Ile is privately owned but public entry is tolerated. With the main objectives ashore likely to be The Restaurant at L'Hotel du Fort, noted for its seafood, and the general store, much of the island tends to be undiscovered by visiting yachtsmen. From the top there are spectacular views over the Sound and some

Hotel du Fort   General store

The Granville ferry alongside the slipway

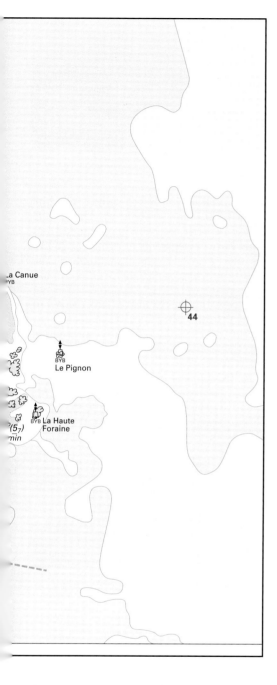

TIDAL INFORMATION
Chausey Sound 48°52´.14N 01°49´.09W

MHWS	MHWN	MLWN	MLWS
13.0	9.9	4.9	1.9

Standard Port St Malo
Difference on St Helier –0014

At 11m or more, Chausey's tidal range is one of the largest in Europe. To avoid the mayhem that can occur at HW springs, when, with the exception of Grande Ile and a few pinnacles, the area is open sea, it is better to make an initial visit on a moderate tide. At LW the scene is transformed into a dramatic landscape, leaving a few pools in which to float.

Streams generally conform to the pattern outside, that is easterly on the flood and NW'ly swinging to SW'ly on the ebb. Within the archipelago there are variations.

S of Grand Ile lighthouse
The flood stream sets ENE'ly from HW–0410 to HW+0250 attaining a rate of 2 knots. It turns SW'ly HW+0250.

In The Sound
During the flood and the first hours of the ebb, the stream sets N up The Sound. At half ebb there is a reversal to the S following which there is a brief period of slack before it returns to the N.

Caution
At large spring tides, accelerated rates in The Sound may attain over 5 knots, making dinghy work hazardous. It can also be a wet business when wind and stream are opposed. At such times it is better to wait aboard or ashore for conditions to moderate before crossing The Sound.

launch pays frequent visits and foreign yachts should fly their national and the French courtesy flag and be ready to show passports and registration documents.

Approaches to the Sound of Chausey
SHOM chart 7134 shows 12 channels serving the archipelago. Five of the most commonly used are described in this guide. They are aimed on The Sound.

When making the first visit use the straightforward southern entry.

Some key marks:

L'Etat

L'Enseigne BW column

Grande Ile LtHo

La Chapelle

L'Ancien Sémaphore

fascinating corners, such as a patch of typical Normandy countryside with minature fields and woodland (*bocage*) at its centre.

The lighthouse and Le Fort at La Pointe de la Bretagne make an interesting visit. The most convenient beach is at Port Marie.

Nature reserve
The area E of a line from Grande Ile LtHo and L'Enseigne beacon tower is a bird sanctuary. No landing in this area is permitted from April to June. This does not apply to L'Ile Aneret (Grande Ancre) 1.1M ENE of Grande Ile lighthouse .

Entry formalities
Chausey is not an official port of entry and there are no permanent customs services. However, *les douanes*

FROM THE SOUTHWEST

(Plan page 147)

Inbound from the direction of St Malo or from the north, westabout the archipelago, the final approach to Grande Ile will be on an ENE heading. Use Transit C1 (2.3m):

le Tonneau
E cardinal buoy

Ile Longue

065°

C1 065° ⊕46 The gap in Ile Longue in line with Le Tonneau E cardinal beacon will clear S of both La Cancalaise (dries 3.6m) with its beacon and the Roches de Bretagne (dries 5m)

When 200m from this beacon, steer E to leave it 100m to port and join the main entrance from the SSE as described below.

FROM THE SOUTHEAST

The approach from the direction of Granville is straightforward but if navigating on the first hours of the ebb, guard against being set N towards the edge of the reef. Grande Ile LtHo should be held on a bearing of no less than 280°. (See *Main entry to The Sound* below.)

Grande Ile LtHo

280°   Les Épiettes

PASSAGE À L'EST DES EPIETTES (Dries 2.3m)

(Plan page 147)

This route passing within 30m of the S end of Ile Longue is used by locals coming in from Granville. It is not recommended below half tide.

The marks are as follows:

292°

C3 292° The right hand (E) side of the old semaphore in line with Rocher Tourette. This rock is painted white and on top is a stone cross

FROM THE NORTH

SE

La Grand Entrée (dries 3.5m)

(Plan page 142)

This approach is favoured by Jersey yachtsmen. The line from Demie de Pas LtHo S of St Helier to La Grande Entrée passes close E of both the NE Minquiers and Les Ardentes E cardinal buoys. Departing at or just after LW St Helier ensures that you carry the best hours of the southeasterly stream and arrive well before the stream turns NE at HW St Helier–0130.

The deadline for crossing the extensive banks down to the Sound is about 2 hours after local HW. If late, go westabout or, light permitting, take the alternative circuitous route to the Sound by the Chenal Beauchamp, starting from La Petite Entrée.

Conspicuous in the sprawling plateau of rocks is Grande Ile LtHo (see previous page). Approach with this on a bearing of 165°. By the time L'Etat W column to the E is bearing 090° you should have aligned the first set of marks:

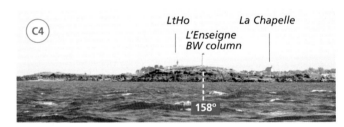

LtHo   La Chapelle
L'Enseigne
BW column

158°

C4 158° ⊕41 L'Enseigne BW column midway between Grande Ile LtHo and La Chapelle

On this line you will pass close E of La Pointue E cardinal beacon and 100m W of Les Longues W cardinal beacon. When the next mark, L'Etardière E cardinal beacon, is almost abeam, be ready to turn SSW onto the next transit which leads over the extensive sandbank.

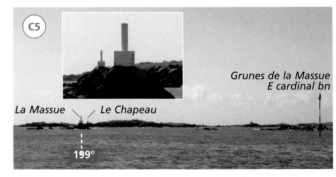

Grunes de la Massue
E cardinal bn

La Massue   Le Chapeau

199°

C5 199° Le Chapeau and La Massue columns (white) in line

When 50m from Grunes de la Massue E cardinal beacon look SE to identify La Saunière W cardinal beacon and beyond it Le Cochon E cardinal beacon. The next transit leads over the shallowest part of the channel, a sandbank drying at up to 4.8m.

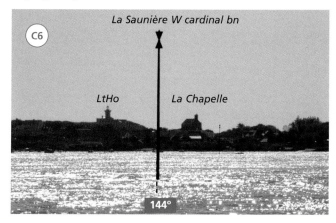

C6 144° *La Saunière W cardinal beacon midway between the lighthouse and La Chapelle*

Hold until 120m short of La Saunière beacon, then course should be altered to starboard to leave it 15m to port. Then take up the final transit:

C7 141° *Grande Ile lighthouse in line with Le Cochon E cardinal beacon*

Pass between Le Cochon beacon and La Grande Fourche W cardinal beacon. This is the gateway into the Sound anchorage.

LA PETITE ENTRÉE AND CHENAL BEAUCHAMP (2.3m)

(Plan page 142)

The deep-water Chenal Beauchamp through the eastern half of the archipelago may be entered from the N at La Petite Entrée W cardinal beacon. This is 0.85M W of La Pointue E cardinal beacon of La Grande Entrée. It terminates at La Tournioure isolated danger beacon SW of Les Huguenans. The Chenal Beauchamp is a succession of cardinal beacons which in the N half are well apart and easily misidentified. Good visibility with the aid of binoculars is essential.

At one point the channel passes through a gap barely 100m wide.

Streams

Throughout the length of Chenal Beauchamp allowance should be made for streams of up to 2 knots. These set NW for 9 hours starting HW St Malo–0500 then SE for 3 hours, but be prepared for variations.

The entry transit is as follows.

C8 ⊕42 174° *Gde Ile lighthouse in line with the W face of Grand Ramont (14m), identified by its strip of sand*

This will leave La Petite Entrée W cardinal beacon 50m to port.

The final entry into Chausey Sound from the north

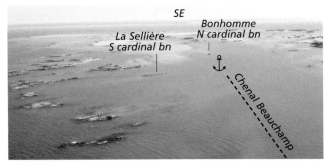

The northern part of the channel is a vast area with few reference points

When 200m SSW of La Petite Entrée beacon take up a heading of 115°. Identify La Sellière S cardinal beacon to the E and further ahead Le Bonhomme N cardinal beacon. The transit is:

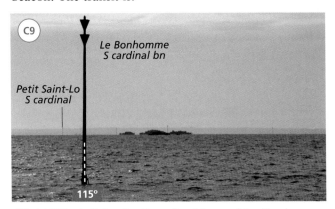

C9 115°Petit Saint-Lo S cardinal bn and Le Bonhomme S cardinal beacon in line

800m along this line, look ENE for a breast mark telling of a slight change of course to starboard onto 121°.

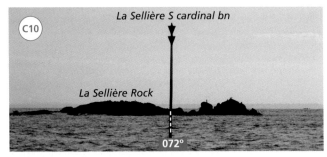

C10 072° La Sellière Rock in line with La Sellière S cardinal beacon

The next transit is as shown.

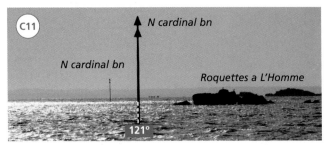

C11 121° The two N cardinal beacons off Roquettes a L'Homme (dries 10.7m) are aligned (here shown open for clarity)

This will lead into the narrow gap between Grand St-Lo N cardinal beacon and the SE of the two cardinal beacons guarding Roquettes a L'Homme. Once through the gap, alter course SE with stern transit as follows.

C12 319° La Sellière (9m) in line with the right (E) side of La Petite Mauvaise (9m)

This line leads into the Beauchamp anchorage described above.

Before clearing out to the S, identify the following three marks:

1. La Culassière (10m), an isolated rock that looks like an inverted yacht hull with its rudder at the W end.
2. L'Etat, the prominent white column on the NE edge of the archipelago (see page 143).
3. Caniard du Sud, if uncovered, is a large clump of rock to the N that dries 12m.

Take up following stern transit:

C13 002° La Culassière midway between Caniard du Sud and L'Etat

This transit is held all the way S to the exit at La Tournioure isolated danger beacon. This may be passed close (10m) either side but there is more room to the west.

The southern entry to the Sound lies 1.7M to the E.

Chenal Beauchamp from the south

This entry, known as La Passe Sud de Beauchamp or Chenal Des Roquettes à L'Homme, follows the route described above in reverse. Approach with Transit C14:

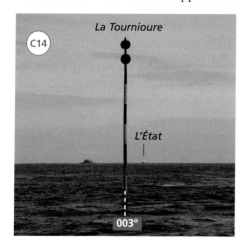

C14 003° L'Etat white column in line with La Tournioure isolated danger beacon

MAIN ENTRY TO THE SOUND OF CHAUSEY (0.3m)
(Plan page 147)

The key is early identification of Les Épiettes starboard buoy which is 300m E of the SE tip of Gde Ile, Pointe de la Tour.

Position 0.25M SE of the buoy and enter on the marks as follows.

C15 332° ⊕45 L'Enseigne BW column in line with Crabière light beacon, only visible with sufficient height of eye

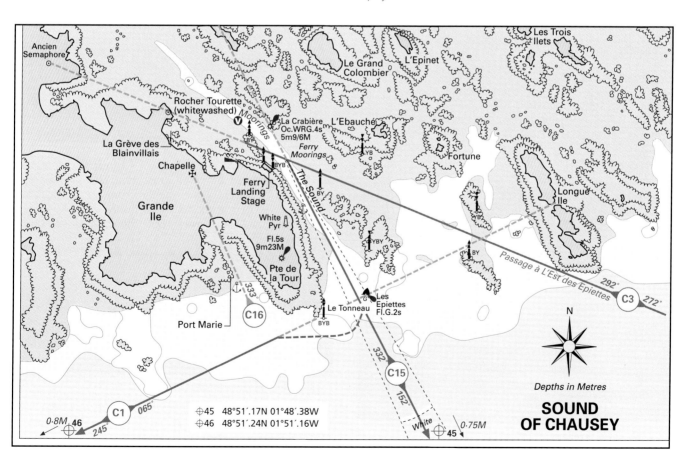

⊕45 48°51′.17N 01°48′.38W
⊕46 48°51′.24N 01°51′.16W

SOUND OF CHAUSEY

Depths in Metres

This line leaves Les Epiettes buoy close to starboard and crosses a sandbank NE of the LtHo over which there is 0.3m at CD. It may be necessary to borrow 25–30m to the E to clear this.

Just short of Crabière light beacon, which should be left 50m to starboard, the entry channel ends and the anchorage begins.

ENTRY TO CHAUSEY BY NIGHT

The only possible night entry is by the main entry to The Sound from the SE as described below.

Approach with Grande Ile light (Fl.5s.39m23M) on a NW'ly bearing. Identify Les Epiettes (Fl.G) and La Crabière Est (Oc.WRG.4s5m9-6M).

Enter in the W sector (329°-333°) of La Crabière Est light. This will leave both Les Epiettes and La Crabière Est 50m to starboard. The anchorage is a sombre place after dark with unlit obstructions, so a good searchlight is a necessity.

Anchoring and mooring

THE SOUND

The Sound from the S

Anchorage

In winds between S and W, this anchorage in the lee of Grande Ile is sheltered but can be swelly over HW in strong to gale force winds from this direction. It is exposed, particularly at HW, in winds between NW and SE.

A short-term anchorage with good holding in sand may be found abeam the white pyramid N of the LtHo and clear of the leading line (see plan and air view on page 147).

La Grève des Blainvillais

Anchoring further into in the Sound is inadvisable due to rocky areas, numerous private moorings and fishing gear. There may also be insufficient room to swing when the stream turns. The safest option is to use the visitors' fore and aft moorings laid by Granville Yacht Club. These are located at the N end of The Sound. At LW Springs most will dry out, so attention must be paid to depths. Further S opposite the slipway is a large white conical steel buoy marked Ponts et Balises. With a minimum depth here of about 2.6m, this tends to be used by larger deep draughted yachts. In certain conditions it may cause damage to topsides.

The heavy moorings SE of La Crabière light beacon and opposite the ferry landing stage are used by the Granville Ferries. They may be used after the last ferry has left for Granville providing the mooring is vacated before the first ferry arrives the following morning.

Mooring alongside the slipway is prohibited.

Drying out

La Grève des Blainvillais, 300m NW of the slipway, has a beach of flat, firm sand, although there are isolated boulders. Above it are the miniature houses once occupied by stone quarriers.

Port Marie

48°52'.12N 02°49'.46W
(See plan page 147)

This narrow bay on the S coast of Grande Ile below the lighthouse is used by small craft as a fair-weather day anchorage. It offers some shelter from winds between NW and NE. Part of the bay is cordoned off for bathers.

It is fringed with rock but the bottom is sand. Approach with:

C16 *La Chapelle on a bearing of 333°.*

It is possible to remain afloat if the S end of Longue Ile is visible behind Pointe de la Tour, the SE point of Grande Ile.

ANCHORAGES IN THE CHANNELS

(See plan pages 142–3)

There are numerous idyllic anchorages around the archipelago offering total seclusion over the LW period or useful pit stops while waiting for the tide.

In Chenal Beauchamp

From S–N the recommended anchorages are:

W of Les Huguenans 48°52´.29N 01°46´.41W

The heavy mooring buoy 200m NW of La Tournioure was not in evidence in 2005. Anchor in this position or further E around islets of Les Huguenans (see view) with reference to the chart.

Les Huguenans from the NE, a popluar haunt for bilge keelers

The Beauchamp Anchorage

48°53´.30N 01°46´.53W
SE of La Mauvaise (10m)

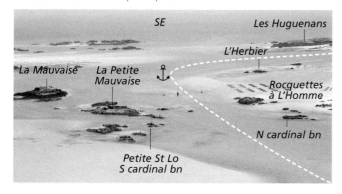

WNW of Le Bonhomme S cardinal beacon

48°53´.98N 01°48´.52W

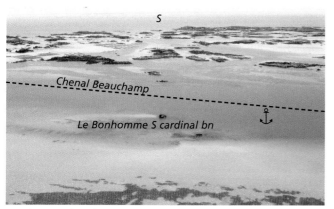

Anchor with reference to SHOM chart 7134 (see also air view on page 146).

In La Grande Entrée

NNW of L'Enseigne BW column
48°53´.95N 01°50´.54W

This is a useful anchorage just N of the sandbank if waiting for sufficient water to cross the banks further S in the channel.

The antique 'bisquine' *La Cancalaise* is a frequent sight in Chausey waters. She now carries charter parties

ILES CHAUSEY

Appendix

Tidal Streams

Arrows show direction.
Figures show the mean rates of flow in knots at neaps
followed by springs.

Sources of information:

British Admiralty Tidal Stream Atlas
SHOM Courants de Marée
Local research
R. Adams

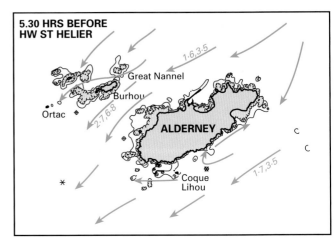

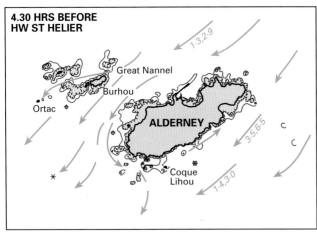

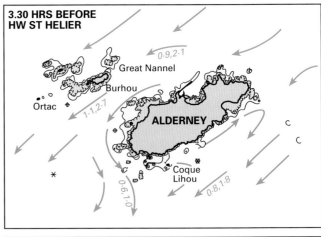

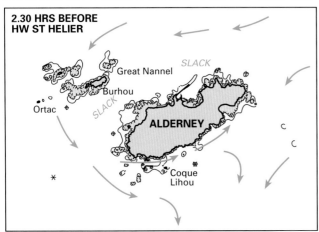

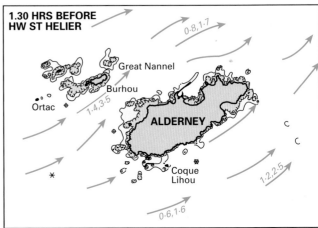

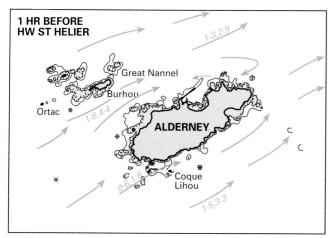

1 HR BEFORE HW ST HELIER

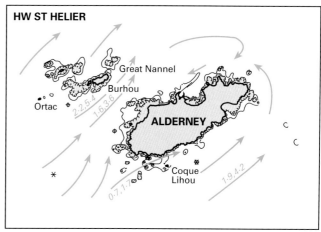

HW ST HELIER

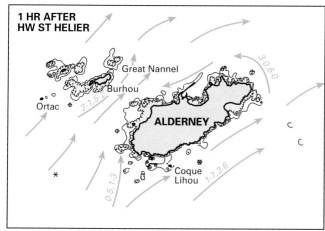

1 HR AFTER HW ST HELIER

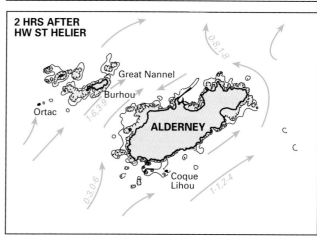

2 HRS AFTER HW ST HELIER

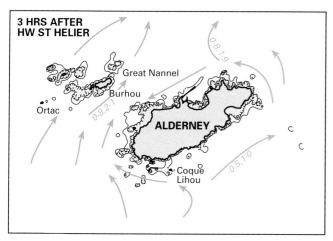

3 HRS AFTER HW ST HELIER

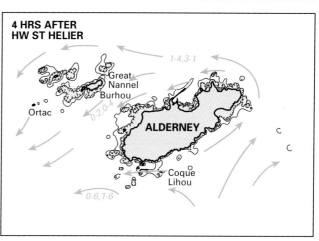

4 HRS AFTER HW ST HELIER

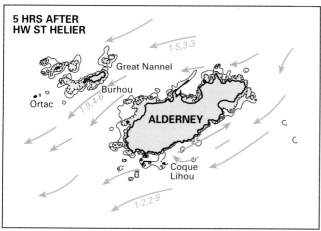

5 HRS AFTER HW ST HELIER

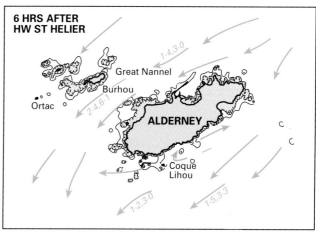

6 HRS AFTER HW ST HELIER

APPENDIX

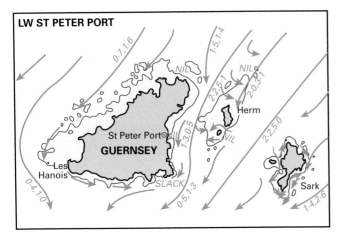

LW ST PETER PORT

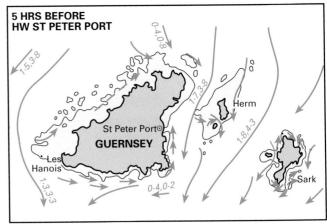

5 HRS BEFORE
HW ST PETER PORT

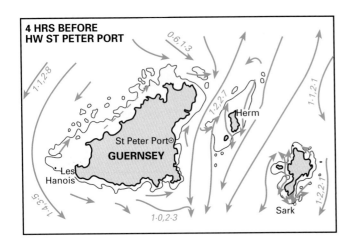

4 HRS BEFORE
HW ST PETER PORT

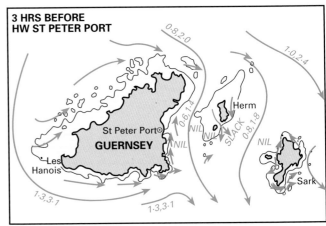

3 HRS BEFORE
HW ST PETER PORT

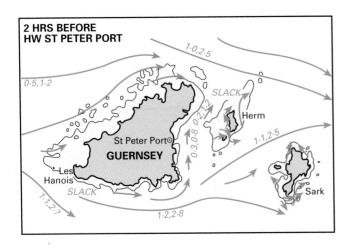

2 HRS BEFORE
HW ST PETER PORT

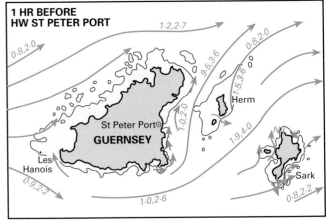

1 HR BEFORE
HW ST PETER PORT

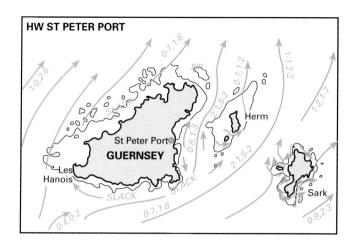

HW ST PETER PORT

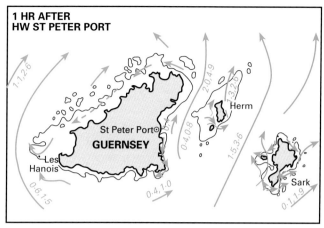

1 HR AFTER
HW ST PETER PORT

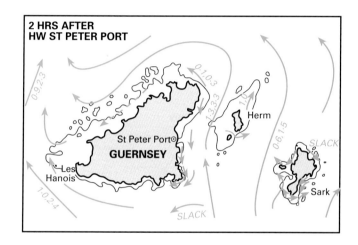

2 HRS AFTER
HW ST PETER PORT

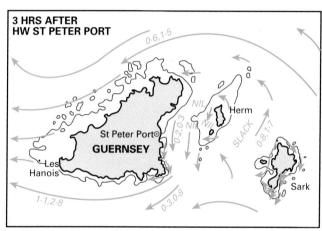

3 HRS AFTER
HW ST PETER PORT

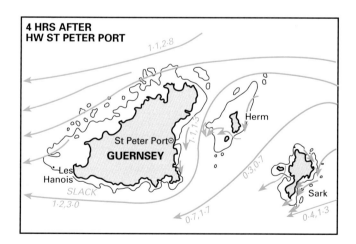

4 HRS AFTER
HW ST PETER PORT

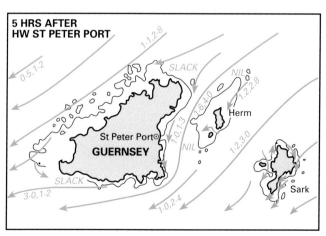

5 HRS AFTER
HW ST PETER PORT

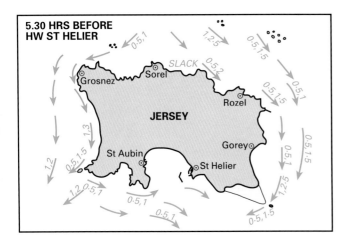

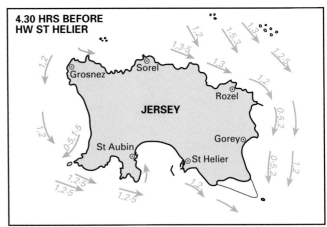

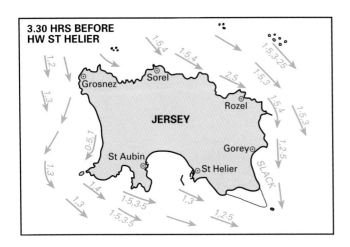

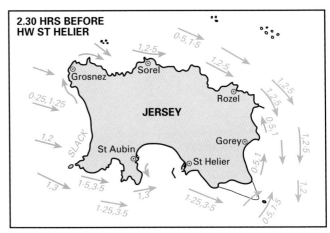

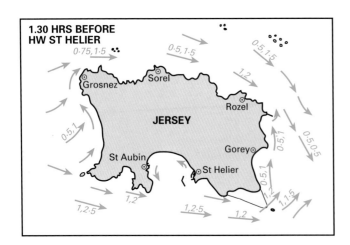

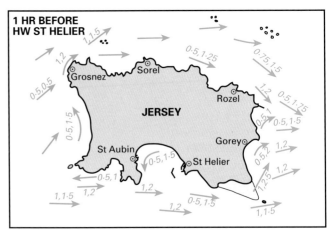

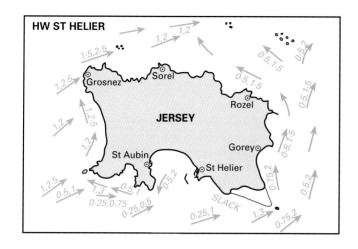

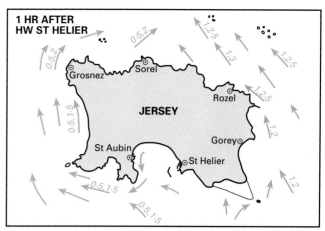

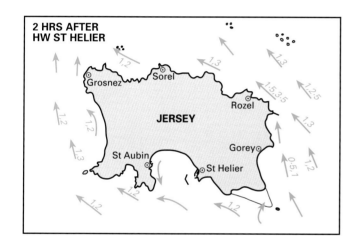

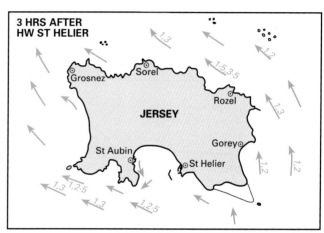

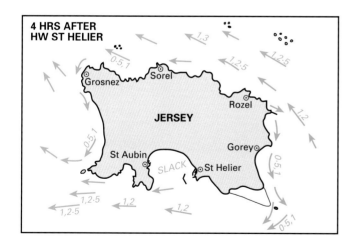

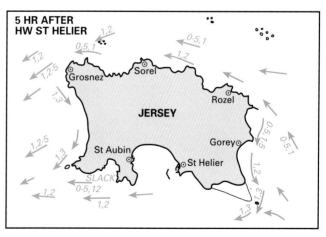

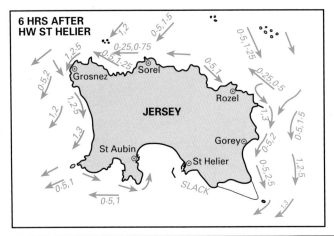

Sark

The 12-hour clocks show the general direction of the tidal stream at various positions around Sark. The DEROUTE clocks are for the stream clear west and east of Sark (ie off the plan).

Example: at the Pércheresse the stream runs SE from HW to HW+3, then NW from HW+3 to HW+6, SE again from HW+6 to HW−2 and finally NW from HW−2 to HW.

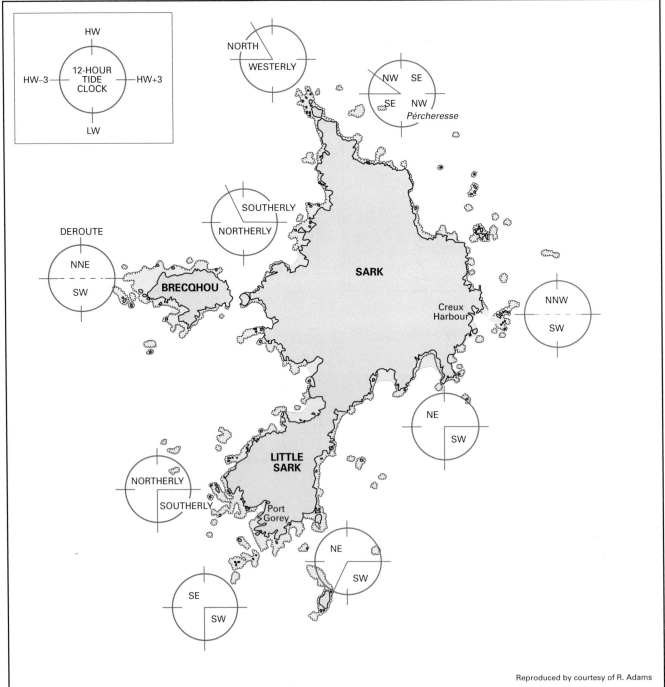

Reproduced by courtesy of R. Adams

Further reading

Channel Islands
North Brittany and Channel Islands Peter Cumberlidge
A People of the Sea Edited by AG Jamieson & Roy
   McLoughlin
Alderney
The Alderney Story The Alderney Society
Guernsey
The Sea was their Fortune Roy McLoughlin
Guernsey. Round the Island John Frankland
Transit Pilot Guernsey Herm & Sark Le Messurier &
   Petit
Herm
Herm Island John Frankland
Herm My Island Home Jenny Wood
Sark
Sark. Round the Island John Frankland
Jersey
Jersey Pilotage Frank Lawrence (Navitron Ltd)
Les Ecréhous
Les Ecréhous Warwick Rodwell
Iles Chausey
Iles Chausey. Abcdaire Gilbert Hurel, Jean-Loup Eve,
   J-C Tordai
*Pilote Cotier St Malo Iles Anglo-Normandes,
   Dunkerque* Alain Rondeau

Noire Pute

Channel Island rock names

Rocks and coastal features have long held great significance for Channel Island mariners. Their names are often descriptive of their appearance, their character or just whether they were regarded as a friend or foe to the seafarer. They are mostly of Celtic, Latin and Norse origin.

In recent history the complication of three languages in the islands – French, English and the local patois Jérriais and Guernesiais – has created some confusion for cartographers. It is not uncommon for rocks to be known by a French and an English name.

French	*English*
Aiguillon	A sharp point or sting
Amont	Upper or upstream
Ardente	Reddish or 'she who boils'
Aval	Lower or downstream
Baveuse	Foaming rock
Bec	Bill or point of land
Bequet	Point of land
Bigorne	Two pointed heads or pickaxe
Boue	An offshore rock on which waves break
Bouilly, Bouillon	On the boil, excited
Burron	Small hut
Caîne	A chain of rocks
Caramé, Karamay	Grim, rugged
Conchée	Rock covered by bird lime
Conchière	A shell used for signalling, or corner
Conière	Inglenook or corner rock
Coq	Black
Corbière	A place of crows, ravens or cormorants
Coupe	The highest point in a group of rocks
Corbière	A place of crows, ravens or cormorants
Cracheux	The spitter
Crapaud	Toad
Creux	A crevasse or cave halfway down the cliff
Croute	Croft, small enclosed field
Demie	A rock visible at half tide
Dirouilles	Mischievous dwarfs
Échiquele	Chequered
Écrevière	A place for lobsters or shrimps
Ecureuil	Squirrel
Épé	A sword
Équierrière	A haunt of cormorants
Étacq	Stack
Étoc, Étot	Stump
Fara	A beacon, lighthouse or passage between rocks
Faucheur	The reaper
Ferrière	Iron rock
Four, Fournier	Oven, furnace
Fourdré, Fourché, Frouquie, Fourquie	Forked or jagged-topped rock
Fruquier, Fourchiaux	Forked with twin peaks
Godin	Happy rock
Goubinière	Hands cupped to form a bowl
Gouffre	Abyss, chasm

French	English
Goulet or Gouliot	Narrow opening or pass
Grève	A sandy beach, scooped out from a cliff foot, also a shoal, sand bank
Grosnez	Grey cape
Grouin	A cape like a snout
Grunot/Grune	A flat topped rock usually surrounded by deep water and just below surface at low tide
Guet (soft 'G')	Watch (house)
Herbeuse	Grassy
Hocq	Cape, headland, spur of rock
Homet, Hommet, Houmet	A little island; used of smooth rounded islets, rock or boulders of no great height
Hurel	Stony
Jumelles	Twins
Jument	Mare
La Noire	Black
Le Vieux, La Vieille	The old man or woman
Les Cloches	The bells; perhaps rocks once belled (maintained) by the Church or resembling bells
L'Hôpital	A rock where sick seamen were landed
Lit ès chiens	Dog's nest
Longin, Longy	The long one, or one you can coast along
Maurepos	A ground swell, bad anchorage
Moie, Moye, Mouaie	Cape shaped like a heap
Mouille, Mouillière	Soaked or an anchorage, also Mussel rock
Moulet, Mulet, mullet	Mullet
Pêcheresse	Fishing rock
Perelle or Rocquaine	Rocky coast
Pierre	Rock
Pignon	Gable
Pignonet	A small gable end
Pipette	A small pipe
Pont	Bridge, used of a flat rock bridging a gap or channel
Plat	Flat area
Plaquière or Platière	Ledge
Quenon or Quignon	Hunk or lump
Rigdon	Exhilarated dancing
Rochelle, Rochette	Small rocks
Roquet, Rocquaine	
Rond	Round
Ronez	Rock cape
Rougeraie, Rougeret, Rouguet, Rousse	Reddish
Ruaudière	A place of eddies or currents
Sablonnière	Sandpit
Salerie	Fish salting ground
Selle rock	Saddle rock
Sercul	Tail of Sark
Sillette	Rocks on the horizon, reminiscent of a furrow
Silleuse	Rock over which sea breaks
Tête	Head or headland, of a rock above its neighbours
Troupeurs	A line of cavalrymen
Usurie	Doorway, little door
Verclut	The green cleft
Vraiquière, Vachère, Vraiquière	Where vraic (seaweed) collects or covered with vraic

Transits, bearings and striking marks

ALDERNEY

	WP		
A1	(2)	262°	Casquets Lt Ho open to N of Burhou
A2		063°	W. pyramid bn near Roque Tourgis Fort open to N of Fort Clonque
A3/10		055°	W. pyramid bn near Roque Tourgis Fort open to S of Fort Clonque
A4	(3)(4)	005°	Gt Nannel open E of Burhou Is
A5		080°	N side of Chateau a L'Etoc in line with N end of breakwater
A6	(4)	137°	Turret on Essex Castle over gap in slope below Ft Albert
A7	(5)	142°	Bn on the foreshore ('the ball') in line with Bn (triangle) E of Ft Albert
A8		210°	W. pyramid on Douglas Quay in line with St Anne's Ch spire
A9	(6)	215°	Leading Lts in line
A3/10		055°	W pyramid bn near Roque Tourgis Fort open S of Fort Clonque
A11		035°	Old Telegraph Tr (85)
A12		303°	Ortac open to S of Garden Rks
A13		050°	Roche Pendante is just touching the left (N) edge of L'Etac de la Quoire
A14		007°	W pyramid open left (W) of L'Etac de la Quoire
A15		350°	W pyramid open right (E) of L'Etac de la Quoire
A16		258°	All the Noires Putes are open S of Coque Lihou
A17	(7)	313°	West wall of Fort Albert in line with the Nunnery (E end of Chat de Longy)
A18		322°	The Nunnery is just open of the W side of the bay
A19		240°	The innermost Cocque Lihou open E of L'Etac de la Quoire
A20		289°	Quenard Pt Lt Ho over the yellow house with black roof and a chimney at each end
A21		225°	Quenard Pt Lt Ho open to S of the bunker on Fort Homeaux Florains
A22		215°	Quenard Pt Lt Ho in line with Fort Homeaux Florains
A23		272°	Gt Nannel open N of all The Grois Rks
A24		107°	St Anne's Ch spire on the right (S) edge of Rocque Tourgis and in line with white pyramid
A25		154°	Coupe open W of the Les Etacs (Garden Rks)

GUERNSEY

	WP		
G1	(9)	208°	St Martin's Pt open of Brehon Tr
G2	(8)	223°	Belvedere House in line with Castle Cornet breakwater white mark
G3	(10)	198°	Roustel Bn Tr in line with Brehon Tr
G4	(13)	004°	Vale Mill over middle shed of a group of three (green) at St Sampson
G5		350°	W. Rk Lt open to E of Castle Cornet
G6		304°	St Peter Port pierheads open
G7		265°	Green church spire over Victoria Marina Lt Tr
G8		270°	QE2 Marina leading marks
G9/15		276°	Beaucette Marina leading marks
G10		286°	St Sampson clock tower in line with white band on S breakwater head
G11A		295°	Vale Mill in line with the flat topped Jumelle
G11B		290°	White post in line with the gable of a house
G12		206°	White patch on S edge of Castle Cornet open to E of Castle Cornet
G13		020°	Platte Fougere Lt Ho midway between Bequets & Bectondu
G14		222°	Mont Crevelt Tr above the N head of Bectondu

	WP		
G9/15		276°	Beaucette Marina leading marks
G16		146°	Corbette d'Amont Bn Tr midway between Herm & Jethou
G17		343°	Grandes Brayes open to the E of Rocque Vieille
G18		092°	Platte Fougere Lt Ho in line with Rocque Vieille
G19		210°	Martello Tr in line with Vale church spire
G20		173°	Bn (B) on the end of the pier off Fouse Pt in line with Victoria Tr
G21		122°	Vale Mill closed behind Martello Tr 10 on Mt Chouet
G22		186°	Radio Mast in line with Cliff Rk
G23		233°	House on Lihou on W side of Moulière
G24		106°	Red roof (N end) in line with Vale church spire
G25		233°	La Pecheresse on with Corner Rk
G26		141°	Torteval Ch in line with N side of Fort Grey Tr
G27		215°	Round Rk just open to S of Nipple Rk
G28		023°	Saddle Rk on Lihou Is in line with Black Rk
G29		095°	Apex house in line with N side of Fort Grey Tr
G30		148°	Red roofed house in line with Portelet Pier Bn
G31	(15)	010°	The W'most rock off Lihou Is over the E edge of Nipple Rk
G32	(15)	092°	Lookout Tr (89) near La Corbière Pt
G33		095°	L'Etac (65) S of Sark open S of Pte de la Moye and midway between the Pte and Grande Lieuse
G34		298°	Hanois Lt Ho midway between Gull Rk and Herpin Rk
G35	(14)	000°	Corbière Lookout Tr (89) bears N
G36		303°	The Martello Tr above Saints Bay is well open of the southern most mast Tas De Pois d'Amont
G37		353°	Petit Bot Martello Tr bears 353
G38		026°	Brehon Tr is open E of Longue Pierre bn
G39	(11)	312°	White Rock Lt Ho open S of Castle Cornet Breakwater Lt Ho

HERM

	WP		
H1		074°	Vermerette bn in line with white patch on end of quay
H2		095°	Rosière Cottage (above Rosière Steps) open to S of Petit Creux bn
H3		257°	Victoria Tr in line with Petit Creux Bn
H4		282°	Brehon Tr to N of the highest part of Grande Creux
H5/14		308°	Vale Mill open twice its width SW of Corbette de la Mare bn
H6		308°	Vale Mill with Percee (Gate Rock) W cardinal lit bn seen to the E and Epec bn (green with top mark 'E') and lit seen to the W
H7		095°	Gde Fauconniere white bn (pepper pot) touching the S slope of Jethou
H8		321°	Vale Mill by the left (W) side of Brehon Tr
H9		061°	Noire Pute open of southern slope of Grande Fauconnière
H10		280°	Telephone Link Tr with 2 while dishes just to left (S) of Castle Cornet Breakwater Lt Ho
H11		282°	Victoria Tr just to the N of Les Barbées bn
H12		291°	Victoria Tr Over the N end of Castle Cornet
H13	(19)	295°	Brehon Tr well open to the N of Crevichon
H5/14		308°	Vale Mill open twice its width SW of Corbette de La Mare bn
H15		327°	Vermerette Bn open to the right (E) of Percée (Gate Rk) bn
H16		122°	Sauzebourge Pt in line with Corbette de la Mare Rk
H17		078°	Two white drums above the beach N of pier end are aligned

	WP		
H18		350°	Hermetier well open to W of Rosière steps
H19		047°	Selle Rocque open to E of Moulinet (Boue au Port)
H20		264°	Vale Mill over Corbette d'Amont Bn
H21		112°	The highest point of Godin just to N of the highest point of Galeu
H22		055°	Gde Amfroque Bw bn open to the N of Longue Pierre
H23		297°	Tautenay Bn Tr just open to the N of Platte Fougère Lt Tr (if visible)
H24		340°	The left (W) edge of Demie in line with the column like rock Traiffe
H25		230°	Sardinias (2m) bears 230° and is in line with two isolated trees on Herm skyline
H26		028°	Gde Amfroque BW bn over the exposed E end of Les Rosses
H27		150°	Noir Pute on a stern brg of 150°
H28		307°	Platte Fougère Lt Ho in the gully S of Canuette

SARK

	WP		
S1	(20)	133°	E side of Grande Moie in line with Banquette Pt
S2		118°	N face of Noire Pierre in line with N face of Petite Moie
S3		171°	Pinnacle Rk of the Goulet just open of the end of La Maseline Jetty
S4	(21)	160°	All Les Burons are open of Pt Robert
S5	(22)	211°	L'Etac between Les Burons and Sark
S6		329°	La Gorge with its 'head' looking W open to the E of La Grande Moie by a distance equal to the distance between the two peaks of La Grande Moie
S7		218°	L'Etac well open to the E of La Conchée
S8	(24)	344°	Pt Robert Lt Ho in line with Creux Harbour tunnel
S9	(25)	340°	White house above Dixcart Bay over Westward slope of Pt Chateau
S10	(26)	047°	La Conchée well open to the E of Pierre du Cours and Balmée (dries 6.7m) (if above water)
S11		053°	La Conchée & Balmée (if above water) open on the edge of Moie De Brenière
S12		044°	Les Burons chimney in the 'V' of Derrible Pt
S13		202°	Daylight just showing through the hole in Brenière
S14		330°	The beach at the back of the harbour fills the entrance
S15		280°	Cave just open of the pierhead
S16		356°	Gde Amfroque (17) open to the W of La Givaude
S17		357°	Pierre Norman (dries 8.8m) in line with the middle of Gouliot Passage
S18		022°	Bec du Nez just seen through the Gouliot Passage
S19		186°	Moie de la Bretagne open of Moie St Pierre
S20	(27)	070°	Pilcher Monument in line with Sark Mill
S21		070°	Gosselin Fissure over the N edge of Pierre Norman (dries 8.8m)
S22		090°	S edge of La Coupée in line with Pointe de la Joue

PIERRE DU BEURRE PASSAGE

	WP		
A(S11)		053°	La Conchée and Balmée on E edge of Moie de Brenière
B			Key marks viewed from Point X
C			S end of Jethou in the bottom step of Petite Baveuse
D			Boue Joseph
E			The heach at Port Gorey is open
F			The S point of Guernsey
G			The chimney of Moie de Viet is on the peak of L'Etac

	WP		
H		013°	Gouliot Passage is open (the peak of Moie de St Pierre is open its width to W of Moie de la Bretagne)
I			The beach at Port es Saies is open

JERSEY

	WP		
J1		045°	Gt Rock of the Paternosters open of Grosnez Pt
J2	(37)	098°	The lookout Tr on Noirmont Pt open S of Le Fret Pt
J3		135°	White patch on Jument Rk between the two heads of Les Jumelles
J3B		000°	The Lookout Tr on NW tip of the Island bears due N with Frouquie rk if visible well open of the headland
J4		050°	La Rocco Tr with the dam open its width to the N
J5		290°	La Corbière Lt Ho open S of white painted La Jument Rk
J6	(36)	082°	Greve d'Azette Lt Ho in line with Dogs Nest Bn
J7		044°	Fort Regent signal mast just open S of breakwater end
J8	(35)	341°	The BW vertical stripes on the sea wall between twin heads of Gros du Chateau
J9		338°	Elizabeth Castle b'water end on and in transit with Platte Rk Bn
J10		350°	Demie de Pas Lt Tr aligned with power station chimney
J11		023°	2 thin day dayglo R columns in line
J12		106°	Dayglo red marks in transit
J13		339°	Mon Plaisir House in line with with St Aubin Fort
J14		000°	Martello Tr 2 on E side of Grosse Rk
J15		254°	N pierhead Lt on white mast
J16		006°	The E end of St Brelade's Bay Hotel above white patch on end of jetty
J17		000°	The middle of Beauport beach bearing N
J18		334°	Pinnacle Rk below red roofed hut on skyline
J19		000°	Janvrin Tr aligned with white tank on roof of flats behind
J20		290°	La Corbière Lt Ho open of La Moye Pt
J21		292°	Noirmont Pt Lt Tr well open S of Demie de Pas Lt Ho
J22/26		293°	Icho Tr open SW of La Conchière rk
J23		333°	La Coupe turret over St Catherine b'water house
J24		327°	Archirondel RW Martello Tr in line with Kempt Martello Tr
J25		353°	Karame Bn in line with St Catherine b'water
J26/J22		293°	Icho Tr open SW of La Conchière Rk
J27	(32)	304°	Gouray ch spire over white patch on pierhead
J27B		298	Gorey leading lights
J28	(30)	172°	Le Fara E cardinal bn open of St Catherine b'water end
J29		250°	Fort William red-roofed house just open S of Gorey pierhead
J30	(31)	230°	Grouville Mill open S of Mt Orgueil Castle
J31		290°	Belle Hougue Pt open of Tour de Rozel
J32		250°	Conspic buff coloured gable open of white patch on pierhead
J33		250°	The right (W) side of Ft Lester over white patch on pierhead
J34	(29)	168°	The root of Bouley bay pier open of Vicard Pt
J35	(29)	128°	La Coupe Turret well open of N edge of Tour de Rozel
J36		223°	Bonne Nuit harbour leading marks
J37		182°	E wing of Hotel des Pierres open to right (W) of Tr
J38		205°	Tr almost obscures Hotel des Pierres

LES ECREHOUS

	WP		
E1	(38)	022°	La Bigorne midway between Gde Galère (4) and Sablonière (2)
E2		330°	A black board in line with Marmotière flagpole above vertical white stripe

PLATEAU DES MINQUIERS

	WP		
M1	(39)	160°	Jetée des Fontaines de Bas RW bn in line with Maîtresse Ile flagstaff
M2		200°	Grune Tr bn with 'T' topmark
M3		165°	Rocher du Sud Bas bns in line
M4		081°	Rocher Blanc bns in line
M5		007°	Rocher NE RW bn in line with La Grande Gauliot bn pole with open diamond topmark
M6			The most S'ly chimney on Maîtresse Ile on with the toilet
M7	(40)	345°	Rocher du Sud Bas bcns in line
M8		067°	Récif Le Coq bn is just open N of Petit du Sud Bas rocks, if uncovered
M9		NNE	The huts on Maîtresse Ile open to W of the northernmost Rocher du Sud Bas bcns.
M10		NE	Flagstaff on Maîtresse Ile open W of Les Demies (Demics) bn
M11		339°	Flagstaff on Maîtresse Ile in line with the toilet

ILES CHAUSEY TRANSITS

	WP		
C1	(46)	065°	The gap in Ile Longue in line with Le Tonneau E cardinal
C2		VIEW	Approach from SE
C3		292°	The right hand (E) side of the Old Semaphore in line with Rocher Tourlette
C4	(41)	158°	L'Enseigne BW column is midway between Gde Ile Lt Ho and La Chapelle
C5		199°	Le Chapeau and La Massue white columns in line
C6		144°	La Saunière W cardinal bn midway between Gde Ile Lt Ho and La Chapelle
C7		141°	Gde Ile Lt Ho in line with Le Cochon E cardinal bn
C8	(42)	174°	Gde Ile Lt Ho in line with W face of Gd Ramont
C9		115°	Petit Saint-Lo S cardinal bn and Le Bonhomme S cardinal bn in line
C10		072°	La Sellière rk in line with la Sellière S card bn
C11		121°	The two N card bns off Roquettes a L'Homme are aligned
C12		319°	La Sellière in line with the right (E) side of Petite Mauvaise
C13		002°	La Culassière midway between Caniard du Sud and L'Etat
C14		003°	L'Etat white column in line with La Tournioure isolated danger bn
C15	45	332°	L'Enseigne BW column in line with Crabière Lt bn
C16 dear		333°	La Chapelle

Violet Channel buoy

Waypoints (WGS 84 Datum)

ALDERNEY

WP	Transit	Reference	Brg° from	Distance	Lat	Long
1		Quénard Pt Lt Ho E	090	3.8	49°43′.75N	02°03′.90W
2	A1	Quénard Pt Lt Ho NE	053	1.5	49°44′.65N	02°08′.10W
3	A4	Fort Clonque	210	1.6	49°41′.42N	02°15′.22W
4	A4/5	Great Nannel	186	0.8	48°43′.46N	02°14′.90W
5	A7	Braye B'water hd NW	347	0.97	49°44′.76N	02°12′.00W
6	A9	Braye B'water hd NE	042	1.0	49°44′.56N	02°10′.65W
7	A17	Essex Castle	126	1.15	49°42′.38N	02°09′.10W

GUERNSEY

WP	Transit	Reference	Brg° from	Distance	Lat	Long
8	G2	Roustel bn Tr	270	0.1	49°29′.27N	02°28′95W
9	G1	Tautenay bn Tr	001	1.2	49°31′.30N	02°26′.80W
10	G3	Platte Fougère Lt Ho	063	1.0	49°31′.27N	02°27′.78W
11	G39	Lower Hds S Card buoy	180	0.2	49°25′.64N	02°28′.55W
12		Castle Cornet Lt Ho	039	0.29	49°27′.53N	02°31′.16W
13	G4	St Martins Pt Lt Ho	155	0.64	49°24′.72N	02°31′.30W
14	G35	La Corbière Tr	182	0.9	49°24′.37N	02°37′.20W
15	G31/32	Hanois Lt Ho SE	140	0.93	49°25′.39N	02°41′.28W
16		Hanois Lt Ho W	270	2.0	49°26′.10N	02°45′.17W

HERM

WP	Transit	Reference	Brg° from	Distance	Lat	Long
17		Grande Amfroque bn tr	090	1.75	49°30′.56N	02°21′.93W
18		Noire Pute E	090	0.5	49°28′.21N	02°24′.25W
19	H13	Noire Pute SW	209	1.1	49°27′.25N	02°25′.84W

SARK

WP	Transit	Reference	Brg° from	Distance	Lat	Long
20	S1	Bec du Nez bn NW	322	0.53	49°27′.50N	02°22′.67W
21	S4	Bec du Nez bn NE	042	0.56	49°27′.50N	02°21′.60W
22	S5	Pt Robert Lt Ho	050	1.2	49°26′.95N	02°19′.34W
23		Blanchard E card buoy	090	0.5	49°25′.35N	02°16′.65W
24	S8	Creux Harbour	164	1.0	49°24′.88N	02°20′.20W
25	S9	L'Etac E	085	0.9	49°24′.17N	02°20′.68W
26	S10	L'Etac SW	242	1.0	49°23′.63N	02°23′.39W
27	S20	La Givaude	205	0.7	49°25′.25N	02°24′.40W

JERSEY

WP	Transit	Reference	Brg° from	Distance	Lat	Long
28		Désormes W card buoy	270	0.1	49°18′.94N	02°18′.13W
29	J34/35	Belle Hougue Pt	030	0.7	49°15′.91N	02°05′.38W
30	J28	St Catherine b/water hd N	356	1.0	49°14′.32N	02°00′.75W
31	J30	St Catherine b/water hd E	087	1.4	49°13′.40N	01°58′.51W
32	J27	Gorey pierhead	125	1.8	49°10′.80N	01°59′.10W
33		Violet ch buoy	180	0.1	49°07′.70N	01°57′.14W
34		Canger Rk W card buoy	270	0.5	49°07′.34N	02°01′.13W
35	J8	Demie de Pas Lt Ho	193	1.0	49°08′.00N	02°06′.50W
36	J6	La Corbière Lt Ho S	202	1.8	49°09′.14N	02°16′.00W
37	J2	La Corbière Lt Ho W	255	1.0	49°10′.53N	02°16′.48W

LES ECREHOUS

WP	Transit	Reference	Brg° from	Distance	Lat	Long
38	E1	La Bigorne Rk	202	1.3	49°15′.94N	01°55′.65W

PLATEAU DES MINQUIERS

WP	Transit	Reference	Brg° from	Distance	Lat	Long
39	M1	Demie de Vascelin buoy	090	0.1	49°00′.80N	02°05′.00W
40	M7	Maîtresse Ile	175	2.85	48°55′.40N	02°03′.60W

ILES CHAUSEY

WP	Transit	Reference	Brg° from	Distance	Lat	Long
41	C4	L'Enseigne Col NW	339	2.0	48°55′.53N	01°51′.46W
42	C7	L'Enseigne Col N	012	1.9	48°55′.53N	01°49′.80W
43		L'Etat	000	1.0	48°55′.67N	01°46′.20W
44		Anvers W card buoy	270	0.3	48°53′.87N	01°41′.54W
45	C15	Grande Ile Lt Ho	147	1.2	48°51′.17N	01°48′.38W
46	C1	Cancalais W card bn	180	0.7	48°51′.24N	01°51′.16W
47		L'Enseigne Col W	270	2.6	48°53′.67N	01°54′.32W

APPENDIX

Index